Barrio Dreams

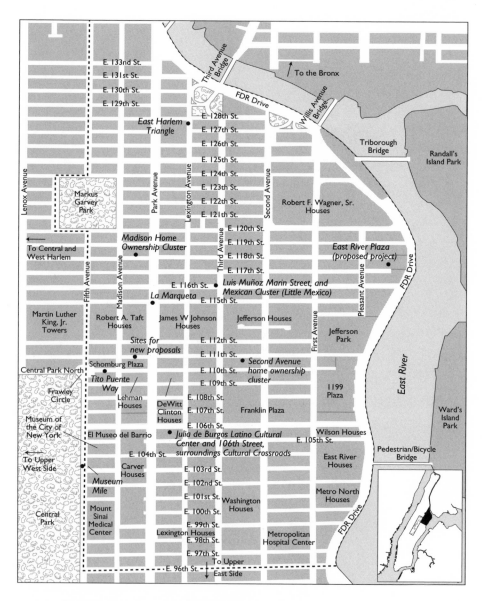

Map of East Harlem. Insert shows its location in Upper Manhattan.

Barrio Dreams

PUERTO RICANS, LATINOS,
AND THE NEOLIBERAL CITY

ARLENE DÁVILA

UNIVERSITY OF CALIFORNIA PRESS
Berkeley   Los Angeles   London

University of California Press
Berkeley and Los Angeles, California

University of California Press, Ltd.
London, England

© 2004 by the Regents of the University of California

Library of Congress Control Number:
2003064572

Manufactured in the United States of America

13   12   11   10   09   08   07   06   05   04
10   9   8   7   6   5   4   3   2   1

Contents

Illustrations

In memory of Delmos Jones

Acknowledgments

Books solidify things. It's unavoidable. El Barrio/East Harlem is happening as we speak in many more ways than I can describe in this text. Yet I take the risk: this book is about a "moment" that I feel speaks about this community's past and its future. As I write the customary acknowledgments, the difficult predicament is not who, but who not to thank and acknowledge. This project benefited from the help, time, enthusiasm, and comments of many residents of East Harlem/El Barrio, including activists, artists, colleagues, and friends, in and beyond its physical and imaginary boundaries, who are too numerous to list. But the help of some individuals was particularly indulgent. I could not but try to thank some of them here, even if this would necessarily fall short from acknowledging the extent of their many contributions to this project. Such is the case with Debbie Quiñones, Erica González, Melissa Mark Viverito, Ismael Nunez, and Rolando Cortés, whose support was continuous and insurmountable throughout the development of this book. To Debbie, my first contact about community politics and the community board, I am particularly indebted and thankful for her vision, insight, and trust. Thanks also are due to John Rivera and José Rivera, Fernando Salicrup, Yolanda Sánchez, Juan Cáceres, Erika Vilkfort, Jerry Domínguez, and Aurora Flores, for their continuous assistance, and most important to East Harlem's Community Board 11. Thomas Lunke, Dorothy Désir-Davis, Javier Llano, and Norma Ojeda were extremely helpful in regard to particular policies, meetings, and for providing valuable contacts. I thank other residents and community activists for their time and their spirit, most of whom are identified by name in these pages—with the exception of those I was unable to contact for permission to use their names.

Many other people contributed in more ways that I can describe. I'm enormously thankful to my friends and colleagues Maureen O'Dougherty, Gabriel Haslip-Viera, Jocelyn Solís, Elizabeth Chin, Ed Morales, and Yasmín Ramírez for providing important feedback and for teaching me so much in the process. Discussions with Juan Flores and artists Juan Sánchez and Diógenes Ballester—from whom I first heard warnings about processes of gentrification in the area in the early 1990s—were also pivotal throughout the years I undertook this project.

Evelina Dagnino's call for "More cultural politics!," as well as fruitful conversations on "cultural hemispheres" and "cultural agency" and "cities and translocal flows," where I had the pleasure of meeting exciting colleagues from the Americas and sharing some of this work, were also enormously inspiring. Thanks to the vision and organizational skills of Marcial Godoy, Rosanna Reguillo, Ramón Gutiérrez, David Theo Goldberg, and Doris Sommer.

Acknowledgments are also due to Julie Sze, who served as research assistant. Segments of this work were also commented on by Felipe Pimentel, Richard Handler, Alyshia Galvez, Sandra Ruiz, Fred Myers, and Raúl Homero-Villa. I am particularly grateful to Monique Taylor, Hector Cordero Guzmán, Steven Gregory, and Luís Aponte-Parés, who generously reviewed the manuscript for the Press. Hector's know-how about important policy and statistical data and discussions with Steven Gregory about barrio politics were extremely helpful. Luís's careful consideration of the politics of space have been an inspiration to many scholars. This work follows his productive footprints.

Lastly, I'm always grateful to my colleagues and students at New York University's American Studies and Anthropology Department for their constant inspiration. I especially benefited from the comments made by Lilcia Fiol Mata, Robin Kelley, Lisa Duggan, and Tricia Rose during a presentation at a faculty seminar, where I presented the earliest version of this work. The feeling of being part of a larger intellectual project was extremely inspirational. My appreciation also goes to my new colleague, Adam Green, who graciously and usefully provided instant feedback during the last stages of publishing this book. Thanks also to Sandra Ruíz and Jan Padios, who provided invaluable proofreading assistance. Comments from students, colleagues, and audience members during presentations at Rutgers University (Laurie Ouellette), University of Florida, Gainesville (Efraín Barradas and Tace Hedrick), and Columbia University (Steven Gregory) were also extremely invigorating as I sorted through the myriad issues this work sought to tackle. I am also indebted to Mariano Desmarás, whose passion for the aesthetics and materiality of space was an inspiration and fundamental to the development of this project. A grant by New York University's Humanities Council facilitated final preparations of the book. Finally, it was a pleasure to have had the opportunity to work again with the editorial team of the University of California Press. My greatest appreciation goes to Naomi Schneider, for her insight and continuous support. The care and professionalism of Sierra Filucci and Nicole Hayward and Kate Warne were unparalleled.

Introduction

BARRIO BUSINESS,
BARRIO DREAMS

"This is not an antipoverty program," repeated New York City congressman Charles Rangel to a beleaguered audience of East Harlemites,
mostly Black and Puerto Rican, in an informational forum on Empowerment Zone (EZ) legislation. Once again, the initiative he himself had
helped design to revitalize distressed inner-city communities through
economic investment and incentives was the subject of much reproach
and criticism. In particular, East Harlem Latinos felt that they and their
community had been neglected by the initiative. But Rangel was
adamant: "This is not about your dreams. This is about business, profit,
and jobs." Only projects that prove to be profitable and "entrepreneurial"
would be considered for funding. But he was speaking at the Julia de
Burgos Latino Cultural Center in March 2002, itself the product of previous struggles, not to mention state distribution programs to quench polit-

1

ical claims. The audience could still remember a time when cultural demands commanded economic resources and political valence. But there was little that could be done. Coffee and biscuits had been served, the meeting was called back to order, and break-out sessions were about to start. Some sat anxiously through the forum while others swiftly departed in protest.

One of the central contradictions in East Harlem is the treatment of culture as industry to attract jobs, business, and profits and the simultaneous disavowal of ethnicity and race as grounds for equity and representation. Meanwhile ethnicity and race are in fact the bases on which urban spatial transformations are being advanced and contested. The resulting struggles around space, representation, and identity not only reveal strategies of contemporary Latino cultural politics but also the place of culture in the structuring of space.

result of racialized space

This book examines the cultural politics of urban space in New York's East Harlem (also known as El Barrio or Spanish Harlem) in the context of rapid gentrification and social change. I foreground gentrification and the neoliberal policies that favor privatization and consumption alongside the increasing "Latinization" of U.S. cities. These processes are overtaking cities throughout the United States and beyond, and are vividly at play in New York City, a global center of culture and consumption, where Latinos, at 27 percent of the population, now constitute the biggest minority group. Put simply, Home Depot, Starbucks, and Soho-like museums are coming to El Barrio, confronting residents with disparate and competing agendas for their future. Spurring these contests is an increasingly tight real-estate market, which has attracted new residential and commercial tenants to predominantly Black and Latino Upper Manhattan neighborhoods such as Harlem, East Harlem, and the South Bronx. State and federal government policies, such as the Upper Manhattan EZ, have served as catalysts for outside development, displacing in the process local businesses and residents.[1] Even the politics of multiculturalism have arguably helped erode the borders that once maintained these communities as ethnic enclaves, rendering their once despised differences into potential ethnic or historical attractions. At issue is the meaning of the ostensible "Latinization" of U.S. cities when the displacement of Latino populations is simultaneous and even expedited by

competition btwn big companies & local businesses

this very process. At stake is whether El Barrio remains primarily Latino, becomes gentrified, or—in the eyes of many, and wistfully offsetting this binary vision—develops into a gentrified but Latino stronghold.

In part, these dynamics are not at all new. Latino/a communities have long been outcomes of struggles between developers and residents' resistance practices for space (Acuña 1988; Villa 2000; Leclerc et al. 1999). This is true of East Harlem, a major target of urban renewal policies since the 1940s. After all, gentrification—whether called renewal, revitalization, upgrading, or uplifting—always involves the expansion and transformation of neighborhoods through rapid economic investment and population shifts, and yet it is equally implicated with social inequalities (Delaney 1999; Logan and Molotch 1988; Neil Smith 1996; Williams 1988). While a complex and multifaceted process, it is also characterized by the re-signification of neighborhoods to be rendered attractive and marketable to new constituencies through the development of museums, tourist destinations, and other entertainment venues that characterize global cities like New York (Zukin 1995; Judd and Feinstein 1999; Lin 1998). I suggest, however, that the specificity of contemporary processes of gentrification and neoliberal policies pose challenging questions about the operations of culture in the spatial politics of contemporary cities, and about the growing interplay between culture as ethnicity and as marketable industry. Moreover struggles over El Barrio can help reveal the place and prospects for Latinos in the neoliberal city, particularly in communities where they have had a long history and continue to be a visible majority.

I am especially concerned with the intersections between current development initiatives and people's dreams and aspirations to place. I suggest that veiled in culture—and intricately invested in issues of class and consumption—proposals for tourism, home-ownership programs, and even the EZ become implicated with people's ethnic and class identities in multiple and contradictory ways. As such, they prompt questions about the intersection of culture, ethnicity, class, and consumption in development debates, while underscoring that so-called race-neutral policies are never devoid of racial and ethnic considerations. For instance, central to current transformations in El Barrio is the cleansing and disassociation of the area from its marginal past, processes that many residents have in fact contributed to as part of their upwardly mobile aspirations for themselves and for El Barrio. By supporting consumption and entertainment projects, such as museums and home-ownership programs, residents are furthering gentrification and increasing prices in East Harlem, thereby hindering their own future claims to the area. A closer look at people's embrace of these projects, and of the same discourse of marketing and business that seem to threaten El Barrio and its history, however, shows motivations and aspirations at play that are different from those promoted by current developments. For one, it is the prospect of bridging culture as industry and as ethnicity that heartens residents' efforts, that is, a longing to align economic empowerment with particularized identities. Despite neoliberalism's supposedly race- and ethnicity-free tenets, dreams of economic empowerment are thus never devoid of distinct racial and ethnic aspirations. People's engagements with contemporary projects reveal as much about the intricacies of gentrification and the neoliberal policies that currently fuel it as they do of this community's history and aspirations (cultural, political, economically, and otherwise) in a rapidly changing landscape. This work sorts through similar disjunctions in order to critically assess the workings of the neoliberal city in light of East Harlemites' continuous claims for representation and place.

Strategies of marketing and re-signification are as central to the transformation of landscapes as they are to people's negotiations and contestations of space. Culture will thus surface as an important resource of development, and as a significant challenge. In this way, I wish to complicate dominant frameworks used to talk about gentrification and displacement, where culture and discourses of identity are primarily seen as defiant challenges to gentrification, not as resources that can be situationally put to its service. In particular, I explore how Puerto Rican and Latino culture and discourses of Latinidad figure as both objects of and challenges to entrepreneurial strategies and processes of gentrification.[2] These are dynamics that have reverberations wherever "Latinized" cities are pitted against processes of gentrification, where there is little choice but to maneuver among entrepreneurial-based urban developments, whose control, this book shows, is beyond people's everyday influence.

My focus on Latinos is purposeful and part of a growing literature intended to disturb the dominant tenet of urban studies, where issues of race and ethnicity are consistently subsumed to a black-and-white paradigm that veils the complex multiethnic/multiracial dilemmas of contemporary cities. Public discussions of gentrification in Harlem, for instance, continually subsume East Harlem into Harlem, erasing the significant number of Latino populations in the greater Harlem area, not to mention the centrality of El Barrio's Latino history among Puerto Ricans and Latinos, who, at more than 52 percent, are the largest population segment in East Harlem.[3] Indeed, the meaning of East Harlem to Latinos, especially to Puerto Ricans, is similar to African American perceptions of Harlem, the "Black capital of the world," even if this meaning is not as widely known beyond the borders of El Barrio. Geographical definitions of East Harlem, however, vary according to political or planning designations, though for the purposes of this work East Harlem will be defined as it was understood by most of my informants: bounded by Ninety-sixth and 142nd streets, Fifth Avenue, and the East River.[4] This is a section that is included in the Manhattan Community District designations, but is not defined solely on these administrative bases.[5] But beyond its geographical limits, El Barrio is defined in relation to its Puerto Rican, and increasingly, Latino history, as well as in relation to West and Central Harlem, the well known Black culture stronghold to the west, and in relation to the upscale and mostly white neighborhood of the Upper East Side to the south. These rigid racial/spatial identifications prevailed in people's discussions even though in practice these boundaries were always more fluid. This work focuses primarily on Puerto Ricans and Latinos and their claims to El Barrio, but as I am also intent on elucidating the intersection of race, ethnicity, and processes of gentrification, I will also touch on intra-Latino relations, and relations among Latinos, African Americans, and other residents of El Barrio. I am concerned mostly with the specificity of current racial, ethnic, and spatial conflicts in the area, which I suggest become exacerbated by the cultural bases of many contemporary development initiatives at the very time that intraethnic and racial alliances among minorities are most impending and most needed.

El Barrio/East Harlem is a key site to examine these dynamics, given the area's renown as a symbol of Latinidad and its contested public meanings disseminated in the social science literature and in the media at large. A community with a long, multicultural immigrant history, as formerly a Jewish, Eastern European, and Italian enclave, East Harlem's Latino/a identity spans the early 1900s and peaks in the 1950s with the massive immigration of Puerto Ricans spurred by the island's industrialization program and the government-sanctioned migration of destitute agricultural workers into the States (Andreu Iglesias 1984; Sánchez-Korrol 1983). Soon thereafter East Harlem became a chief example of ghetto culture, an identity consolidated through representations in the media and in the social sciences literature. The archetype ethnic enclave, or the "island within the city" and the paragon of Puerto Ricans' "culture of poverty," East Harlem is also the site of numerous anthropological studies of lower-income urban enclaves, as well as of journalistic exposes of crime, urban blight, and poverty.[6]   *pg 216*

Conversely, El Barrio is also the nostalgically celebrated barrio of Puerto Rican fiction writers, and the site of transnationally important Puerto Rican events, such as Puerto Rican festivals and landmarks ranging from *casitas* (brightly colored "little houses" evoking Caribbean architecture) to murals to fiction, each serving as a recourse of identity for Puerto Ricans in and beyond New York.[7] El Barrio is also home to key images of "urban" Latino culture, often appropriated as background in Jennifer Lopez music videos or *Sports Illustrated* modeling shoots, and most recently, the backdrop to Fox's controversial new ghettocentric Latino-themed comedy show *Luis*. Most important, the area continues to serve as a reservoir of immigrants and vulnerable workers. It is home to one of the largest concentrations of Mexicans, the fastest growing immigrant group in the United States. The neighborhood's past and present thus provide key sites in which to explore the re-signification of ethnicity and marginality as well as the different interests now vested in struggles over El Barrio/East Harlem, which involve claims to physical space and the shaping of the past, present, and future meanings of the area. Such struggles are already evident in the emergent names circulated for the area, each registering contesting claims to space, a common index of the gentrifying process (Mele 2000). Names as varied as "Upper Yorkville"

From industrialization to Ghetto Culture to Culture of poverty and "Upper Carnegie Hill," which link East Harlem to the bordering up-scale neighborhood of the Upper East Side, or alternatively, "Yukieville," which mocks such attempts, increasingly complement the more traditional and still debated names of El Barrio, Spanish Harlem, and East Harlem. This work will use the area's official and colloquial name of East Harlem and El Barrio interchangeably, though a recurrent concern is to sort through the politics and the claims embedded in the growing preference among Puerto Rican and Latino residents for "El Barrio" as part of political statements of assertion in the face of gentrification.

Adding to my interest in East Harlem is the recent development and expediency of social transformations in the area amid continued poverty and inequality. Some numbers are illustrative here. Following a consistent decline since the 1970s, East Harlem's population grew for the first time throughout the 1990s to stand at 117,743 in the 2000 census; the number of housing units built in the area also increased. And while still lagging behind the medium household income for New York City ($38,293), East Harlem's medium grew to $21,295. This represents the most significant rise in a figure that had been lagging in the low and mid-teens for decades. Similar increases are seen in residents' levels of educational attainment: Although lagging behind greater Manhattan rates, high school graduation rates (56 percent of the population in 2000) show steady increases since the 1980s. The inequalities are particularly stark the closer one gets to the affluent Upper East Side, with some census tracks displaying among the greatest income gaps in the entire city between the affluent and the poor (Scott 2003). Once known as a decaying neighborhood, East Harlem is no longer an overflow of vacant lots and buildings. Nevertheless, poverty rates in the area have remained high, at 36.9 percent in 2000, as opposed to 21.2 percent for the city, with 36.7 percent of population in income support, as opposed to 19.3 percent for the entire city, and unemployment at 17.1 percent as opposed to 8.5 for the city. These numbers are likely to show increases in years to come as a result of New York City's growing fiscal crisis and ensuing cuts in social services. A major target of urban renewal policies, East Harlem has one of the largest concentrations of public housing in New York and the fewest number of homeowners: 93.6 percent of the population are renters, among the highest numbers in Manhattan. Overall, East Harlem's population is highly vulnerable to diminished social welfare and the privatization of government services and highly susceptible to shifts in rents and to changes in public housing legislation.[8] Such is the context in which these chapters unfold.

NEOLIBERALISM: CULTURE, CONSUMPTION, AND CLASS

There is now a significant amount of work on the many interrelated global, social, and economic forces affecting transformations in urban environments and the processes of gentrification. Neil Smith, in particular, has been central in assessing how housing rental markets create rent gaps that trigger cycles of disinvestment, reinvestment, and gentrification; "frontier" metaphors are crucial to sustaining these developments (Neil Smith 1996). Research has pointed to the characteristics of different housing stocks available (for instance, brownstones versus tenements), and how a neighborhood's history may influence its ensuing development (Plunz 1990; Abu-Lughod 1994). Attention has also been focused on the role of governmental policies as catalysts for gentrification (Sites 1994; Smith 1996). New York City policies favoring the privatization of public land and housing stock, for instance, have been extremely influential in East Harlem. Indeed, spatial transformations involve varied and complementary processes affecting the built environment: social control through legal/juridical implements and ideological control through cultural and informational institutions and representations. These are all part of the barrioization processes impacting everyday barriology, recently described by Villa (2000), always at play though taking on distinct manifestations in everyday economies. Unchanged is their unequal nature: far from a natural process, gentrification is fueled by specific policies and forces favoring some groups, forces, and entities over others.

I am especially concerned with neoliberal policies favoring the deregulation and privatization of social services, including public housing, education, welfare, the arts, and thereby favoring the middle classes and a consumption ethos that is increasingly pressuring residents in El Barrio. By "neoliberalism" I am referring to the rubric of economic and urban development policies that favor state deregulation, that is, a decrease in state involvement accompanied by privatization and free market approaches, all in the guise of fostering more efficient technologies of government.[9] Since the 1980s, similar policies involving tax incentives to the private sector, as in today's EZs, have consistently replaced publicly financed community-based development strategies as the dominant urban development strategy. The preeminence and diversity of these policies is evident today, ranging from those encouraging partnerships between nonprofit and private entities, as in the merge between nonprofit companies sponsoring private developers in housing projects (discussed in chapter 1), to those that aim at reshaping nonprofit organizations along business lines, as in the EZ's Culture Industry Investment Fund (discussed in chapter 3). Likewise, they may involve the transfer of managerial and decision-making services to private corporations, as in the involvement of for-profit educational corporations in the development of charter schools (discussed in chapter 4). In each case, a business mantra and discourse of sustainability, viability, profits, and results trump those of social equality, promising much while leaving East Harlem's residents with higher rents and fewer services, though never with fewer dreams for themselves and for El Barrio.

Within this larger context, I am especially concerned with the material uses of "culture," and with the claims to space established and contested on its bases. Neoliberalism is often connected with homelessness, poverty, residential segregation, and other indexes of inequality, yet "culture," a well-known instrument of entrepreneurship used by government and businesses, a medium to sell, frame, structure, claim, and reclaim space, is closely implicated in such processes and always in demand of closer scrutiny (Fincher and Jacobs 1998; Gregory 1999; Sassen 1998; Rotenberg and McDonogh 1993; Zukin 1995). I place culture in quotation marks to foreground the variety of manifestations within the range of cultural entrepreneurial strategies and discourses promoted by corporations, residents, and government policies. These are not fully problematized and distinguished in the literature, where culture is oftentimes conflated with such disparate domains as heritage, architecture, high art, advertising, malls, and entertaining venues, in ways that do more to veil than to expose the different dynamics affecting its production, circulation, and consumption. Obviously, *culture* is an extremely contentious term, and my purpose is not to document each and every one of this concept's reverberations or definitions.[10] Instead, I call attention to two central treatments, both of which are constituted and deployed materially and discursively to frame and contest space, and are recurrent in debates over gentrification, as they are throughout U.S. cities. First is the equation of "culture" with manifestations of ethnic or racial identity, such as Black or Puerto Rican or Latino, and treated as a goal or an end in itself that can and should be safeguarded, promoted, marketed, or undermined in regards to specific interests. This is culture as articulation and "boundary of difference" (Appadurai 1996) among other accounts of culture that treat it not as a given but as socially constituted, objectified, and mobilized for a variety of political ends. Second, "culture" is treated as an object of entertainment and industry and a conduit of progress and development devoid of distinct identifications, though always enmeshed in specific ends. This is the definition at the heart of Zukin's insightful discussion of the symbolic economy of finance, media, and entertainment that dominates contemporary urban economies (Zukin 1995), akin also to Yudice's description of culture as an "expedient resource" for socioeconomic amelioration (Yudice 2003). This is "culture" masked in attending discourses of globalization and treated as a medium of uplift, industry, entrepreneurship, and progress. The parallels with the abiding tension between particularizing and universalizing definitions of culture—the former evoking plurality and difference and the latter a civilizing project, or more specifically for the case at hand, an entrepreneurial project—will not be lost to anthropologists.

These different treatments of culture are easily more complementary than contradictory. Even when mobilized for opposing ends, they can become equally caught up in the same dynamics of privatized development. After all, manifestations of ethnicity and cultural difference within a given state are never entirely free of its dominant ideological canons, which, this work shows, increasingly prioritize what I describe here as "marketable ethnicity." What is very different, I suggest, are the aspirations and identities that sustain such different uses of culture and the claims and politics that are communicated by these different treatments. I contrast, in particular, the goals and objectives of marketing culture for economic development that favors ethnicity cleansed from ethnic memories and politics with those that are part of larger assertions of El Barrio's identity of place in resistance to gentrification. Part of persistent struggles over the use- or exchange-value of space, which are always at play in gentrifying contexts, these contestations remind us that people and places are never easily reducible into commodities, even in a heightened privatizing context (Logan and Moloch 1988). I further expose the inequalities regarding who can or cannot participate more or less easily in the economy of culture, as will be evident when I contrast the ease and profitability of racially unmarked developers and projects with the difficulties encountered by East Harlemites seeking economic control of their culture. In other words, I seek to expose the hierarchies that are fostered and maintained in the creation of value, and to complicate class with processes of racialization, and vice versa. My goal then is not to impugn marketing and consumption—realms I have elsewhere recognized to provide openings and spaces to marginalized groups (Dávila 1997, 2001a)—but rather to delve deeper into the politics behind the marketing of space. In contrast to the uncritical promotion, celebration, and emphasis on culture as a tool of local/national and even global economic development, I expose the contradictions and inequalities that characterize the production of marketable ethnicity. Ultimately, I show that despite the growing emphasis on the marketing of culture for economic empowerment, not all manifestations of culture are so easily rentable or consumable. In fact, El Barrio's "collective symbolic capital" (Harvey 2001) revolves around a marginalized identity that is not generally considered profitable to all parties involved in its economic development, but rather poses a hindrance to be overcome.

This predicament is clearly evident in debates over the application of the Cultural Industry Investment Fund Heritage Tourism initiative, a component of the Upper Manhattan EZ legislation. Geared toward transforming Upper Manhattan communities into tourist destinations with

cultural, entertainment, dining, and recreational attractions, this initiative has been an impetus for current discussions about how and in what
ways the area should be marketed and redefined for these ends. In reality, however, "culture" surfaces here as a veil of industry, and lacking in
cultural industries and entertainment infrastructure, Upper Manhattan
residents, particularly East Harlemites, have faced difficulty in obtaining
approval for smaller initiatives that promote the ethnic and historical
identification of their neighborhood. Discourses of economic growth,
marketing, and business, even when mobilized in preservation of El
Barrio's Puerto Rican and Latino history and identity, are never free of
contradictions.

In seeking to understand these disjunctions I start by acknowledging
that the ascendancy of neoliberal discourses and policies alongside a lack
of development alternatives have begotten especially beneficial conditions in which to align the interests of capital with the aspirations of
particularized groups. In this tenor, current urban entrepreneurship initiatives will decidedly be questioned in relation to the new forms of privatized governmentability on which they are predicated as well as foster.
Specifically, I highlight the preeminence given to consumption-based
developments within these policies, that is, to developments whose
access presupposes acquisitive power, furthering exclusions around
those with resources and those who lack them. But most significantly,
however, I point to how these policies reproduce a distinct worldview, or
the belief in what Jean and John Comaroff have recently termed a "millennial capitalism," because it "presents itself as a gospel of salvation; a
capitalism that, if rightly harnessed, is invested with the capacity wholly
to transform the universe of the marginalized and disempowered"
(Comaroff and Comaroff 2000, 292). This occurs simultaneously with a
decrease in government services, total disbanding of welfare and support
services for the poor, rendering neighborhoods like East Harlem ripe for
furthering privatization as the only recourse for social services and entitlements. In other words, I consider the material context of contemporary
transformations, but given the particularities of the current neoliberal
moment, I primarily foreground the symbolic realm and its multiple
entanglements in the selling of El Barrio.

Nothing is more central to these dynamics than issues of class and consumption. This coupling, as contemporary research repeatedly explicates, is extraordinarily relevant given consumption's preeminence for defining and projecting class identities and aspirations (Daniel Miller 1995; McCracken 1988). For as many debates as have been sustained and triggered by the concept of class, we know that class is foremost about social inequalities, and about the distinctions that are mobilized to express and maintain the boundaries that sustain them. Ethnographic studies of class have documented that contrary to the dominant view that class distinctions become irrelevant, leveled in advanced capitalist economies, people do operationalize and define class distinctions in myriad ways and actively perform and discuss class on a daily basis (O'Dougherty 2002; Prince 2002b; Jackson 2001). But even when people are not willing to discuss class or define themselves in this manner, such as by favoring nationalist or panethnic forms of identification as Puerto Ricans and Latinos, this does not imply that they do not experience, perform, and define class memberships through their actions or that it does not affect their outlooks and aspirations. Consumption is critical to such operations, though I suggest not solely in terms of actual acquisition, which is always affected by income and purchasing power, but also in terms of position, outlook, and openness to specific types of consumption. Here I am in agreement with Maureen O'Dougherty's observation that analyses of middle classes "suffer from excessive realism and inattention to the social imaginary. Unlike class in theory, a good part of the middle-class experience seems to be immaterial, a state of mind" (2002, 9). This is where the realm of dreams and the imagination come in. As we shall see, consumption-based developments (charter schools, home-ownership programs) were repeatedly equated with choice, entertainment, and upward mobility, associations that in turn coalesced with people's upwardly mobile aspirations, many times independently of whether people could realistically purchase these "benefits." I call attention to these disjunctions, not to impute Puerto Ricans' and Latinos' desire to consume, or even less to invoke the tired and totalistic critiques of consumer culture as the greatest threat to social equity. As Elizabeth Chin (2001) explains, the involvement of disenfranchised groups in consumer culture has long been pathologized as aberrant or apolitical, rendering any critique of consumption that is blinded of the structural forces that mediate such consumption largely misguided. In this vein, my goal is to extrapolate the intersection of culture, class, and consumption, foregrounding the premises consumption seemingly entailed for the attainment of dreams and visions of place, particularly of the past and future of El Barrio. These dynamics affected people's stances to different projects, including their reasons for staying in, or for leaving or relocating to, El Barrio. Thus following Gregory (1998), I am also concerned with whether contemporary projects and urban policies are aligned with globalization, progress, localized pasts, and identities, and with how these framing patterns affect the ways in which people maneuver among the many state, private, and local forces affecting livelihood, the built environment, and even their identities. Conversely, I explore whether East Harlemites are articulating their identities and advancing their concerns as Puerto Ricans, Latinos, or in class, community, place, or global terms. I suggest that these modes and positions reveal the orthodoxies about culture, identity, and development, and about the area's state and future that are currently being advanced and contested in East Harlem.

Since my primary focus is on Puerto Ricans, I should note that as U.S. citizens—part of the island's colonial history—their migration to the United States and to El Barrio has been constant and ongoing, though many have migrated back to the island or moved elsewhere beginning in the 1960s, peaking in the 1970s, and continuing throughout the 1980s (New York City 1994). Changes in New York's economy, such as a move toward service jobs providing fewer opportunities to unskilled workers, have been linked to this trend (Cordero-Guzmán et al. 2001). A key, though less-documented, impetus for this out-migration that is especially relevant to this study is the dominant association of El Barrio with urban blight and of upward mobility with moving away from El Barrio to Puerto Rico or the suburbs of Connecticut, New Jersey, Florida, and elsewhere, leading to the decentralization of the Puerto Rican community. As such, it is important to keep in mind that El Barrio's role as the symbolic stronghold for Puerto Ricans is intrinsically bound up with the contradictory evaluation that ethnic neighborhoods have historically commanded among the upwardly mobile. Similar dynamics are documented for the Black middle class in West and Central Harlem (Monique Taylor 2002). Interestingly, while the Black middle class has been the subject of important studies, the Latino middle class is only beginning to receive comparable scholarly consideration, a void that is undoubtedly tied to the hyperprivileging of "culture" and language as a defining element of Latinidad.[11] Lessons from studies on issues of class and gentrification among Puerto Ricans and Latinos in Chicago and on the Black middle classes, including some focusing on neighboring Harlem, however, are illustrative here. These include: (1) the importance of appreciating internal diversity; (2) their ambivalent position to ethnic-and racially specific communities coupled with the overt and covert racism that often motivates relocation and interest in these very communities; and finally, (3) the continuous conflation of racial and class identities mediating the relative value of "status" (Jackson 2001; Patillo-McCoy 2000; Pérez 2001; Ramos-Zayas 2003; Gregory 1998; Prince 2002a; Monique Taylor 2002). Similarly, these works point to the relevance of class and cultural capital as important variables shaping how Puerto Ricans experience, consume, and interpret El Barrio. In particular, the ways El Barrio is experienced by Puerto Rican and Latino intellectuals and activists and the most destitute workers can sometimes converge but at other times be sharply at odds. These positions have implications for people's awareness of, and experiences with, the state's distribution policies, with the promises seemingly offered by new entertainment and consumption venues, and with their stance toward different development projects and transformations in the area.

THE ECONOMY OF RACE

Feeding the current interest in the transformations of U.S. cities is the realization that cities are central to understanding the cultural politics of multiculturalism, the formation of new forms of participatory politics, and the potential realization of a just multicultural society (Holston and Appadurai 1999; Gregory 1998; Sanjek 2000; Sassen 1998). These issues are especially brought to the forefront by Latino populations, given their rapid growth, their concentration in cities, and their public visibility as the "new majority" in places like New York. However, not until recently have scholars paid attention to Latinos in their study of contemporary transformations in the global metropolis. The result is the problematic disjunction that currently exists between Latino studies, urban studies, and the anthropological literature on the city (Davis 2001). Which is not to say that Latino scholars have not been informed by urban studies literature, but that the latter have less often taken Latinos or Latino studies into account. Consider, for instance, that while some of the most theoretically influential studies on gentrification have focused on New York City, most notably, the Lower East Side, seldom have these studies focused on the fate of Latinos or the uses of Latinidad, even when Latinos have maintained a historical and continued presence in the areas under study (for example, Abu-Lughod 1994; Mele 1998).

There is nevertheless a growing literature examining the city as the space of Latinization, pointing to how urban economic and political transformations affect or contribute to such processes (Cordero et al. 2001; Davis 2001; Lao and Dávila 2001; Cruz 1998; Jones-Correa 1998; Haslip-Viera 1996; Pérez 2001; Portes and Stepic 1993). Rather than as background to larger studies, cities and neighborhoods are increasingly considered as spaces/places in and of themselves, whose social structuring should be studied in relation to the range of wider social processes affecting Latinos' place in the broader society (Ševčenko 2001; Aponte Parés 1998, 1999; Villa 2000). Most specifically, work on Latino Los Angeles has alerted us to the local and global processes affecting urban community development and the politics of space (Leclerc et al. 1999; Valle and Torres 2000). Work in Chicago, where Mexicans and Puerto Ricans have historically lived side by side, has also revealed the intra-Latino relations that are increasingly central to their politics and exchanges with the many state and private forces involved in urban policy planning and community development. In particular these writings have exposed some of the struggles these groups have engaged in to claim their right to space and to their communities, showing the centrality of discourses of Latinidad, race, and ethnicity to these claims (Flores-González 2001; Pérez 2001; Ramos-Zayas 2003; Toro-Morn 2001). A similar interethnic focus is demanded by the context of East Harlem, a neighborhood that has been undergoing rapid change and a growing diversification of its Latino populations, rendering it, as other New York neighborhoods, into a key site for analyzing the inclusions and exclusions of contemporary Latino politics.

An important point worth considering here is the meaning of power and politics on which the debates are being waged. Students of cultural politics are well aware that the institutionalized settings for debating issues of urban planning and policies—such as community boards, public hearings, and the EZ workshop with which I started this work—are not the only spaces for defining politics. In fact, this work shows that they are questionable for bringing about participation and representation of minority populations. Neither are they conducive to examining racial and ethnic convergence among groups, or to exposing their give and take and cooperation. As an important and growing literature on intra- and interethnic relations shows, these dynamics have long been present though they are oftentimes most evident in the realm of popular culture and everyday life (Burgos 2001; Flores 2000; Rivera 2003). However, institutional spaces are not only the ones that most affect and translate to access to urban policies and economic resources, but also those least likely to be the subject of ethnographic and critical analysis. Readers are therefore warned. Competition and particularized ethnic assertions, not cooperation and openings, far abound in these pages, all connected to the institutional space and neoliberal context where these discussions take place. Examining these spaces is central, I believe, not only for elucidating the specific challenges posed by neoliberal policies to particular ethnic and racial groupings, but most important, for fostering and maintaining future coalitions.

Pivotal in this regard is the exchange between Puerto Ricans and African Americans. As said, Blacks and Puerto Ricans share important points of interaction, activism, and collaboration at the level of cultural creation and political activism in New York City and beyond (Burgos 2001; Cruz 1998; Flores 1993, 2000; James 1999; Rivera 2003). Because of their African legacy, many Puerto Ricans stand at the crossroads of U.S. racial/ethnic boundaries in ways that make it difficult, if not oftentimes irrelevant, to differentiate between the two, as is also the case with

Dominicans and other Caribbean and Black Latinos. Puerto Ricans' colonial status and history of racialization in the city also render them a
racialized minority closer to African Americans than to other Latino
groupings in the city's racial and ethnic hierarchy, a position increasingly
shared by Dominicans (Flores 2000; Grosfoguel and Georas 2001; Urciuoli
1996). This is why, against what I call marketable ethnicity, I have repeatedly made reference to treatments and manifestations of race and ethnicity in El Barrio without clearly differentiating among these two social
constructs. I recognize that idioms of race and ethnicity signal opposing
forms of insertion into the nation: ethnicity is recognized to index a
"safer" form of inclusion, whereas race is always about hierarchy and historically persistent and unredeemable difference (Omi-Winant 1994;
Williams 1989; Urciuoli 1996). Yet the valence of these distinct categories
is ultimately predicated on the ability of particular groupings to incorporate into normative conflations of race/class/nation that have historically
limited the "safe" incorporation of the least assimilable, and hence more
racialized groupings. Such is the case, I argue, for my primarily Puerto
Rican and Latino/a informants and for the particularizing idioms of identity (be it around ethnicity or nationality) they deploy against the preference for more marketable and safe manifestations of culture. This is so,
notwithstanding that on account of class, cultural capital, citizenship status, education, color, and race among other variables, different members
of these groupings are more or less subject or likely to free themselves
from particularized practices of racialization and political and economic
subordination.[12] My usage of "Black" and "white" responds to this reality. In this text I capitalize "Black" but not "white" because "Black" and
"Latino" operate in a similar manner in East Harlem: as marginalized
identity categories blurring ethnic and national identifications—as well
as other social differences of class, education, citizenship status—that,
while historically and socially prescribed, are politically activated to
denote associations, establish political alliances, and wrest shrinking resources within the neoliberal city.[13]

Yet Black and Latino relationships have never been exempt from contention, tensions that a general lack of documentation have made even
more difficult to ascertain, understand, and supersede.[14] Writers have

repeatedly documented how racial and nationalist ideologies at play in Latin America and the United States have affected Black and Latino relations in the United States (James 1999; Jones-Correa 1998; Herbstein 1978). Most relevant to this work is an area that is well recognized to have mediated relationships between Blacks and Latinos since the 1960s: the consolidation of cultural pluralism and distributive programs (Jennings and Rivera 1984; Torres 1995; Aponte Parés 1999). By providing the infrastructure for local control of resources, ethnic-based distributive programs were pivotal to the development of Puerto Rican politics in New York, and to the control of local electoral politics by Puerto Rican politicians in East Harlem throughout the 1970s and 1980s. The consolidation of the racial-based paradigm has polarized the groups' relationship since the start of urban renewal projects and still mediates debates over space and development in the area.

In the past decades, however, while both groups continue to lag behind whites, Latinos have achieved considerably less power and influence in New York City electoral politics relative to Blacks (Sales and Bush 2000). Again, these are not mutually exclusive groups or categories, as shown by the growing circulation of the categories of white non-Hispanic or Black Latino after the last census. Nevertheless, important differences have been documented in the electoral realm, where as a group, New York Latinos are repeatedly shown to lag in political representation relative to their numbers.[15] On this issue, writers point to African Americans' earlier involvement in the city's economy and local politics, their attainment of federal and government jobs, and their development in the city of strong politically indigenous institutions, such as Black churches, social agencies, housing groups, and local economic development corporations (Torres 1995; Falcón 2001). Issues of language and citizenship have also impaired Latinos' political power, especially among recent and first generation immigrants. Last but not least, the U.S. dominant Black-and-white racial binary, where Asian Americans and Latinos continue to be rendered forever foreign, is also not unrelated to the existing exclusions and lack of recognition Puerto Ricans and Latinos have attained at the level of electoral politics. All of these factors coalesce in the lower voter registration and turn-out patterns of Latinos vis-à-vis "Blacks" and "whites."[16] This situation is evident in East Harlem where at the time of this writing, African Americans held leadership positions in all areas involved in urban development (the chair of the community board, the district councilman, borough president, and congressman are all African American), bringing about important tensions between these communities. A caveat here, and a little-known fact instructive of the complex exchange between Puerto Ricans and African Americans, is that two of East Harlem's most important politicians, Assemblyman Adam Clayton Powell IV and Congressman Charles Rangel, are in fact—or at least locally reputed to be—of mixed Puerto Rican and African American parentage. However, each has nonetheless become strictly associated with different constituencies: Rangel is the preeminent and nationally recognized Black politician, while Powell, who was born in Puerto Rico, is locally recognized as Puerto Rican. However, as the son of the legendary Black Harlem politician Adam Clayton Powell Jr., Powell is also situationally associated with both constituencies.[17]

Relations between Puerto Ricans and other Latinos are not less complex. As one of the oldest Latino subgroups in New York City, Puerto Ricans are considerably familiar with Latinidad, a category that they have long helped further and use strategically for political purposes. Yet the use and subjective acceptance of categories so invested in cultural struggles never correlates so easily. The case of Puerto Ricans in El Barrio, for instance, shows that those most implicated in struggles to create what are now primarily conceived as "Latino" institutions and spaces are also the most compromised when subsumed into a Latino construct, particularly in the current neoliberal context so adverse to politicized ethnic claims. Still, Puerto Ricans are not the only ones mistrustful of Latinidad in El Barrio. This will be evident in my discussion of Mexican residents, who I chose to focus on because of their rapid population growth and visibility in El Barrio. For example, the section of 116th Street that has been named after Puerto Rico's first elected governor, Luis Muñoz Marín, is now brimming with primarily Mexican businesses and flags, a vivid example of the rapid transformations in the area's demographics and landscape. These transformations have been accompanied by tensions between Mexican and Puerto Rican populations, traced to their different

histories, citizenship status, and/or self- conception as residents, racialized minorities, or temporary immigrants (Bourgois 1995; González 2000;
Robert Smith 1997). The relationship between Mexicans and Puerto
Ricans, however, echoes that of Blacks and Puerto Ricans, at least in
regards to a history of cooperation and competition. Pressures to adjust
to dominant categories of Latinidad, on the other hand, make Mexicans
and Puerto Ricans experience analogous political losses as a result of the
area's gentrification.

In this work I am unable to address the myriad variables affecting contemporary relations across Latino groups or between Blacks and Latinos
in El Barrio, but I hope I can nonetheless elucidate aspects of these -
multiple and complex relationships as they pertain to current policies for
urban development, and these communities' continuous demand for
space, representation, equity, and empowerment. One goal is to expose
the effects of the neoliberal context, where in contrast to the 1960s and
1970s, struggles are waged insidiously in the arena of consumption and
national and international recognition in culture and tourism, as minority
communities are being asked to reconstitute their public identity for
tourist aims. In this context, careful considerations of the multiple manifestations of culture and of the objectives and politics for which it is deployed are most needed. Thus while in full agreement and recharged
with current calls to supersede race relations paradigms, in which benefits to one group are seen to entail losses to another, I maintain that a disavowal of race and ethnicity, or of the "messiness" of identity politics, is
not yet warranted. After all, it is not the eradication of race or ethnicity
per se, but their organization, management, and direction that are the
ultimate aims of all hegemonic processes (Williams 1989; San Juan 2002).
And this management can differ widely according to time, context, institution, space, and location; neoliberalism has been known to foster multiculturalism throughout Latin America (Hale 2002), while the celebration
of ethnic difference in U.S. marketing is commonplace (Halter 2000;
Dávila 2001a). Generally in the present context, however, writers have
pointed to the ascendancy of the ideology of color blindness as the dominant U.S. post–civil rights public stance and discourse on race. Accordingly the existence and institutional bases of racial inequalities are denied,

as is the political significance of race derided as exclusionary identity politics (Bonilla Silva 2001; Guinier and Torres 2002). The contradictory disavowal of ethnicity as discourse of political representation in favor of culture as enterprise is intrinsically tied to this position. But so is the rise in nationalist and ethnic revivals in El Barrio that emerge as primary resistance strategies, responses that may simultaneously hamper the prospects for cross-ethnic and cross-racial identifications based on mutual experiences of inequality. Still, I suggest that it is not ethnic politics per se that present the greatest perils to East Harlemites' longing for place. They in fact represent an important recourse against trends prioritizing marketable ethnicity. Instead, I question the ascendancy of neoliberal tenets and logics that not only attempt to erase race and ethnicity as variables of social inequality, but also promote a general distancing from the poor, the destitute, and working classes, and always with little consideration of ethnicity and race. Only by foregrounding this larger framework can the prospects for lasting intraethnic and racial coalitions in East Harlem, or the implications of the so-called Latinization of U.S. cities, be considered.

As is the case for many New York–based Puerto Ricans, East Harlem/El Barrio is a community I have long gravitated to for cultural, political, and social events. The writing of this book is therefore informed and motivated by my previous experiences with a community I consider to be politically and symbolically important for the history of Puerto Ricans and Latinos both in New York City and beyond. Yet the material for this book is necessarily more narrow. Specifically, I draw on ethnographic research carried out intermittently from May 2001 to December 2002, which is based on attendance at community board meetings, public hearings, and activities of different cultural and civic organizations; I have also interviewed past, current, and new residents of East Harlem, focusing on gentrification and change.[18] I conducted follow-up interviews throughout the summer of 2003. All quotations cited were made during this time unless otherwise noted. In particular, I focused on sites of strategic importance for looking at current development initiatives in El Barrio, and for exposing the nuanced discourses and operations of power as manifested in decisions over development. The community board, whose volunteer members are appointed by the borough president and by the local city councilman, was especially relevant as the local representative body to the city on matters of land use, zoning, municipal service delivery, and planning. It is in these forums that developers present their proposals, that politicians address East Harlem as a "community," and that invitations to other events, such as hearings, electoral debates, and cultural activities, are circulated. In this way, what follows is not an account of East Harlem's many layers of undocumented histories attesting to the different ethnic groups, political movements, and trends evolving inside it. I do not pretend to represent the totality of East Harlem's history, whether at the level of representations or practices; nor is this a much needed history of Puerto Rican politics in the area, though traces of those stories will surface here. Instead the book is organized around a series of interconnected chapters focusing on a range of sites where current struggles over space are simultaneously, even if disparately, taking place from debates over housing policies to tourism to advertising. My goal, nonetheless, is that the book will provide an entry point into contemporary struggles over space and representation taking place in traditionally Latino/a neighborhoods like El Barrio and will perhaps be an incentive for others to take on more historical and ethnographic work on the largely undocumented history of Puerto Rican and Latino/a neighborhoods in and beyond New York.

I start with a brief overview of Puerto Ricans' struggle for housing equity in East Harlem to establish how a key index of gentrification—a diminishing market for affordable housing—is affecting their dreams of place in the area. I pay close attention to how the area's history and cultural identity is being deployed by developers and residents and how, despite their differing aspirations for the area, they end up advancing a similar development vision and ideology. New governmental policies favoring the privatization of land and property simultaneously intersect with and depart from Puerto Rican and Latino dreams of empowerment and tap into these dreams in multiple ways.

Chapter 2 establishes the symbolic value of East Harlem as a putatively "inalienable" space for Puerto Ricans and Latinos in and beyond El Barrio in order to delve deeper into the stakes of current development strategies from the perspective of my primarily Puerto Rican informants. Space is never immutable or fixed, but an outcome of social relations and processes of social contest to stabilize meaning and particularize identities, that is, to secure "the identity of places" (Massey 1994). This chapter discusses how these dynamics take place in El Barrio, such as through its historical representation and objectification as a Latino space, and through the work of Puerto Rican activists intent on marketing and promoting El Barrio as a direct response to the area's gentrification. The ensuing inclusions and exclusions that result from definitions of "community" are part of these place-making strategies, which I nevertheless suggest are key resources against attempts to de-ethnicize the areas that accompany most current developments. Conceptual linkages of culture and place, that is of "Latin culture" and "El Barrio," are never the sole product of processes of cultural objectification, but of material inequalities and historical exclusions in housing policies, jobs, and services that have long shaped ethnic and working-class enclaves throughout U.S. cities. By calling attention to the symbolic and representational processes that have tied race, ethnicity, and place in East Harlem within the public imagination, I do not deny the multiple material processes shaping El Barrio as a Latino space, but rather, account for the value of these representations in the symbolic economy of contemporary cities.

Chapters 3 and 4 describe two cultural projects that foreground the multiple reverberations of culture in contemporary development initiatives: the Cultural Industry Investment Fund of the Upper Manhattan EZ legislation; and the failed Edison Project, which involved the development of East Harlem's first corporate headquarters, the move of the Museum for African Art from Soho to East Harlem, and the development of a new charter school. Both of these projects aroused considerable contestation over the identity and public representation of East Harlem, providing good examples of the different endeavors that increasingly favor marketable ethnicity, not as a medium of inclusion or assertion but of co-optation or economic development. Specifically, these chapters expose how culture-based development initiatives adroitly build on and dissipate discourses of heritage, culture, quality, and national recognition in ways that triggered racial tensions while furthering the gentrification of

Figure 1.   Flag flying above El Barrio's landscape. In the background is "Barrio Renacimiento" (Barrio Rebirth), a mural by Manny Vega, 1980. It was painted next to a former community garden on 103rd Street that has since become an empty lot awaiting future development. Photo by Rebecca Cooney.

the area. Discourses of Puertorriqueñidad and Latinidad operated both in the strategies for obtaining acquiescence to these projects and as a basis for rejecting them as ethnicity surfaces as an always lingering and strategic component in debates and approval of these projects.

El Barrio's Mexican residents were not part of the public hearings and debates I attended, and while central to current events in El Barrio, they were largely absent from urban development debates. This situation speaks to the exclusionary bases of the planning process, and to the national and transnational scope of their concerns and politics as recent immigrants, a pattern well documented in the social science literature (Cordero et al. 2001; Jones-Correa 1998; Smith and Guarnizo 1998). Yet immigrants are also actively, and necessarily, involved in urban politics, and in forging intraethnic alliances, even if these are often tested by the transnational character of their politics and the type of concerns at the center of Mexicans' struggle for empowerment. Chapter 5 centers on this growing community: how it stakes claims to particular spaces and the alliances it makes in East Harlem. This population is also affected by neoliberal policies, though not solely those exerted upon the city by private developers or government policies, but also by the transnational policies of two nation-states for whom immigrants are both a resource and a peril. By examining debates over control of the New York Mexican Independence Parade (Desfile Mexicano de Nueva York), this chapter proposes that as recent players in urban cultural politics, immigrant groups help recharge ethnicity as political recourse and ends by considering some of the conditions and goals in which such claims may be more or less effective in the neoliberal city.

Chapter 6 examines street art and outdoor advertising in relation to the marking and marketing of Latinidad in El Barrio. It highlights a central aspect of the ethnicity/business cultural quandary that accompanies processes of gentrification: that when properly marketed, culture as ethnicity continues to be a vital recourse for particular culture industries, such as ethnic-driven advertising. It is the different ends to which "culture" is deployed, the politics that are advanced and the people and interests that are involved in the different economies that it sustains, that we should listen and pay attention to as we sort through the intricacies of contemporary cultural politics in the neoliberal city. Lastly, I offer some final words, an attempt to synthesize what the disparate projects discussed in the book may suggest about the place of culture and identity in the execution of and resistance to neoliberal strategies.

ONE Dreams of Place and Housing Struggles

"This neighborhood will be lost unless we make it ours. Look at Loisaida, that's gone," Nazario said. "All those white yuppies want to live in Manhattan, and they think Spanish Harlem is next for the taking."

Ernesto Quiñonez, *Bodega Dreams*

In *Bodega Dreams*, Ernesto Quiñonez's novel set in El Barrio, the hopeful protagonist Willie Bodega dreams of building a Latino professional class born and bred in El Barrio that, through cunning and politics, would lead all Latinos toward economic and political empowerment. A former Young Lords activist, Bodega had learned that it is only by Anglo rules, by stealing through "signing the right papers," by accumulating property, money, and power, that Latinos can get ahead in El Barrio. Foremost, Bodega is keenly aware that the 1960s are over. The government is no longer pouring money into El Barrio; white yuppies are moving in, and if Latinos want to protect their legacy and their turf, they will have to buy it, building by building. So he sets out on a buying spree with illicit funds that are put into a good cause with the help of a lawyer friend who has contacts with the city's Housing Department. But his dream—to become the second largest "slumlord" in the city of New York—comes to a quick end when he is killed by his deceitful lawyer, who is intent on taking over Bodega's reign. The lawyer is soon exposed, however, and the buildings are reclaimed by the city, leaving the briefly "empowered" Latino residents vulnerable but hopeful, propelled by Bodega's dream for a brighter future.

Written in 2000 by a young writer raised in El Barrio by Puerto Rican and Ecuadorian parents, who has expressed publicly his wish for an empowered Latino middle class to combat gentrification, *Bodega Dreams* provides a vivid display of the stakes involved in the current neoliberal moment. The context it speaks to is one where the purchase of place is presented as the only alternative for lasting power, even when the feasibility of such a dream is quickly fading. Rents are rapidly increasing, and buildings that a decade ago would have been abandoned or sold cheaply are being coveted by nonprofit investors and private speculators alike. Renamed Upper Yorkville, Upper Manhattan, or Upper Carnegie Hill, names intended to further link it to the affluent and bordering Upper East Side, East Harlem is now one of the last open frontiers for development in the city, and local residents are feeling the crunch.

Contributing to this situation is the rapid decline in federal and state housing assistance, which has greatly eroded the safety net for the urban poor in El Barrio. East Harlem has the second largest concentration of public housing units in the city, and among the largest number of households on public assistance; up to 62 percent of its population is dependent on publicly subsidized housing, making this area particularly susceptible to federal and state policy changes on public housing.[1] Two major trends have been particularly harmful to East Harlem residents. The first is the move at the federal level from direct subsidies for the construction of new affordable housing toward the fading measures such as the politically vulnerable tenant vouchers and subsidies. The second is the trend toward privatization. In New York City, this is evident in government housing policies favoring private ownership and expedited transfers of the city's housing stock to private and nonprofit developers while maintaining little responsibility over housing management and maintenance.[2] The results are higher rents and less affordable housing.

Obviously, the lack of affordable housing is not limited to East Harlem. Citywide, there is an eight-year waiting list for public housing, more than 224,000 households are waiting to receive Section 8 (federally funded) vouchers to subsidize their rents, while one quarter of New Yorkers spend more than half of their income on rent, well above the recommended cap of 30 percent (Housing First 2001). My concern here is with the urgency and potential meaning of this crunch for the identity and demographic composition of East Harlem in light of the area's growing status among developers and apartment hunters and the upwardly mobile, Bodega-like, class aspirations of Puerto Rican community leaders and activists. In this regard, I consider the seemingly puzzling fact that despite growing concerns about the invasion of "fake bohemians" and white yuppies to the area, development had attracted more enthusiasts than open critics. Many bemoaned the changes, but few cries against gentrification were being heard as "development" surfaced both as the threat and the solution.

Arguably, with some exceptions (such as the contested development of Pathmark Supermarket in the 1990s), East Harlem's development has been relatively less tangible and therefore less threatening to residents compared to that of Central and West Harlem, which is front-page news in the real estate and arts sections of local papers. This explains the excitement with which many residents received the first *New York Times* article linking East Harlem's gentrification to a "Puerto Rican rebirth in El Barrio" (Berger 2002). I would suggest, however, that East Harlem's relative prodevelopment stance can be found in the widespread embrace of a particular privatization ideology that coincides with residents' upwardly mobile aspirations while being actively conducive to the area's gentrification. Lefebvre's (1995) conceptualization of planning as ideology is relevant here: all "policies have their system of signification"; that is, they are sustained by particular ideologies that help reduce the social and historical to a distinct logic for the managing of space. A dominant planning ideology engages and accommodates both the marginal history of this community and the class-based visions of neighborhood empowerment—wherein private home ownership and consumption-based housing (housing development geared to private ownership) are equated with the promise of mobility. These associations were dominant among the different interests fueling development in the area, such as nonprofit and private developers and community activists, even though they were accompanied and promoted by different visions of community and views for East Harlem's future. Thus, for many Puerto Rican leaders, disassociating this area from its marginal history is seen as a pivotal step in their larger middle-class dream of Puerto Rican empowerment through property and the purchase of place. Theirs is a vision of El Barrio as a predominantly Puerto Rican or Latino neighborhood, anchored by a strong middle class, not unlike the dream of Willie Bodega. This upwardly mobile vision for El Barrio, however, is conveniently aligned with development enthusiasts operating in the area, although for the latter, the area's Latino identity is something to be underplayed, superseded, or else treated as a selling point, if neatly packaged into a larger multicultural identity collage.

The result is the widespread circulation of a consumption based ideology, contradictorily sustained by public policies and politically appealing discourses of "neighborhood revitalization," "community empowerment," and "nonprofit development."

HOUSING POLICIES AND STRUGGLES, PAST AND PRESENT

Housing and empowerment have long been inexorably connected in East Harlem and in government policies that appealed to people's housing aspirations and longing for place. East Harlem was a prime target for federal slum clearance under the Federal Housing Act of 1937, which led to the construction of densely populated public housing projects and to the displacement of its residents, among them Puerto Ricans who had settled in the area since the early 1900s. As Sánchez-Korrol notes, by the 1930s there were Puerto Rican settlements from around Ninety-seventh Street to 110th Street, around northern Central Park to about 125th Street, and from Third Avenue on the east to Eighth and Manhattan avenues to the west, with the largest concentration around 116th Street (Sánchez-

Korrol 1983, 61–62).[3] These areas were still shared by Irish, Italians, Jews, and African Americans at the time, though by the 1950s they were becoming primarily Puerto Rican, first around 110th and 111th streets between Park and Madison avenues, and later around the sections of 106th Street, bordering Fifth Avenue on the west and Park Avenue on the east (Meyer 1989).[4] These are the same areas that under urban renewal saw the construction of massive development projects as early as 1941, with the construction of the East River houses that inaugurated the high-rise model for public housing, and peaked throughout the 1950s and 1960s, causing widespread displacement among East Harlemites. In a pattern that surfaced in the mid-1940s, African Americans displaced Puerto Ricans by moving south and to the east from neighboring Harlem, while Puerto Ricans displaced Italians by moving to the east. Overall the area lost 17 percent of its population in the 1960s (Sexton 1965).[5] I found no statistics accounting for the number of Puerto Ricans displaced by these developments, but their numbers were likely to be great, as indicated by estimates from 1959–61, when Puerto Ricans accounted for up to 76 percent of the people displaced from various urban renewal sites in the city.[6] In fact, stories of displacement are not rare in El Barrio, where residents were soon sensitized to the effect of changes in the landscape on their future. Almost repeating a Jacobean lament for the displacement that followed on the heels of urban renewal, people recalled a vibrant community of tenements, stores, friends, and neighbors all swiftly displaced by the projects.

The "projects," as public housing is commonly known, have since become associated with urban blight, crime, grime, and poverty. Yet they were initially intended for the "submerged middle classes," those "worthy" of help, not the minority, unemployed, or "untraditional" large, extended families. Through this discriminatory admissions policy, Puerto Ricans had to struggle for due and equitable access to public housing, which became a marker for class distinctions among East Harlemites through housing policies that included interviews for tenant suitability, apartment inspections for hygiene, wait lists for apartments, and other forms of tenant surveillance. Sánchez's study of Puerto Ricans in public housing from 1945 to 1980 notes that not until civil strife and protest in the late 1960s and 1970s did Puerto Ricans begin to gain parity in their entrance to public housing, which initially tended to favor whites and African Americans over Puerto Ricans, who were seen as a transient and vulnerable population not worthy of permanent welfare aid.[7] According to this study, Puerto Ricans were not as far behind African Americans as tenants in public housing in East Harlem as they were in other parts of the city. Still, public housing did increase the number of African Americans in East Harlem, particularly in the housing stock constructed along Madison and Park avenues between 112th and 115th streets along the highly contested borders of East and West Harlem.[8] This development still informs the perception that the projects increased Blacks' presence within "Puerto Rican areas," ignoring the strains upon African Americans likely exerted by the swift growth of the Puerto Rican population in the 1950s. In fact, different public housing buildings are still regarded as more or less "Black" or "Puerto Rican" based on long-time perceptions of who dominated these projects at their inception. Such notions attest to how strongly public housing admissions, both then and now, are intertwined with racial/ethnic politics in the area.[9]

A common concern voiced by Puerto Rican activists is that "our community" should have access to the housing stock that was built in "our community." Central to consolidating such concerns was the War on Poverty programs of the 1960s, which provided Puerto Ricans with local access to resources. As is well known, antipoverty programs led to the growth of ethnically organized public social-service infrastructures that helped further the consolidation of a politicized and bureaucraticized Puerto Rican leadership in the area. Their emergence coincided with and fed the ethnicity-based political strategies and policies that pervaded the then dominant ideology of "cultural pluralism" during this racially charged time (Herbstein 1978; Torres 1995).[10] Distribution of public funds on the basis of ethnicity became the medium through which Puerto Ricans could stake control, not only to counter the white establishment that had so discriminated against them, but also to demarcate themselves from African Americans, whose concurrent struggles over turf and space in West Harlem had been a model for Puerto Rican activists, despite the two groups colliding in East Harlem (Aponte-Parés 1999). Most directly,

however, these programs represented a blunt challenge to the social services organizations, such as the East Harlem Protestant Parish, Union
Settlement, and James Weldon Johnson Houses, which dominated important sectors of East Harlem's civic structure, and though much less so,
continue to be influential in El Barrio. All led by white leaders, mainly
clergy men and social workers, these institutions are remembered for
their patronizing attitude toward Puerto Ricans and the poor, and attributed by some with stalling the development of indigenous leadership.[11]
Bob De Leon, a longtime resident and political activist and director of
a social-service organization, whose family had come in the 1920s and
who both witnessed and participated in El Barrio's transformations,
remembered:

> My family came during the twenties, and I was raised here, and there
> were a lot of *gente blanca,* but they were not *blanco* [white]. They were
> ethnics: Irish, Italian, and Jewish. Those differences mattered, but now
> it is all white and Black. I went to the service and came back in the midst
> of the civil rights movement. And everyone was involved. We were
> young and we were going to end poverty forever. "Community Control"
> was the banner, and we got control of the poverty funds to the chagrin
> of the whites. For them we were sheep to be led, but never leaders.

He recalled the 1960s as a time when there was a variety of groups, from
gangs to community groups to social clubs, caught in the movement for
social empowerment and community autonomy. But the War on Poverty
was predicated on community-based disbursement of funds, which were
easily centralized, and in East Harlem soon led to one of the strongest
welfare-funds-driven political clans in the city. Its anchors included former assemblyman Angelo Del Toro, in office from 1974 to 1995, and his
brother William; the brothers Raul and Roberto Rodríguez, the latter a
city councilman from 1980 to the mid-1990s; Roberto Anazagasti; and
state senator Olga Méndez, in office since 1978.[12] Through political office
in the city council and the state assembly and control of the two entities
disbursing antipoverty funds—Massive Economic Neighborhood Development, founded in the late 1960s and later reformed as the East Harlem
Council for Community Improvement; and the East Harlem Community

Corporation, established in 1967—this Puerto Rican power bloc achieved almost total control over development and political activity in East Harlem throughout the 1970s and mid-1980s.

The story of the political power attained by Puerto Ricans through control of federal funds for local development merits more attention than I am able to provide here, except to note that its legacy is still strongly felt in the area. After some of its core members were publicly discredited and accused of bribery and mismanagement of funds, the power bloc came to be seen by some as the area's "poverty pimps," blamed for fostering patronage, stealing and wasting scarce poverty funds, and tainting the political integrity of the Puerto Rican community. As one critic noted, because of them, "People dismiss us as a plantation run by the Del Toro brothers . . . Puerto Rican politicians in East Harlem have not been taken seriously since."[13] Others, however, sternly defended them, believing they were wrongly persecuted as a reprisal for creating the first Puerto Rican power bloc in Manhattan. Among the defenders are those who benefited from their access to state management contracts and resources, receiving jobs, incomes, contracts, services, and housing. Moreover, many of the East Harlemites who became politically active during this era are still heading social service and housing organizations (such as East Harlem Multiservice and NERVE, or Nuevo El Barrio para la Rehabilitación de La Vivienda y Economia, Inc.) and are recognized leaders (in entities such as the former local New York City Public School Board and the East Harlem Chamber of Commerce) or are district leaders. Others are important figures in nonprofit groups and private housing development in the area. Most important, many of these pioneer political figures have friendships and contacts with long-time elected officials such as Olga Méndez and Charles Rangel, whose almost unchallenged permanence in office since the 1970s assures the continuity of networks of support and patronage. The legacy of the 1970s is also felt in the importance of social service and nonprofit institutions. I had been encouraged to interview their directors first, and they are always represented in local community and political affairs. At the same time, and echoing the ascendancy of neoliberal politics, these earlier leaders and their political gains were also viewed with deep suspicion by many for promoting reliance on nonprofit institutions and programs in which political power is forever vulnerable and transient. As a local businessman put it, echoing what others said in different ways: "What happened was that Puerto Ricans got only programs. We got elected officials and worried only about public monies and programs to put family and friends to work. That's it, no bricks and mortar and no real power. That's East Harlem's history for thirty years."

The War on Poverty funds provided little money for housing development, and it would not be until the rise of federal programs in the 1980s that Puerto Rican leadership would tap into government funds to develop housing. Still, the few projects developed at the time stand as legacies to the struggle over the control of federal and state monies for "Puerto Rican–controlled housing."[14] Speaking about one of these projects, Roberto Anazagasti made a point of noting the large backyards, stoops, and *escaleras*, with railings that had been designed by Tres Hermanos (Angelo Del Toro Housing Development) to evoke the tenements where Puerto Ricans used to hang out prior to the construction of projects. Interrupted by a call from a potential tenant, I witnessed one of his self-described operations to further the stakes of Latinos in El Barrio. The call was from an undocumented Salvadoran family from Queens, to whom he explained that he was unable to house them in his Section 8-restricted building. But, stating that his primary objective was to keep East Harlem "Latin," he quickly instructed them to write him a letter stating that they have children and are at risk of homelessness, promising them that he would get them housing. Such strategies are now infrequent in an era when outside agents, not local brokers, control housing development in the area.

But Puerto Ricans' struggle for affordable housing has not been waged solely on the public housing front. For the most part, they countered countless private "slumlords" whose tactics of abandonment, disinvestment, and retrieval of services had, by the 1970s, turned East Harlem into a prime example of urban blight. This massive abandonment and disinvestment followed a citywide pattern stemming from a wave of owner abandonment in the 1960s and 1970s that hit the city's poorest communities particularly hard (Sierra 1992). At this time, hundreds of buildings

[margin note: War on Poverty]

[margin note: Private slum lords]

Figure 2. Congressman Charles Rangel and Roberto Anazagasti, general manager of NERVE and a longtime political figure in El Barrio, chat during a public meeting. Photo courtesy of East Harlem.com.

became part of the city's centrally managed stock, making the city the "reluctant landlord" to thousands of East Harlemites. Another major policy was triggered by this development. By the 1980s, rapidly declining federal housing funds, plus the city's inability to keep its housing stock, led to the development of what is still the largest municipal housing plan executed under any city administration. The Koch administration's ten-year housing plan was to dispose of thousands of abandoned and tax-delinquent buildings that the city had accumulated by handing them out to private and nonprofit developers and tenants. Similar disposition programs have since been in effect, though renamed by different city administrations (Braconi 1999).

Like other urban renewal programs the ten-year housing plan has been criticized for displacing the poor and for the unevenness of revitalization. What is certain is that the plan had important consequences for current development in East Harlem. Specifically, it furthered the "neigh-borhood revitalization hypothesis" (Van Ryzin and Genn 1999), the idea that government housing programs should work in tandem with com-munity-based, nonprofit, and profit-making organizations, which greatly stimulated the public housing sector. Most of the thirty-some social ser-vice and housing nonprofits involved in developing housing units in East Harlem were created after the mid-1980s (Manhattan Community Board 11, 2000). The plan also furthered the current concern among East Harlemites over the development of mixed- and middle-income housing to remedy what they perceived to be the misuse of their neighborhood as a dumping ground for special needs and low-income populations. Cen-tral to the ten-year plan was the development of an economically inte-grated community through a combination of mixed-income housing and home ownership programs as a means of creating truly "revitalized" communities.[15] In East Harlem, however, most of the housing developed under the Koch ten-year plan was constructed or rehabilitated under fed-eral programs such as Section 8, federal senior housing, or special needs housing, mostly under the sponsorship of community-based agencies with different orientations and histories, including religious, social ser-vice–based, and tenant groups. Local residents felt those types of hous-ing overburdened their community with social, economic, or needy pop-ulations. One resident explained this as follows: "The problem is that poverty-appeasing programs failed to meet the needs of the middle class. We were raised in the projects, and there is all this housing for the elderly, for battered women, for people with AIDS, but our children are college educated and they have nowhere to live." Similar statements were repeated by district leaders and representatives from entities like the Community Board, the East Harlem Chamber of Commerce, and the up-wardly mobile, educated, and politically connected Puerto Rican leader-ship of El Barrio. One leader of a social-service organization stated, "I grew up in the projects, but if you were getting ahead, you could not live here. You had to leave El Barrio. They did not think that we Latinos could make money. So all they built was public or special-needs housing. Like myself, I left and bought property in New Jersey." As many residents were quick to note, there were no middle income or home ownership programs as there were in other parts of the city. As a result, the promotion of mixed income and middle-income housing rang a politically correct tone to residents who have long felt that El Barrio has been discriminated against as a dumping ground for special needs housing. Fueling these kinds of statements was controversy over the 2000 census, in which Puerto Ricans in New York were shown to be declining in numbers while remaining among the poorest of the poor. The lesson many residents took from such news was that upwardly mobile Puerto Ricans had left the city, and that for the community's survival, this exodus had to be stopped.[16]

HOUSING AND URBAN FLIGHT: ON THOSE WHO STAYED AND THOSE WHO LEFT

Puerto Rican migration to the United States has been constant and ongoing, as well as circular in nature, as has been so well documented by Puerto Rican scholars (Duany 2002; Flores 1993). Since the 1960s, however, many Puerto Ricans have purposely left New York, driven out by changes in New York's economy and a move toward service jobs that provided fewer opportunities to unskilled workers. Upward mobility was synonymous with leaving El Barrio for Puerto Rico, Connecticut, New Jersey, the Bronx, or just about any suburb. Many had no intention of returning. Consider the comments of Roberto, a labor union leader who was born and raised in El Barrio and became a first-time homeowner in Westchester in his mid-fifties:

> Most of us, and with that I mean my friends from El Barrio and I, who got education and jobs, don't share the sentimentality of El Barrio. It's only the people that never lived there that do. I saw a lot of brutality. Even if I had a choice to buy property, I would never go back. Because El Barrio will always be El Barrio, not the Puerto Rican Barrio, but the barrio of other immigrants and the poor. What I miss is the family, because we all lived close to each other in El Barrio, but I don't miss the violence, the brutality, the welfare agency, the stigma, and the poverty.

This self-described "lack of sentimentality" about El Barrio is quite revealing. Unlike the views harbored by Puerto Rican intellectuals and

[handwritten margin notes: "lack of sentimentality" (left margin); "Upward mobility" (bottom left)]

the middle classes, the working poor in the area had fewer opportunities for empowerment and upward mobility. It appears that acquisition of cultural and economic capital can fuel romantic views of El Barrio, but it can easily distance one from it, if for different reasons.[17] Anna Morales, a social worker, was raised in El Barrio, and her family decided to stay. She spoke of the pressure exerted on her family to leave and the price she paid for staying. She recounted the many who left to look for what she described as "the American dream in Puerto Rico":

> I remember people would knock on the door to say *adiós* [gets tearful]. People who had saved a little money would leave. There [in Puerto Rico] you had the factories and Mom could stay home and take care of the children, and houses were very cheap, and you did not have to be afraid of gangs and drugs. Once a child had reached puberty they would pack up and leave. There was no mold there, just chickens and cows and animals. Some of them have come back to visit, and I show them the buildings where they used to live, and they don't believe it. They never thought that this would take on any value. For so many years we were not visited by our own families. We were isolated. They looked down on us. Upward mobility meant going back. My family implored my mother to take us, her two daughters, away. They would not understand that this was our community.

In this light, the flight of Puerto Ricans from El Barrio was never based solely on the type of housing available, but also stemmed from a range of factors, foremost among them the real conditions of poverty and the stigma or dominant association of El Barrio with urban blight. These are associations that were in turn strengthened by Puerto Rican nationalist discourse, where urban New York life and its by-product, "the Nuyorican" (U.S.–born/bred Puerto Rican), were taken as tantamount to polluted culture, always opposed to the supposedly authentic culture of the island. In other words, El Barrio was one place you left lest your children became polluted or corrupted. These views have been documented in recent studies of Puerto Rican immigration. Gina Pérez's study of out-migration from Chicago to San Sebastián, for instance, shows how migration is constructed as an economic decision, and return (primarily to Puerto Rico) is associated with community, place, home, and nation (Pérez 2000). Consequently, migrants become directly embedded in the same discourses that forever render them polluted and suspect since mobility is always associated with return. But class and cultural capital have always been factors in the ways Puerto Ricans experience and interpret El Barrio. In contrast to poor and working-class Puerto Ricans born or raised in El Barrio, many Puerto Rican intellectuals move and establish roots there as assertions of their commitment to the area's preservation and upliftment. This situation directly echoes Monique Taylor's research on gentrification in Harlem. Middle-class and educated Blacks played a central role in the gentrification of the area, though this trend is not seen in these terms but rather as an act of Blacks' assertion and upliftment. By moving to Harlem, maintaining steady jobs, and becoming involved in neighborhood events and community groups, new residents positioned themselves as "examples" and champions of the greater goal of making Harlem into the Mecca for Black people in the city and beyond (Taylor 1994). A similar stance mediates perceptions of Puerto Rican newcomers to the area, notably of those who are deemed able to contribute political, cultural, or intellectual capital. Local professionals moving to the area, for instance, are oftentimes the center of attention, celebrated in the pages of local newspapers and becoming the object of local hearsay. Yet it is important to recognize that the departure of the upwardly mobile does not entail their complete divorce from the area, but rather a repositioning of their relationship with it. Felix Leo Campos, a self-described Nuyorican filmmaker who continued to gravitate to East Harlem and to identify himself with the cultural life of El Barrio, even after his family moved to the West Side during his youth, put it this way:

> For many, East Harlem was the ghetto, and the idea was to leave. But though people moved to the South Bronx and other parts of the city, their cultural life was in El Barrio. They have a Puerto Rican Day Parade and parties in the Bronx, but [it] is never the same as the one in El Barrio, because El Barrio *es la cuna de los Puertorriqueños* [the cradle of Puerto Ricans] . . . and I have lived in Harlem and the Bronx, and I still have never felt as good as I felt in El Barrio.

I heard similar comments from other East Harlemites who had moved, or whose parents had moved, in search of greener pastures, and who now saw El Barrio with nostalgic eyes and maintained active connections with the community. The Old-timer Stickball players, who meet annually in a block party on 111th Street, are a good example. Players, most of them born and raised in East Harlem and many of them professionals now living in Puerto Rico, Florida, California, and beyond, return annually to play and meet family and friends in a ritual celebration of assertion and continuity with El Barrio. Visitors to the annual 116th Street Festival on the weekend of the Puerto Rican Day Parade, gathering thousands of Puerto Ricans from outside the city, provide another example of recurrent visitors, akin to the transnational visits to Puerto Rico or the "home country" so common among generations of immigrants. Nevertheless, when prompted, few of those who left affirmed forthrightly that they would trade their Westchester or San Diego homes for a Barrio apartment. Cheaper housing was mentioned as a factor attracting them to the suburbs, but so were better schools, social infrastructure, and services.

Thus Puerto Rican flight from East Harlem did not arise simply from the need for affordable housing. Furthermore, the mere promotion of mixed income housing will not assure Puerto Ricans' continued presence in the area. Housing is central, yet it is only one of the many variables informing Puerto Ricans' decision to stay, leave, or return to El Barrio. Its use as a dominant explanation for Puerto Ricans leaving the area is thus better understood in relation to the attending discourses furthering privatized development. This is evident in the recurrent explanation regarding public housing. Specifically, the promotion of middle-class housing was accompanied by attacks on public housing, seen by many as a barrier to the permanent settlement of Puerto Ricans in the area and, contradictorily, as a bulwark against development by and for others. The statement of a social worker and administrator of a work-training program, who had been born and raised in the projects and still had family there, is evocative of this position: "Concerns over gentrification are ill-founded. The projects will stop whites from moving to El Barrio. Who's going to want to live next to the projects? The projects kicked our people from El Barrio. I was born and raised in the projects, but the problem is that there is nowhere to go after the projects."

Rolando Cortés, an MTA worker, who bought and renovated two buildings in the 1980s when Puerto Ricans were reluctant to buy property, and is now a landlord and a recognized local expert on real estate in the community, was even more bold in his association of public housing with the sad fate of Puerto Ricans in El Barrio: "You won't believe it, but when I bought property here my friends thought I was crazy. I see low rents as part of a master plan to keep Latinos from buying property in El Barrio. Puerto Ricans were paying as little as seventy five to one hundred dollars for rent. The current thinking was, Why buy when we live so cheaply?" Rolando is well aware that prices are rising and now sees property sharing, or pooling of resources, as the only recourse for purchasing property in East Harlem. His goal is *"atraer la gente buena"* (whom he defined as the "positive assets to the community"), socially conscious Latinos who keep rents low for other Latinos. He connects the "positive assets" with the quick dissemination of information on newly available properties, though fewer and fewer properties are now obtained through such informal networks.

Undoubtedly, public housing poses a structural barrier to development. It interrupts cross-streets and avenues throughout El Barrio, blocking traffic, cutting off pedestrian flows, and forming pockets of low-income housing. Public housing also creates tangible and intangible barriers of race and marginality that insulate the area from the rest of Manhattan.[18] Less evident, however, is the precariousness of public housing; instead of serving as barricades to development, the "projects" could potentially be catalysts to gentrification. The 1998 Quality Housing and Work Responsibility Act is the most significant federal public housing reform since 1988. It deregulated public housing authorities, granting them greater flexibility and little oversight. Its ultimate goal was the abolition of public housing. The legislation provided for rent increases, the halt to construction of new housing units, and the promotion of new forms of private and public initiatives. One stark reminder of the vulnerability of high-rise public housing projects can be found in Chicago, where the Chicago Housing Authority razed the Robert Taylor Homes and targeted them for mixed- and middle-income redevelopment (Venkatesh 2002). Other blatant measures have taken their toll in heavily police-scrutinized neighborhoods like El Barrio: public housing tenants could be evicted if a family member or guest was arrested on drug charges, another dimension of the Rockefeller Law mandates, which have placed myriad Blacks and Latinos behind bars for minor drug use and nonviolent offenses. Contrary to the view of many East Harlemites, the days of public housing as public, and hence as a protective haven against gentrification, may be numbered.

GENTRIFICATION AND THE PLANNING PROCESS

East Harlemites' support for development can be traced to the close alignment between residents' dreams of upward mobility and consumption-based developments in the area. Briefly, the dominant view is that public housing, social services, and all that is associated with the gains and struggles of the past hampered rather than strengthened the present stakes of Puerto Ricans in El Barrio, opening up the way to privatization and consumption-based developments. It is important to note, however, that this ideology is constituted through the veil of community involvement and participation that reverberated in other areas of East Harlem's planning process.[19] This is why, in countering studies of gentrification that emphasize private landlords and the market, I probe into public policy and the nonprofit housing sector, which is also directly implicated in furthering privatization, particularly in communities like East Harlem where the nonprofit sector has been a dominant development agent.

Consider, for instance, East Harlem's *New Directions* (2000), a planning document developed by the local community board over a period of ten years in consultation with representatives of local institutions and staff from the New York City Department of City Planning. It forms part of Section 197-A of the city charter, allowing communities to detail their recommendations for future development. Though it has yet to be approved by the city's Planning Commission, as required by the charter, the document stands as the legitimating source for residents' vision of future development; it is widely circulated in board meetings and cited by development consultants and local leaders to both direct and challenge local development. In fact, as of 2001, East Harlem was one of the few community boards that had conducted this planning process, which in itself indicates community leaders' concerns over development.[20]

By allowing communities to recommend their own planning vision, the document is recognized as a double-edged sword, a tool to assert community views as well as to render the area more vulnerable to investors (Bressi 2000). After all, it is not enforceable by law nor is it an autonomous local development, but rather it is directed at, and ulti- mately validated by, the Department of City Planning as a means of facil- itating development by having clear directives and a consensus plan with the appearance of community support. What the process does pro- vide, however, is a venue for community involvement and an entry point into the generalized vision for planning that favors the goals of develop- ment and privatization. The plan's recommendations for housing, for instance, draw heavily from a study conducted by George Calvert, the former director of Hope, one of the largest nonprofit housing developers in the area, who chaired the final preparations for the plan. This study, "A Call to Action: Rebuilding Main Street in the Village of East Harlem" (Calvert 1998) is widely quoted in *New Directions*, and, in contrast to the dry wording and formulaic format of the document, is explicit in its enthusiasm for private development.[21] As it reads: "Businesses are com- ing in: Pathmark on 125th Street is underway, Home Depot at 118th Street in the East Harlem Plaza site is moving through approvals . . . workers all over the city are looking for apartments. East Harlem's cultural heritage is drawing national attention. . . . Household income levels are increasing in East Harlem" (8). His is a vision of East Harlem as a community quickly coming of age, primarily because of the work of private corpora- tions and developments, whose effects in terms of pollution and quality of life are never mentioned. East Harlem is presented as an open com- munity, a home to "workers from all over the city," a vision that priori- tizes housing but not necessarily for locals. A similar outlook is evident in *New Directions*, whose recommendations in terms of housing, urban renewal, and design overwhelmingly favor middle-income and mixed- income housing and home ownership. It calls for the renovation of all "occupied and vacant city-owned buildings." In fact, the plan recommends that all city buildings, occupied or vacant, be disposed of, while providing few provisions for sustaining, conserving, and rehabilitating the existing public housing stock, except to encourage management alternatives such as their privatization.[22] In other words, *New Directions* is an ode to state-subsidized private development transformed into "community recommendations."

Yet considering that similar programs have been rejected by many community activists, including some involved in the 197-A planning process in the mid-1980s, their inclusion as "community recommendations" is better seen as a triumph of planning ideologies favoring privatization than as community consensus. Indeed, when the New York Housing Partnership first sought to build small homes for private ownership in the area, on land that had previously been cleared for urban renewal, community activists stopped the initiative through a lawsuit by the local Legal Aid Society and the Puerto Rican Legal Defense and Education Fund. Residents had also protested proposals to develop a TV studio on the same East River site now coveted by Home Depot, which led to an influx of speculators to the area. Francisco Díaz, now a private development enthusiast and corporate consultant, who was then one of the antigentrification activists, recalled: "I remember that this was the first time that I heard the word gentrification. Prices were skyrocketing, and everybody wanted a piece of East Harlem, all based on rumors of Procter and Gamble and a TV studio coming to the area." The studio plan never materialized, but residents had been forewarned. Gloria Quiñonez, a retired lawyer and resident, who was at the forefront of the lawsuit to stop the New York Housing Partnership's homebuilding plan, explained:

> It was our position that this land had been cleared of low-income people with the promise that they would be able to return to new affordable housing. The city hoped that the people had lost the collective memory with respect to that land clearing through urban renewal. Our argument was very simple. We were talking of city-owned lands that belonged to everyone in the community, that were of the people, and that by definition could not be sold to the highest bidder. We felt strongly that the only appropriate development in those lands is affordable housing geared to the people of this community, who are low income.

backfire

People liked it

Gloria's comments speak to the diversity of stances among Puerto Rican middle classes, not all of whom embraced private-driven developments so wholeheartedly. A lack of development choices, however, presented little room for dissent. Indeed, the first home owners' project was halted, but not for long.[23] As Gloria went on to note, the plan may have even backfired: "We stopped the development, but then there was no development, no housing for anyone, and now people are clamoring [for] development."

It is in this context of no pending development that the Cacique and the Nueva Esperanza Houses, the first private homes constructed on public lands, were built in the late 1990s, with little criticism and much fanfare. Both were sponsored by Operation Fightback, a housing nonprofit led by a Puerto Rican housing advocate. The transition toward this type of development was eased by investing the houses with an "indigenous" feel. With empowering names evoking the Puerto Rican indigenous Taino leader Cacique and Nueva Esperanza, or "new hope," these homes were presented by their sponsors as a needed development to consolidate the community and protect it from gentrification, furthering much hype about the possibility of home ownership for upwardly mobile families in East Harlem. The success of these first homes led quickly to more programs. East Harlem is the site of six new developments under the Housing Preservation and Development's (HPD) Cornerstone Program, under which twenty-three hundred new middle-income and market-rate housing units will be created in Upper Manhattan, financed primarily by private sources.

I am not seeking to critique homeownership, an important goal of grassroots housing movements, particularly among minorities, who have been historically discriminated against for loans with which to fulfill this staple of the middle-class dream. Instead, I point to the growing inaccessibility of most of these projects, veiled by the current hype over "affordable housing." Sponsored by federal and state monies, their construction requires specific income and tenant eligibility guidelines. They are entirely out of the reach of the poor and those most in need of housing. For instance, 2001 income requirements for a three-person family are $26,600 for very low-income housing and $42,550 for low-income housing. Neither category is affordable to East Harlemites, whose 2001 median household income was $14,882. This situation has not gone unchallenged by local residents. As one stated, "These developments are supposed to be for affordable housing, but they want incomes of twenty to twenty-five thousand dollars for a studio, and, for two adults, twenty-eight to thirty-five thousand dollars. Who are they talking about, from which community?"

Moreover, most new state-subsidized construction is primarily for middle-class and home ownership programs, undoubtedly out of the reach of most local residents. A good example is the lot between 119th and 120th streets and Madison Avenue, sold by the city for fifteen dollars and due to be privately developed into a "standard old fashioned co-op" that will admit buyers earning up to 250 percent of the $59,100 median income for a family of four, or $147,750 (New York Times 2001). These home ownership programs are open to anyone who meets eligibility requirements, applies by the deadline, and is selected by a lottery. A two-income working family applying for a one-bedroom apartment has as much chance to be selected as a professional couple applying for a three-bedroom: both are equally eligible so long as they meet income eligibility requirements that can be as high as 250 percent of the maximum area median income. These constructions are no longer aptly described as "Gilded Age private philanthropy for the deserving poor" (Plunz 1990), as they were initially regarded, but rather as subsidies for young professionals to conquer a quickly refurbished ghetto. They are increasingly out of the average working person's reach. All the while, property prices are rising rapidly, and city-owned properties are disappearing quickly.[24] During an action that gave rise to much talk by residents throughout the summer of 2001, five city properties were sold for record prices, including one for one and a quarter million dollars. Among the sites was a lot on 111th Street and Third Avenue, which some residents had hoped would be given to the International Salsa Museum. Such news confirms that outside developers had already heard the call for development, quickly reducing the chances for local control, as East Harlem was no longer the vacant land full of government buildings up for the taking described in New Directions. This is the context that frames the concerns

[handwritten margin note: state-subsidized housing for middle-class not local residents]

of Puerto Rican community leaders with regard to staking a claim in El Barrio. At issue was the involvement of Puerto Ricans in the new development initiatives, and the same old debate of whether "our community" would be housed in the new structures.

THE WHO BEHIND "OUR PEOPLE"

Government-subsidized projects always function under income guidelines and tenant eligibility requirements. But within these guidelines, the struggle over turf was ongoing, though the playing field has quickly eroded. As a Puerto Rican resident noted, "If we can't stop speculators from coming in we can at least make sure Puerto Ricans buy and relocate in the area." The problem, however, is that while Puerto Rican nonprofits and developers were partly involved in some of the early home ownership projects, such as Cacique, most housing development has been spurred by larger nonprofits, such as Hope, while most of the current development is dominated by HPD-designated private developers. The marketing of different projects, and the stipulation that the community be somewhat represented as tenants, provided a last chance to assert local control of these projects. This was the case with the Nueva Esperanza project, where aggressive marketing by a Puerto Rican developer resulted in a mostly Puerto Rican and Latino tenancy, the majority of which were from East Harlem. The developer estimated that 90 percent of the applications had come from East Harlem and that 65 percent of the homeowners were Latinos. As he said:

> We are required to do a seminar, to print newspaper ads, and to look
> for people who are qualified, but we did far more than that. We did
> a lot of hand-holding to make sure that *our* people would qualify [my
> emphasis]. Because there are qualified, qualifiable, and not qualified
> people. People just look at the qualified. Why waste their time? Someone
> who is not from this community will not take the time.

These strategies, however, did little to subdue contentions over "who" constitutes "our people."[25] The clannish times of the past surfaced in El

Barrio among many who felt slighted by the new constructions. The comments of a Black Puerto Rican woman and public housing resident represent the sentiments of many who felt left out. She was unaware that there was an open application process for the new houses, or that it was a city-subsidized project: "What you see are the Calderons and the Allendes living in these houses, but who's ever heard of an everyday Maria Rodriguez getting a home?" The informant was referring to some of the politically important family names in the area; I was unable to confirm whether they had indeed bought a house or were renting from the development. The point she made, however, reflects a common perception in this community: clannishness and political patronage are still at play, excluding many Puerto Ricans who are neither able nor allowed to realize the ethnic/class aspirations of those who have wrested some political or economic power.

Ironically, perceptions of clannishness are fostered by the fact that the only tool left to combat what an activist called the "cultural gentrification of the area" may be the maneuvering of rules that are ultimately unbeatable. Indeed, even development enthusiasts complained of receiving inadequate notice of new housing developments, deadlines for the application process, and eligibility requirements. Anxiety over the new construction was amply visible during community board meetings, when marketing agents for different projects announced seminars and housing workshops to what always seemed to be anxious audiences. Most important, the financial and eligibility requirements of home ownership projects restricts who can or cannot be helped by Puerto Rican housing enthusiasts. There was little option but to deliberately rely on a narrow and class-based conception of "Puertoricanness." After all, the requirements for these new projects could only be met by the "right people"—people who had the cultural, class, and economic capital to meet guidelines aimed at attracting the few "deserving" among the housing needy.

Given this, critics saw home ownership programs as part of a master plan to further divide the community, and ultimately reghettoize it. An African American member of the community board put it in simple terms: "We forget that all the hoopla is really about low-quality housing with low floor ceilings. They are badly planned, with cheap, prefabricated materials. Where are the theaters, the entertainment, the offices, mom-and-pop stores, the services that bring community development if East Harlem becomes a 'bedroom' to the city?" Rumors also circulated that "the stakeholders" of El Barrio (that is, people with political contacts) were accumulating the few brownstones and more valuable properties, leaving only prefabricated homes to be acquired through the market. These rumors notwithstanding, the struggle to increase the presence of locals in these programs was ongoing, even though most developers did not play by the "right rules."[26] The most qualified—not qualifiable—tenants are what developers are after, and there is little to be done about it. The Puerto Rican leadership's dream of upward mobility and turf control is not shared by institutions and developers, for whom the area is coming of age as a sanitized community, perhaps "multicultural," but never "Puerto Rican."

Perhaps the best example of this trend is provided by Hope, the oldest and most visible and influential nonprofit developer in East Harlem. Hope was established in the late 1960s by a group of merchants, community activists, and George Calvert, the minister affiliated with the Church of Living Hope. Initially a small operation that acquired and rehabilitated buildings, Hope grew rapidly in the 1980s by taking advantage of government disposition programs for neighborhood renewal. It became one of the city's most influential and politically connected neighborhood organizations. Today, signs of Hope are visible everywhere: plaques announcing Hope's sponsorship of murals, nearly fifteen hundred units of housing that have been renovated by the group, as well as growing rumors about its effects on the community. El Barrio residents have begun asking whether Hope and, by extension, groups building "affordable housing" are helping or gentrifying the community.

Hope touts the fact that it has been central in making East Harlem an "economically, ethnically, and culturally diverse neighborhood." To stress this point, their thirtieth-anniversary journal, *East Harlem on my Mind*, depicts children of color engaged in some of the cultural and social activities sponsored by Hope against a background of renovated buildings. It is through this and other inclusive strategies, such as the inclusion of Blacks and Puerto Ricans on its staff and board, that Hope has pro-

Figure 3.   New housing developments in El Barrio. Developments like this one
along 110th Street are greatly coveted and are a source of pride among Puerto Rican
residents. Photo by the author.

jected itself as a concerned organization. Hope has received much support from local politicians, who defended the organization in local
forums when residents complained of prohibitive rents. Yet the politicians could not obscure the reality of rising rents, the eviction of many
low-income tenants, many of them undocumented immigrants, and the
drop in tenants from El Barrio as a result of Hope's move toward privatized home ownership and middle-income housing.[27]

Feeding this trend are growing construction costs, along with the increasing competition over a diminishing source of city real estate. This
has forced nonprofit developers throughout the city to enter into ventures with private developers in order to compete for a diminishing
housing stock (Oser 2001). In fact, through a joint-venture partnership
with the Briarwood Organization, a private developer, Hope plans to develop more market-rate apartments to feed its rent rolls with few income
caps. This is a kind of development that, while increasingly promoted by

Results of
Hope

federal and state housing policies, is unprecedented among nonprofit housing developers and will undoubtedly be unaffordable to the families of the Black and Latino kids featured in Hope's anniversary journal.[28]

Hope's executive director, Mark Alexander, who is white but was raised in El Barrio among Puerto Ricans and African Americans—a factor that has helped him make inroads into the leadership of both communities—is keenly aware that his institution is geared toward the production of market-rate housing that may be out of the reach of locals. But he saw few problems with this trend. Embracing the business mantra with which people deflected all criticisms of privatization, he underscored that they are not a social service but a real-estate business. HPD does not require housing nonprofits to maintain information about the ethnicity and race of their tenants. In contrast to the Puerto Rican developer of Cacique Houses, who proudly described most tenants as Latino or from East Harlem, Hope's director was not initially forthcoming about the makeup of its clients. While upholding his commitment to his traditional constituency of Black and Latino residents, he nonetheless admitted that home ownership programs and a less regulated market would result in "more Caucasians" moving to East Harlem. But in his view, this trend was justified by East Harlem's ethnic immigrant history, making it a "transitional" or gateway community used by Irish, Italians, and Puerto Ricans, and that in the future it would be up for the taking. As he noted:

> I recognize El Barrio's importance for Puerto Ricans, but I don't recognize it as the rightful home of only Puerto Ricans. Middle-class Puerto Ricans themselves have voted with their feet, they've become upwardly mobile and are gone. That shapes my view of what we should do in our community. The intelligentsia has long focused on the lower class, and they're not focused on the middle class and those who went up the ladder because they've nowhere to go.

Yet as aligned as his statements may be with the concerns of Puerto Rican development enthusiasts, his vision of East Harlem responds to a very different logic. He, like the Puerto Rican leadership and other nonprofit and government representatives, stressed the need for middle-class and home ownership programs that would encourage people to be upwardly mobile, "to pursue the American dream." But unlike the Puerto Rican leadership, when he referred to "people," he did not mean Puerto Ricans, but the most qualified—not *qualifiable*—tenants. In fact, his goal of achieving a "dynamic," balanced, multicultural community is starkly at odds with the dreams of many Puerto Ricans for El Barrio as a mostly Latino/a community; it seeks to attract working and middle-class whites, the segments that have historically shunned El Barrio as a likely home. Ironically, this strategy echoes compensatory tactics originally devised to reverse the discrimination of minorities in housing. This thinking is now turned against Puerto Ricans and used to justify limits to their entrance to housing in El Barrio, since they would obviously hinder the making of a "balanced," multicultural community.

THE MARKET

I wanted to be around Puerto Rican culture because of the kind memories of my parents. When I moved here the smell of beans or steak and onions or plantains made me smile; the sounds of songs I liked was *conmovedor* [moving]; the inclusiveness of Puerto Rican females was familiar; the respectfulness of Puerto Rican men was memorable, as were people walking by churches and making the sign of the cross.

> Gladys Rodríguez, East Harlem Online
> on "Choosing Where to Live"

They don't tell you they want white kids over Mexicans. They [building owners] say the rents are going up.

> Licensed real-estate broker operating
> in East Harlem

Puerto Ricans' dreams of purchasing (or more likely, renting) space in El Barrio have been relegated to the open market. The many educated

Puerto Ricans, artists, and young entrepreneurs for whom the area has symbolic meaning are starkly aware of the increasingly limited housing environment. Professional Latinos in East Harlem were particularly concerned that many properties (especially rentals) were not being circulated in forums. One complained about the lack of services and amenities in the neighborhood. As she stated, "The prices are going up, but the services are not there. There are no schools. Crack dealers are still around the corner. You can't even find a taxi to pick you up and drop you there. The reality does not meet the prices." In fact, East Harlem's real estate is not advertised in *El Diario* or other Latino and local newspapers; it is more likely listed by downtown realtors, who, many believe, intend to keep Latinos out of the area. Students from New York University were finding vacancies in the school's housing office posted by landlords seeking "worthy" tenants. Moreover, when listed, East Harlem holdings are more often found under Harlem, or Upper Carnegie Hill, names that disassociate the area from its Latin roots; housing was rarely listed as Spanish Harlem or East Harlem. Other landlords were using the Internet. This is how an informant's friend from Paris found a fully renovated apartment for eighteen hundred dollars, which is considerably high for a one-bedroom apartment, but not when considering the twenty-six hundred dollars she would pay for an apartment below Ninety-sixth Street. Another landlord, who was renting renovated one-bedroom apartments for six hundred dollars in 1998, had increased the rent to eight hundred and then to twelve hundred dollars by 2001. Though still inexpensive by Manhattan standards, this represents an almost twofold increase in three years.[29] This is the kind of rent that has long attracted students, artists, and other young urbanites to ethnic neighborhoods while displacing locals.

Christopher Holland, one of East Harlem's newest residents and landlords, is a good example of the kind of investor who is moving to the area and the professional-yet-bohemian tenants they are after. A Soho advertising executive and former resident of the Upper East Side, he saw in East Harlem a convenient community that, in his words, was "prettier than the Upper East Side and had more sense of community." After buying three buildings in the area he, like other landlords, now advertises beyond East

Harlem, through the Corcoran Group, one of the largest real-estate companies in the city. But he also markets his property in poignantly new ways. To educate his market Holland founded Harlemite.com, a Web site that, while still under construction at the time of this writing, already evokes his romantic vision for El Barrio, so central to its re-signification among prospective professional tenants. In Neil Smith's terms, urban pioneers can find new spiritual hope and values in the image of an undeveloped "frontier," a new world of discovery and opportunities (Smith 1996). As the Web site announces: "Harlemite.com celebrates and honors people who nurture their lives in Harlem and fuel the community's spirit in the process of living. Phonies are not recognized. Only those who have Harlem on their mind . . . for real . . . get play. Harlemite.com amplifies the voice, art and visions of those responsible for generating life in Harlem's communities . . . the Harlemites" (http://harlemite.com). In other words, generating life in Harlem is a job for outsiders "with a heart and a vision" to realize. Attitude, not employment or race, is what he looked for in tenants. This is his new neighborhood, and he's selecting his neighbors, not just his tenants. But at fourteen hundred dollars a month (in 2002) for a one-bedroom (plus a rental fee), jobs and race will undoubtedly be factors helping to determine his future tenants.

As a response to East Harlem's furtive rental market, my respondents spoke of strategies to maintain informal rental networks to ensure Puerto Ricans and Latinos are not as affected by these trends. Erica González is a member of the community board and the Mujeres del Barrio and is active in numerous other initiatives. She moved to El Barrio soon upon graduating from college:

> I found my apartment through friends who were leaving to the island. They told me about their apartment. They were looking for someone who was committed to this community. They saved it for me, and I have tried to do the same for others to circulate among Puerto Ricans and nongentrifiers. . . . We once went building by building making an inventory of all buildings that had a "for rent" or "for sale" sign, to circulate among young professional Puerto Ricans, all part of a strategic trend so that those who have money can buy or at least make sure that we rent to our own.

This paucity of rentals is compounded by the profits that East Harlem landlords have historically wrested from immigrant tenants. East Harlem is heavily dominated by a few landlords who have owned property for more than thirty years and who, having profited from one working group and immigrant population after another, see little incentive to change since they already have a dependable base of vulnerable and "industrious" tenants. One landlord, reputed to own one-third of East Harlem, considered "gentrification" a threat to his business since higher rents are predicated on rehabilitation and repairs and investments, which he has little incentive to make. This landlord's East Harlem office does not even advertise in the real-estate pages, but relies largely on word of mouth, which works fine since there is little turnover. His tenants, who he described as being primarily Koreans, Chinese, and Mexicans, stay put, sharing with friends and family or acquaintances, taking additional roommates as needed. He also gets occasional students, referred primarily through nearby Mt. Sinai Hospital but, as he explained, he houses them in the better apartments to assure that "they are safe." For him, the system works fine; his buildings do not have to comply with any standards, and his "desirable" tenants, as he called them, are not about to complain to housing authorities about the conditions of their buildings.

It is impossible to continue here without a mention of asthma. Its high incidence in East Harlem and the entire Harlem area has received great attention, even attracting the interest of Senator Hillary Clinton. Many theories abound about asthma, but no one denies that it is directly correlated to poverty, exposure to pollutants, and most of all to poor housing, which is more likely to be infected with vermin, mildew, and other asthma triggers. Not surprisingly, at workshops conducted by East Harlem councilman Phil Reed, efforts centered on prevention and problem solving (how to clean mold, how to force your landlord to make repairs). Residents' concerns to improve housing conditions and to make asthma a priority of public housing authorities remain unanswered.

I did not raise the issue of asthma with this mogul landlord. Considering how blasé he seemed over matters of quality in housing, it likely didn't register as one of his major concerns. In fact, he believed he provided a safety net for a population that needed a place to sleep. Recalling his own immigrant family, he made a point of noting that he had housed the first Puerto Rican immigrants and is now doing the same for the Mexican, Chinese, and Korean newcomers, people who work hard and become very "desirable" tenants. Notwithstanding his good intentions, however, tales of exploitation by area landlords were easily forthcoming from my Mexican informants who complained of arbitrary rent increases, and keepers' fees, and threats of eviction if they complained of bad housing conditions.

What this landlord did not like were welfare recipients. He associated them with Puerto Rican people who never paid their bills, took drugs, and were impossible to evict. Even in this degraded sector of the market, Puerto Ricans find themselves displaced. Upscale developers and residents at the top end and immigrants at the bottom affected those who were supposedly the "most protected": the welfare-dependent housing needy, many of whom are Puerto Rican. They are especially shunned by landlords who can pick and choose their tenants. As a housing activist lamented, referring to the downgrading of Section 8 vouchers among landlords, "Why should landlords take the vouchers and deal with government bureaucracy if they can have cash, there and ready?" Besides, in order to take people through Section 8, buildings have to comply with certain standards that, given the growing housing demand by Mexicans and other immigrants, El Barrio slumlords have little incentive to meet. Thus, in another process exacerbated by gentrification, not only was one class displacing another; one group of the ethnic poor was also being pitted against another.

BODEGA DREAMS OR NIGHTMARES?

Myriad obstacles challenge Puerto Ricans' longing for a permanent place in El Barrio: housing policies that foster privatization and market the area to the highest bidder; development subsidies that target the upwardly mobile and the "deserving middle classes" throughout the city; and landlords who do not even advertise their rentals among the local population, preferring young professionals or more vulnerable immigrants.

For these varied interests, El Barrio is East Harlem, Upper Yorkville, or Spaha (for Spanish Harlem, echoing the trendy abbreviated names for neighborhoods like Soho) and a very different community from that anticipated by the Puerto Rican leadership. East Harlem is envisioned as a multicultural community in which Puerto Ricans are a passing group, and the growing Mexican and Latino population is just a backdrop to current development rather than being a possible target for affordable housing. In all my conversations with people from HPD, the community board, and nonprofit developers, I heard no one mention housing for immigrants or the working poor. What most of these interests do share with the Puerto Rican leadership is a class-based vision of neighborhood empowerment, equating private ownership and consumption-based housing with mobility. This dominant premise of development is one that directly touches their dreams and aspirations, but not without entangling them in their own continued dislocation or in the breakdown of their Bodega-type dreams of empowerment. This is one of the many contradictions of policies that emphasize privatization in the neoliberal city as they play out in the contested intersection of class, culture, and the marketing of place. Visions of community are plentiful; scant are the opportunities to bring life to these visions.

TWO "El Barrio es de Todos"

PREDICAMENTS OF CULTURE AND PLACE

Like many ethnic urban communities, El Barrio has historically been the focus of interests as varied as missionaries, reformers, social workers, anthropologists, developers, artists, museum professionals, and planners—a legacy I now follow. Even while researching this book, I observed the sizable number of students and professionals scouting the neighborhood for a variety of scholarly, business, and research purposes. There was the reporter taking pictures of a drunken man in the street, no doubt to use as an example of urban grit; the art enthusiast taking pictures of *casitas* on 115th Street; the TV crews scouting ad locations; as well as the many writers, myself included, writing on El Barrio, or filming or documenting Puerto Rican, Nuyorican, and Latino life.

These representations attest to the historical linkage of culture and space in El Barrio, underlying an important predicament for its residents

59

in the face of gentrification: whether it is by pathologizing, romanticizing, promoting, or even minimizing its Puerto Rican and Latino presence, representations of El Barrio/East Harlem continue to reference its Latino image in multiple ways. Of special interest, then, is not solely its construction as a Puerto Rican or Latino stronghold, but rather the different uses and deployments of this junction of culture and space. Consider for instance one of several events held by universities and cultural institutions around the gentrification of Upper Manhattan communities. The event, held at St. Cecilia Church by the Lower Manhattan Cultural Council (LMCC) in the spring of 2002, was titled La Rosa del Barrio, drawing from the song "There is a Rose in Spanish Harlem," popularized by Aretha Franklin. The LMCC invited a group of primarily Puerto Rican artists, art administrators, and musicians as guest speakers, celebrating East Harlem as a "Latin" community. A similar event was held by the LMCC at the Studio Museum in Harlem, but it gathered a mostly African American crowd of artists and community activists, reinscribing the pervading ethnic and racial boundaries around Latino East Harlem and Black West Harlem. This was the case even when the event's overall premise was transformation and diversification, which simultaneously invalidated the area's ethnic identity, as was done by the well-intentioned coordinator of La Rosa's panel that night. She asked participants to redefine their meaning of community by accepting diversity and change. She asked them to recognize and acknowledge that gentrification could have positive effects and, most emphatically, to acknowledge that we live in a "globalized world," where difference and change were the order of the day.[1] The result was a presentation of how Latinos in this "Latin enclave" are responding to the processes of "inevitable transition," a perspective that underscored the simultaneous reinscription and denial of this linkage of Latino/a culture with space, or, more perceptively, the different uses to which the concept of a "Latin barrio" can be put to play.

This chapter considers the linkage of culture, space, and gentrification. Namely, my concern is El Barrio's Puerto Rican and Latino identity from the perspective of my primarily Puerto Rican informants, as well as the deployments of this identity, especially in response to processes of gentrification. This involves calling attention to the objectification of culture in relation to gentrification and change.[2] By "objectification of culture," I mean its reduction and linkage to particular traits, conventions, or, more appropriately here, spaces, a well-documented aspect of managing a particular "culture" and its bearers and thereby expediting modernization and social transformation.[3] These are the same dynamics that play out in numerous tourist, nationalist, and multiculturalist contexts, all of which presuppose the existence of a bounded and identifiable "culture" that can be showcased and deployed for a range of political, social, and economic ends. This is why I maintain that discourses of Latinidad can be central to both processes of gentrification and to local resistance to these forces. Similar processes are evident in Central and West Harlem, whose identity as the "Black capital of the world" has been pivotal to its marketing to outside developers (Jackson 2001; Monique Taylor 1994). It is not surprising, then, that public assurances that Harlem is undergoing a "second renaissance" come at the very time that EZ legislation is selling the area to outside corporations and fueling rapid demographic transformations. Assertions of identity are, after all, central to the marketing of place, and neither process is devoid of contradictions.

By looking at La Rosa event participants, I will also introduce primary informants who, in different ways, shared and helped shape this vision through their work and participation in Puerto Rican and Latino cultural and political networks. This was not a homogenous group but one that shared similar immediate concerns and, most important, functioned as "place makers," brokers, and interlocutors for this community, aiming to secure El Barrio's "identity of place" (Massey 1994). These are processes that were invariably accompanied by distinctions and hierarchies of belonging and entitlement to space among residents, even among the conglomerate of Puerto Ricans invested in El Barrio's Puerto Rican and Latino identity. Yet, these distinctions notwithstanding, I suggest that attempts at promoting El Barrio's past and present as a Puerto Rican and Latino area constitute an important response to the area's gentrification. Even if they are unable to challenge the policies expediting transformations in El Barrio, these cultural practices help to at least confront the de-ethnicization of the area and the erasure of Puerto Ricans' memory that accompany these processes. Most significant, and in light of the role that marketing plays in the re-signification of space, these practices of place-making by Puerto Rican activists also promote alternative logics for the evaluation of culture and a different approach toward its marketing to those increasingly at play in El Barrio. Namely, rather than marketable ethnicity, that is, cleansed ethnicity that is palatable to economic developers, their goal is cultural assertion. This is the claim that a different definition of community should prevail; one that accounts for a past of social struggles, as opposed to that favored by developers and neoliberal policies.

THE LINKAGE OF CULTURE AND SPACE

Participants in La Rosa were selected through recommendations and previous contacts of the LMCC, which explained the predominance of artists and arts administrators on the panel. But an ad in the local Spanish newspaper *Siempre* and a public announcement by the parish of St. Cecilia Church, along with word-of-mouth and formal invitations, provided a more diverse audience of local residents and Puerto Rican community leaders, and hence a good introduction to the characters and identities of some of my primary informants. As one of them stated in self-recognition, the group gathered many of *"los mismos de siempre,"* that is, a core of people with a history of collaboration, and of mistrust in some cases, but overall, many of the same people recurrently speaking for, organizing in behalf of, or publicly vouching for El Barrio.

Panelists included Fernando Salicrup and Marcos Dimas, artists and codirectors of the Julia de Burgos Latino Cultural Center, who have been active in the East Harlem artistic scene since the late 1960s and have directed the center since its opening in the mid-1990s. There was also Joe Cuba, salsa musician and board member of the International Salsa Museum; Melissa Mark Viverito, a new East Harlem resident from the Vieques Solidarity Network and Mujeres del Barrio (Women of El Barrio); as well as artist Diógenes Ballester, YerbaBuena musician Tato Torres, and author Raquel Rivera. Also present was Jose Rivera, the founder of East Harlem Online and one of the few Latino staff members at EZ; and the artistic director of Mixta Gallery and a new homeowner in El Barrio, Tanya Torres. Meanwhile members of the audience included Gloria Quiñonez, retired lawyer and civic leader; Debbie Quiñones, from the

Cultural Affairs Committee of Community Board 11; Ismael Nunez from the East Harlem Historical Society; Father Skelly from St. Cecilia; a representative of Edison Project; district leader Felix Rosado; and other residents, speaking from a variety of positions, all in agreement about the rising rents and the threat presented by the "many whites" renovating tenements and moving to the area. Altogether, attendees included new and old residents of El Barrio, people who had been born and raised in the neighborhood, and those recently attracted by cheaper rents relative to Manhattan and by home-ownership opportunities. There were also a few non-Barrio residents invited by the organizer as part of a list serve distributed to interested parties in cultural policy and programming throughout the city. This wide exposure of the event, including two sets of cameras that visibly followed participants whenever they spoke, rendered the event more of a public display than an intimate discussion. A skeptical artist insisted to me that the tape would end up in someone's basement. Others wondered if their images would be used to get money for more museum-type community programs they don't need.

Some of these frustrations were addressed in the discussion, during which people quickly began raising concerns about gentrification and changes in their community, perhaps inspired by their immediate experience, which to some was an obvious extension of these processes. The audience, made up primarily of Puerto Rican residents, reacted to the organizer's repeated request that speakers define what they meant by community and acknowledge El Barrio's growing demographic diversity. Echoing repeated statements by media and politicians, the request was quickly challenged. Predictably, participants used the event as an opportunity to assert El Barrio's significance as a Puerto Rican and Latino stronghold, vividly exposing the threats they felt were being exerted on them by processes of gentrification. Hence the response of Tato Torres, the leader of the Puerto Rican and Caribbean music group YerbaBuena, to the organizer's prompts that panelists account for the area's growing demographic diversity:

I think that when we live in the building, I live in one community; when I live in El Barrio, I live in another community; when I live in Yorkville, I live in another community. I have to go back to who I hang out with, where I spend my money. So literally, you live on the same block, same building, same floor but can live in two different communities. But is there anybody here that says to their friends, "Yeah, I live in Upper York-ville," like you see in the newspapers? That community is not going to be the same kind as mine. And that's really important.

In other words, while acknowledging El Barrio's demographic diversity, Tato asserts that although many different communities live in El Barrio, it is still El Barrio. Different communities may live next to each other in East Harlem, he notes, yet "living in El Barrio" is ultimately defined through practice—"Who I hang out with, where I spend my money"—that is, a matter of participating in particular networks, namely Puerto Rican networks of politics, entertainment, and consumption. Most emphatically, however, Tato's words reaffirm that newcomers could come into this neighborhood, but never be part of El Barrio; that El Barrio is *not* Upper Yorkville. In other words, not only should El Barrio be defined as a Puerto Rican and Latino community first and foremost, its history should be asserted and promoted, not erased by processes of change. Another attendee stated this more forcefully when he appealed to El Barrio's role as repository of Puerto Rican traditions:

El Barrio is the first place where Puerto Ricans flourished. This is where salsa music was born, where Los Rosarios de Cruz [chanted rosaries] are still sung, and little ladies make *pasteles.* Now everyone wants a piece of East Harlem. But we can never forget that this is the Ellis Island of the entire Latino community. Everyone has come through El Barrio. This is where we became politically active in New York.

These associations of culture and place are central to understanding El Barrio's significance as a Puerto Rican and Latino space. Namely, for residents and for many Puerto Ricans in and beyond El Barrio, this identity is not solely based on the numerical dominance of Puerto Ricans and Latinos in the area, but rather on their having historically worked, waged struggles, and imbued space with meaning and memories. This—in addition to the range of interests, from advertisers to politicians who have a vested interest in this identity and continually feed it through public representations—has undoubtedly heightened the political and economic value of such representations, not unlike similar constructions of culture and place recently discussed for Harlem, or "Harlemworld," or Black Corona (Gregory 1998; Jackson 2001). As such, the area's symbolic and public significance is seen as transcending and incommensurable with its demographic composition, just as local struggles in El Barrio over the maintenance and future of this community as a "Latin" barrio are never entirely "local." This sentiment is best expressed in the saying *"El Barrio es de todos"* (El Barrio belongs to us all), often said about El Barrio, where *"todos"* implies an "imagined community" of Puerto Ricans both in and beyond the confines of El Barrio, making it emblematic of a "Puerto Rican" and Latino social space.[4] As a member of the community board impassionedly noted: *"El Barrio es la cuna de los Puertorriqueños* [the cradle of Puerto Ricans]. Before there were Puerto Rican communities in Orlando, Hartford, or Alaska, we were here, and we owe it to our children to keep it Puerto Rican, or else Latino."

Cultural geographers posit that space is always socially constituted, and not solely through physical boundaries, representations, or practices, but by the interaction of these various elements. These may sometimes coalesce or oppose each other, but most centrally, are always connected to how we understand, live, and experience a particular "space."[5] This view of space allows one to get a better grasp of El Barrio's social significance, not only in relation to its jurisdictional boundaries—as defined by political, school board, or community board district lines, which in fact are sometimes at odds with each other—but also in relation to the meanings and values vested by its representations and by the social struggles, memories, and histories embedded therein. El Barrio is seen by many of my informants as having "inalienable" value as a space of cultural assertion, a shelter and respite for identity, that should be maintained and protected and is not quantifiable by the standards of speculators in the market.[6] Constructed as such, this value is one that undoubtedly complicates discussions of gentrification in the area, notably by increasing the stakes of this process among many Puerto Rican residents.

Yet inalienable value is never free of political significance, just as the concept of "community" freely deployed by my informants is not absolved of contradictions for implying a homogeneity and consensus in what is always fraught with contingencies. For one, it can serve as a medium of hierarchy, such as among those deemed to have greater or lesser legitimate access to political posts or to the development of projects in the area. Concerns over the maintenance of El Barrio as a place *"de todos"* is a case in point. *"De todos"* clearly has more precise meanings. Notwithstanding the widespread appeals to Latinidad that are increasingly heard in East Harlem, this view places Puerto Ricans as the most-entitled to this space, followed by Latinos. This view can also sustain hierarchies among residents of El Barrio, such as those with the education and money to profit from El Barrio's symbolic "inalienability" and those who lack these advantages. After all, assertions of identity, as the very junction of culture and space, are never free of contradictions. The decisive component is always its specific uses, as well as the contexts framing this use.

In fact, in the context of gentrification, attempts at minimizing or superseding the presence of Puerto Ricans have only raised the significance of this nexus of culture and place. Recall that the growing concern over El Barrio has not emerged in a vacuum. Puerto Ricans' dream of place is increasingly shattered by housing policies and by a housing market that does not favor them. Their experiences with empowerment legislation, in particular, demonstrated the difficulties of cashing in on a devalued culture that accrues little recognition and value from the mainstream society, and that development entrepreneurs and tourist pundits would prefer be transformed or erased. Additionally, real and perceived changes in the level of power Puerto Ricans had achieved, or believed they had achieved in the past but had since lost, contributed to a general sense of disenfranchisement. The latter materialized around two recurrent topics of discussions in my interviews: lack of Puerto Rican leadership and concern with inequities over economic development funds. Both of these issues became racially loaded, inauspiciously pitting Blacks and Puerto Ricans against each other, always with compelling reverberations for development decisions and debates.

As noted, Puerto Rican politicians in East Harlem had attained political dominance throughout the 1970s and mid-1980s, with the concurrent elections of Senator Olga Méndez, Assemblyman Del Toro, Councilman Roberto Rodríguez, and Latino chairs in the community board (such as Harry Rodríguez). They had also wrested control of state and local resources for urban renewal and community empowerment, control in effect assured by their able mobilization of the linkage of culture and place.[7] Roberto Anazagasti would eagerly recall the organization of the blockbuster Fiestas Patronales del Barrio in the mid 1970s in order to contest East Harlem's marginalization from the Model Cities Program, an important urban revitalization antipoverty program. The management and distribution of Model Cities funds had been apportioned mainly to the African American leadership of West and Central Harlem, he explained, but the festival made insurmountably clear from then on that El Barrio was a politically active community in its own right. As said, the ensuing Puerto Rican political bloc of the times was not devoid of critics. Their power was also relative, considering it had always been mediated by other local and state-level politicians. In hindsight, however, Puerto Ricans felt they had lost considerable electoral power since the 1980s, particularly in relation to African Americans, who were then dominant in most local development entities: Phil Reed and David Gibbens as councilman and chairman of the Community Board, respectively, and as members of the community board. In 2001, when there were sixteen Latinos and twenty-three African Americans appointed by the Black councilman and the borough president, rumors circulated about their preference for appointing Blacks over Latinos.

Phil Reed, an openly gay African American Democrat with an impressive history of community activism, was a definite trigger and target of local frustrations.[8] He was openly dismissive, impatient, and even scornful toward any claim based on ethnicity or race. In fact, he was the only Black or Latino councilman who was not part of the New York City Council's Black and Latino caucus. While obviously intended to diminish ethnic conflicts, such disavowals of a given group's claims to El Barrio were predictably distrusted by many Puerto Rican residents and community leaders.

Heightened concerns over the losses by Puerto Ricans in El Barrio should be gauged against the rise of the Republican Party in a historically

Figure 4.   District leaders Harry Rodriguez, Carmen Quiñones, and Felix Rosado at a press conference in Edwin's Café, where they denounced their treatment by the Democratic Party in 2003. Photo courtesy of *Siempre* newspaper.

Democratic district, and privatization policies that did not favor the largely publicly funded Puerto Rican organizations in the area. Charges that the Democratic Party was dismissive of Latinos, particularly of Puerto Ricans, and that the African American leadership took them for granted and was unwilling to back them in leadership positions within the party, were even the subject of a press conference in El Barrio where Puerto Rican district leaders made public threats to leave the party. In 2003, the Democratic Party redrew the district lines for Puerto Rican district leaders Felix Rosado and Carmen Quiñones without their knowledge. District leaders Rosado and Harry Rodríguez requested support from José Rivera, leader of the Democratic Party in the Bronx, a move that suggested the waning of Puerto Ricans' political power in El Barrio and its growing consolidation in the Bronx. For many of my informants, this consolidation was at the cost of Puerto Ricans in El Barrio, who were left out of alliances among Puerto Ricans in the Bronx, Dominicans in Washington Heights, and the African American leadership of the Democratic Party. Evidently then, it was not "Black politicians," but partisan politics—in which many Puerto Rican leaders in the Bronx, and even in El Barrio, strived—that was most implicated with Puerto Ricans' growing disempowerment in East Harlem.

The apathy and skepticism surrounding local electoral politics could be felt in the air. In fact, it was the subject of the 2003 political comedy movie *Vote for Me*, written and directed by Nelson Denis, a former assemblyman in El Barrio (1996–2000). Spoofs of Charles Rangel and Adam Clayton Powell IV are amply recognizable to insiders of East Harlem politics, as is the vehement nationalism of local politics vividly evoked by the vociferous "Viva Puerto Rico" with which a seventy-year-old super wins a seat in the U.S. Congress. Politicians Olga Méndez and Powell were largely absent in public debates, perceived as generally unresponsive to the wider community. Thus, when in a not-so-surprising switch, Olga Méndez turned to the Republican Party in 2002, people believed the change was largely irrelevant. Others disagreed, with good reasons. As Méndez noted in public appearances—in her characteristic populist demeanor that made her a local favorite of admiration, gossip, and hearsay—this move allowed her, and hence East Harlem, greater power and resources from a Republican-dominated state and city government. Coincidentally, Republicans were then eagerly courting the Latino vote, said to be more "fluid" than that of Black voters. Whether East Harlem's neediest would see any of these resources, however, was doubted by most East Harlemites I spoke to; this notwithstanding the great deference received by Méndez. All of these factors contributed to a sense of imperilment in the political realm, fueling in turn activists' concerns about the future of El Barrio. Their worst fears unfolded during debates over the redistricting of city council boundaries for East Harlem in 2002. When New York City's Redistricting Commission proposed reapportioning important sectors of East Harlem in ways that would have reduced the number of Latino voters and removed important symbolic Latino landscapes—such as "La Marqueta," which is also a highly coveted development site—residents had to rise up in heated protest before the commission finally revised the plan. The final redistricting plan, however, just reversed the proposed changes, doing little to accommodate growing concerns over the election of a Latino candidate in the future.[9]

This is the context informing the emergence and the work of a variety of new community groups such as Boricuas del Barrio (Puerto Ricans of El Barrio) and Mujeres del Barrio and media outlets such as *Siempre,* all of which emerged in early 2000. Espousing a Puerto Rican and Latin vision for their community, these groups appealed to Latinidad whenever needed, though the agenda and membership of their groups was primarily Puerto Rican, a stance purposefully intended to contrast and remedy what its members saw as a failing organizational structure among Puerto Ricans. As the largest voting contingent among Latino/as, their position, a member noted, would have major repercussions for all Latino/as.[10] In the words of Melissa Mark Viverito of Mujeres del Barrio, "It's up to us because it's us who vote." Mujeres del Barrio, which was founded by a group of professional women representing different sectors of El Barrio, from housing advocacy, to law, to churches, provides a good example of this stance. Among their goals was challenging elected officials to be accountable to El Barrio, and, most of all, to groom more leaders. With this they meant not only Puerto Rican leaders, but progressive leaders who were responsive and accountable to Puerto Ricans and helpful in furthering a Puerto Rican and Latino/a agenda in El Barrio. Local politicians were "comfortable and unchallenged"; no one questioned destructive projects and policies, said Melissa upon announcing her candidacy for city council—one of at least three Puerto Rican candidates who unsuccessfully challenged the incumbent in 2003. Boricuas del Barrio sponsored events such as "Y Ahora Que? (Now What?): Census 2000, El Barrio and the Latino/a Community" and "We're Still Here, Self Education Seminar," both of which revolved around issues of economic and political empowerment and are indicative of the sense of imperilment mobilizing many Puerto Ricans in the face of gentrification.[11]

The growing emphasis on cultural self-assertion is also evident in disagreements over the name of the community, an old debate heated by the area's gentrification. Activist and church leader Carmen Villegas passionately spoke to this when recalling previous debates in the community board: "There were always people who would correct me when I used 'El Barrio'; they insisted on calling it East Harlem. They never understood the meaning and the symbolism of El Barrio. For us, El Barrio means *la lucha,* that everyday struggle of living, of our culture and roots,

Figure 5. Members of the advocacy group Mujeres del Barrio after a fund-raising event at Julia de Burgos Latino Cultural Center. From left to right: Bettie Gutié, Sandra Talavera, Raquel Villegas, Yolanda Sánchez, Melissa Mark Viverito, Gloria Quiñonez, Carmen Vázquez, and Erica González. Photo by the author.

a testimony of all we had to overcome to say 'El Barrio.'" And this was no small feat. It was never "cool" to identify oneself as Puerto Rican, as I was reminded by more than one long-time resident of El Barrio. Miguel Rivera, an activist tenant of Taino Towers, who came to El Barrio in the 1960s, remembered coming to terms with Puerto Ricans' debased status as follows: "First you have white males, then white females, then Europeans, then Jewish, then African American, then Puerto Ricans. If you were light-skinned Puerto Rican, you'd try to pass for Irish or Italian, and if you were dark skinned, then you tried to pass for African American. Being Puerto Rican was the worst of the worst."

Chroniclers of East Harlem's racial/ethnic landscape in the late 1950s attest to the widespread racism of the time. Then and now, to be categorized as Black was to be positioned at the bottom of the racial hierarchy.

Similarly, embracing one's nationality—in this case, one's Puertorican-ness—has long been a documented way for immigrant newcomers to differentiate themselves from African Americans, even when these distinctions may not be recognized by the greater society. Within the dominant U.S. white/Black binary, however, only "white" or "Black" provided recognized paths toward Americanization, a medium to overcome being marginalized as "Puerto Rican." This identity was a particularly stigmatized identity in the 1950s and 1960s, when Puerto Ricans comprised the poorest and first massive non-European immigrant wave into the city. The scorn toward recent Puerto Rican migrants by more "Americanized," U.S.-born and reared Puerto Ricans, or the tendency of many Puerto Ricans to identify as Hispanic or as members of any other Latin American nationality, speaks to the low status and stigma associated with Puerto Ricans at this time (Padilla 1958; Wakefield 1959, 35–37).

This state of affairs is exactly what the Nuyorican cultural nationalism and struggles of the late 1960s and 1970s were meant to challenge. They did so through the creation of new institutions and through artistic and cultural production anchored in the value of the Nuyorican or New York-based (now synonymous with U.S.-based) cultural expressions and an alternative Puertoricanness that did not conform to island-centric, Hispanocentric definitions of Puertoricanness.[12]

Widespread usage of "El Barrio" and acceptance of a name so identified with Puerto Ricans, particularly by non-Puerto Ricans when done in solidarity, was hence a definite accomplishment. But now that East Harlem was being increasingly subsumed into neighboring Harlem, or else referred to as Upper Manhattan, Upper Carnegie Hill, and Yorkville by developers and new tenants, people felt there was far more at stake. Not only were these names seen to expedite change, many feared that Puerto Rican's history of previous struggles would be undermined with the voiding of El Barrio. Others were far more irate, as the following e-mail response to an East Harlem online discussion shows. This Web site, entirely dedicated to the community—particularly to challenging its image as a "poor" community by showing its richness in "culture, political activity, ideas, ideals, religion, and people"—provides another example of cultural reassertion emerging alongside current developments.

Addressing the request of a number of unnamed Hispanic activists to Councilman Reed that he use "El Barrio" when referring to East Harlem, the respondent, a poet and activist, provides an acute and untempered account of the concerns voiced with more nuance by others:

> What's in a name? History! The African American community has their community in Harlem; the Dominicans are beginning to carve out a space for their people in Quisqueya (Washington Heights). . . . Spanish Harlem is the soul and heartbeat of the Puerto Rican people. . . . In a perfect world, name[s] would mean nothing, but in this world, groups survive by controlling space and maintaining a viable and visible presence. . . . You give up that name, and three things will happen: (1) Blacks will claim East Harlem as "Black territory"; (2) Mexicans will claim it as "New Mexico"; and (3) Latino/a, white, and Black liberals will create a new image to satisfy all groups. . . . Take a good look at the fight for money in the Upper Manhattan Empowerment Zone and one will understand the meanings, etc., etc. I vote for Spanish Harlem all the way. Sincerely, Alberto O. Cappas, President, Don Pedro Enterprises. There is a Rose in Spanish Harlem! (http://www.east-harlem.com/spanish _harlem.htm).

Plainly, winning the battle of names would be no small feat for El Barrio or, better phrased in this case, for Spanish Harlem! Additionally, the message points to the many factors—from Mexicans, Blacks, and liberals to the EZ—that were seen to be implicated with the ubiquitous subordination of Puerto Ricans in an imperfect world, where names signify place and, in turn, power. Evidently, the political valence and the stakes of this nexus of culture and space in El Barrio are both compromised and heightened by the area's gentrification. This linkage nourishes a remembrance of the past, but not without also deterring, at least for now, the kind of openings the past once created in the future.

RACE, CULTURE, AND THE MAKING OF EL BARRIO

It is important to note that the urgency felt by Puerto Rican activists over El Barrio's transformation was not shared by all East Harlemites. Many residents across race and ethnicity, including Puerto Ricans, saw demographic and social shifts as welcome changes that would ultimately increase the value of their investments, or else help improve services available in the area. Residents' attitudes to the threat that gentrification posed to El Barrio's Latino/a identity were also connected to how they saw or positioned themselves against the nexus of culture and place on which this identity is based. The case of African Americans, the area's second largest group, is worth considering. For some African American residents, current changes represented the opening of political and leadership opportunities. Consider the comments of Emma Jackson, a retired African American resident of forty years in East Harlem, who has long been politically involved in campaign advocacy. Like other long-time residents of public housing, who I found had little knowledge of changes in federal housing legislation, she considers herself protected from gentrification. Although she admitted that changes were indeed apace in the community, she insisted that, in contrast to Puerto Ricans, she would be unaffected.

> You have to understand that the average African American in this community does not feel as threatened by gentrification. And this is because of the close proximity with West Harlem. All we have to do is cross Fifth Avenue and you're in Harlem. So, we have never depended culturally on this community. Our churches are in West Harlem. I go to Abyssinian Church. I don't even shop here. We've always done this. The average African American person in my building can tell you everything about politics in Harlem, not necessarily of East Harlem.

Besides, she noted, the whites who are moving to El Barrio are primarily transient young professionals, not families or people invested in establishing institutions and roots, as are Blacks and Latino/as. Whites were well known to stay put, in safe havens; they patronized the new trendy bars Orbitz or Dinerbar or shopped early in the morning at Pathmark. They were yet to be seen as stakeholders to the area. Not all African Americans I spoke with disregarded the threat of gentrification on these bases; Ms. Jackson's claim that she "had never depended culturally on this community" does not mean that she does not have ties, or doesn't participate or is not active in East Harlem. Some of the most widely recognized community leaders in East Harlem are in fact African American women like Emma Jackson, active on the community board, in political advocacy, and other forums. Ms. Jackson herself was actively working toward the creation of a credit union to empower East Harlemites financially. Her statement, however, attests to an understanding of East Harlem that is different from that espoused by many Puerto Ricans in El Barrio: namely, ongoing transformations did not affect cultural and social networks of many African American East Harlemites in the ways it did Puerto Ricans. In fact, she sees openings in current transformations, evidencing the very active exclusions that accompany a history of ethnic politics in the area. In 2002, she even ran for state assembly. In her words, "For a long time, people thought that you have to be a Latino/a to be a leader, and they would say, This seat or this office belongs to a Puerto Rican. But no seat belongs to anyone, that's why we vote."

Other African Americans assured me they lacked the "nostalgia" felt by Puerto Rican residents in the area. Some made a point of clarifying that El Barrio is a particular piece of East Harlem, primarily south of 116th Street, not the totality of East Harlem. Mediating residents' perceptions of East Harlem's Latino/a identity is the fact that despite generalizing references to "East Harlem" or "El Barrio" as an undifferentiated community, East Harlemites—particularly older generations—generally recognized East Harlem as containing three communities: the Triangle, East Harlem's northern part, from 125th Street to 142nd Street; Spanish Harlem/El Barrio, running from 96th Street to 125th Street; and Little Italy, its eastern tip. These divisions evoked the racial/ethnic boundaries stemming from the insulated residential patterns of Italians, Puerto Ricans, and African Americans that congealed in the late 1940s and 1950s. Moreover, within these areas, residents also distinguished different microcommunities marked by class, race, and type of housing. Some housing developments or areas are thus considered to be more Black or Latino/a or middle class, while the organizations, clubs, and socializing taking place within particular housing projects helped to forge social networks that both fed into and bridged interethnic and interracial relations. Consider the comments of Yolanda Gates, an African American member of the community board and a long time resident of the Riverton Houses located on 135th Street and part of East Harlem's Triangle, which is considered a Black stronghold in East Harlem.[13] She used specific housing projects to mark class and a particular "community."

> This community, and I don't mean East Harlem, but this community of housing, of Lincoln and Riverton, has always been primarily Black, however, Hispanics were also part of this community. And the issue was not about race, but class. Two out of three tenants were middle class living in rental spaces and co-ops. Our community was the people who lived here and who you played with. I had a Hispanic friend at 107th and Park, and I remember how my mom expressed concerns that when I visited, I was entering another neighborhood. Her fears were not about my visiting a Hispanic area, but the class card is a different story.

At the same time, the proximity of Central Harlem and the existence of microcommunities within sections of East Harlem do not imply that African Americans do not identify with El Barrio's "Latin" heritage. Marion Bell also gravitates to Central Harlem because of its cultural life; in her words, "All Pentecostal churches in East Harlem are in Spanish." But she noted:

> Many African Americans are unaware of their connections with the Caribbean and don't identify with the culture that's here, but that was never my experience. I went to a store and they called it bodega, but my neighborhood was mine, mine and my girlfriends'. To me El Barrio was the other name for the neighborhood, and it was never a problem that it was a Spanish-speaking neighborhood. As a young person I never felt that I could not be part of East Harlem. Not the young people. We had Spanish girlfriends and boyfriends. I did hear people say, "Don't bring the Black boy home," but then they'd become part of the *familia*. I'm not blind to racism, but for younger generations it was natural to live in this bicultural world. . . . East Harlem is a Latin capital like Harlem is the Black capital of the world, and we would do a disservice to this community if we erased the historical legacy of this land. We already did that to the Native Americans who lived here. Why should we lose another culture?

As her comments show, there is a variability in perspectives over the constitutive boundaries of El Barrio as a Puerto Rican and Latino/a social space, and about the level of inclusion it communicated to its African

American residents, and certainly to other residents for that matter. It is also important to recognize that these boundaries of culture, race, and space are, in practice, far more fluid than peoples' comments suggest. Supporting a Puerto Rican agenda at a public meeting, while later socializing and participating in African American circuits, was not uncommon among Puerto Ricans, particularly those born and raised in El Barrio who have forged social networks through friendships and daily social relations that mediated relationships among groups in ways that could never be captured at the level of community board politics. Furthermore, many Puerto Rican activists, invested in maintaining El Barrio's identity of place, were in fact Black Puerto Ricans, proud of their Black heritage and their identity as Afro-Boricuas. Latinidad and African-Americanness, as Raquel Rivera reminds us, are not mutually exclusive categories among many New York Puerto Ricans, particularly Black Puerto Ricans, whose negotiations of identities challenge both Hispanocentric definitions of Latinidad and Blackness that only takes African Americans into account (2003).

At the same time, I found few Black Puerto Ricans who, while proud of their African heritage, would identify themselves as "Black Latinos"—an emergent category that should be explored in greater detail in light of the continued reticence among Latinos to identify themselves racially, or Puerto Ricans to readily identify themselves as "Latinos." "Call me Puerto Rican" was the headline of an editorial response to a *New York Times* article on how Black Latinos are carving a niche in New York City—if not, call me Nuyorican or Afro-Boricua or any other Puerto Rican–specific category—is what I would hear most from Afro-Boricuas in El Barrio (Navarro 2003; Lopez 2003). In other words, Puerto Ricans' embrace of Blackness was never solely predicated on the use of racially specific categories nor simultaneously dependent on the negation of nationality-based categories. Similarly, a pro–Puerto Rican stance did not necessarily entail acceptance of the dominant Hispanocentric definitions of Puerto Rican identity—favoring light skin, mastery of the Spanish language, or direct knowledge of the island (Flores 2000; Zentella 1997).

Simultaneous appeals to El Barrio and to East Harlem as a "community" implying commonality across class and race, were commonplace, as were situational uses of El Barrio, Spanish Harlem, or East Harlem according to who was present. Black community leaders were as likely to use "El Barrio" among Puerto Rican audiences as Puerto Ricans were to call on "East Harlem" to unite Black and white audiences when summoning support for particular issues. Again, associations of culture and place are not intrinsically exclusionary in and of themselves, but rather convey opportunities and constraints only in particularized contexts. It is in the pursuit of political or economic gain, my informants invariably concurred, that the prospects for forging coalitions and common political agendas, especially between Puerto Ricans and African Americans, are most affected by notions of place, ethnicity, and race. Then, rooted associations of ethnicity and place were attendant, not only in how people saw themselves and others, but perhaps most decisively, in how others could potentially interpret their actions. Perhaps the best example of the heightened racial politics pervading these politicized moments is the 2002 election of community board officers, especially the contest between African American incumbent David Gibbens and El Barrio–born-and-raised Puerto Rican candidate Debbie Quiñones. During an evocative debate with racial overtones, noticeably indexed by spatial references, a Puerto Rican community board member charged that the African American moderator had shortchanged his time for asking questions to the Puerto Rican candidate, while an African American member accused the Puerto Rican candidate of bias. Namely she accused Quiñones of favoring lower East Harlem, "below 106th Street," areas recognized to be "more Latino/a," which Quiñones vehemently denied. She lived on 121st Street—signifying Upper (Black) East Harlem—Quiñones immediately noted. Still, after a very tense public voting roll, all African American members present, with one abstention, gave their vote to David Gibbens, electing him Chairman for a fourteenth term. All Puerto Ricans present, with one exception, sided with Quiñones.

THE PARTIAL 'TODOS'

The construction of El Barrio as a primarily Puerto Rican and Latino/a space does not imply homogeneity among the Puerto Rican culture brokers involved in its making. Important variables to consider here are those of class, education, and place of origin. Thus, just as some residents bemoaned whites, others, such as those with a longer history in El Barrio, criticized Puerto Rican newcomers just as forcefully, despite their Puerto Rican nationality and pro-Puerto Rican leanings. The very passionate intervention by Anna Morales at the La Rosa del Barrio panel is exemplary of these dynamics:

> I probably represent a lot of the things that this community is made up of. I'm a single parent, one child, and I've been raising her alone for the last eleven to twelve years. I was born and raised here, went to schools in the community. So I think I represent those folks who probably you're talking about. So it's kind of weird listening to people, some of whom I know, others I've never seen, telling me about my community and what should happen. . . . A lot of the people coming into this community are complaining about the gentrification, but they're part of the gentrification. . . . It's not just me, there's a lot of other women who are in my position, and trust me, there's a whole bunch of us. And people in politics, you better address us, because I'm telling you, we vote. But with all due respect to everybody here tonight, they do not want to be here tonight. Because we talk about the very professional upper-class professional and then we talk about this other strata of folks, but there's a group of people that I deal with everyday, and you know what, they're fed up. They feel that if they vote they have to say so. There's no accomplishment for them, there's no changes for them, and it's a big group, and I tell you, that big group, by not voting will decide what's going to happen to this community.

I quote Anna Morales's statement at length because it so exemplifies the existing heterogeneity among "Puerto Ricans" that destabilizes simple claims to space based on nationality, along variables as varied as education, professional status, class, and even length of residence in El Barrio. In particular, Ms. Morales underscores that Puerto Ricans are also key agents of gentrification, reminding us of the complexities that permeate discussions even among members of the so-called same group.[14] Like Ms. Morales, some Puerto Rican long-time residents of El Barrio understandably resented the many professional Puerto Ricans now moving to El Barrio when they had long felt derided by the upwardly mobile

Puerto Ricans, for whom leaving El Barrio had been a mark of success. They, not newcomers—be they Puerto Ricans from the island, or U.S. born seeking either to move for the first time or to relocate to El Barrio, or other Latinos—had the greatest claim to this community. It is they who had made El Barrio what it was now by staying put despite previous interludes of landlord abandonment, economic isolation, and urban blight. Others, however, felt that work and commitment to furthering El Barrio were the preeminent criteria for inclusion in networks where "newcomers" from the island were always present. This is not a new process, as attested by Bernardo Vega, the tobacco worker who produced one of the most detailed accounts of Puerto Rican life in New York from 1916 to the mid-1940s. He demonstrated that class and educational differentiation have a long history in El Barrio where writers, poets, and political activists from Puerto Rico and beyond had come together and were central to the making of Latino/a institutions and communities (Andreu Iglesias 1984). Cultural nationalism, involving the preeminence of culture to the maintenance of Puerto Rican identity, continues to be a binding force uniting Puerto Ricans from the island and the U.S. Yet part of cultural nationalism are exclusionary notions of authenticity that also imbue these relationships in multiple ways. Accordingly, "real" Puerto Rican culture is equated with the island and with territorially defined culture, just as transnational Puerto Rican urban authenticity is equated with the diaspora, such as with being born and raised in El Barrio. Neither Puerto Ricans from the island nor those from El Barrio are entirely whole according to such notions, and the ensuing quests for validation are sources of distinction, and oftentimes of hostility and distrust. I call attention to the "lacks" experienced by both Puerto Ricans from El Barrio and the island because much has been said about islanders' supposedly greater cultural capital as "Puerto Rican" on account of enduring nationalist pretenses prioritizing territoriality—that is, being born on the island—or direct knowledge of Puerto Rico (Lassalle and Pérez 1997; Ramos-Zayas 2003). But equally so, El Barrio Puerto Ricans had their own set of cultural knowledge to make territorial and cultural claims to El Barrio. East Harlemites voiced their "authentic" claim to El Barrio by referring to the particular school they attended or the hospital—such as

Metropolitan or Mt. Sinai—where they were born. In interviews they rec-
ollected particular ethnic boundaries—"when it was safe for Puerto
Ricans to cross Italian areas"—and knowledge of spaces once proscribed
to whites and outsiders, such as the Jefferson Houses. Such stances carried little economic rewards, however, as compared to those of economic
capital and education, especially vis-à-vis politically connected stakeholders—who, predictably, were also primarily male.

As has been documented in other Puerto Rican communities, political
activism around the United States' continued colonial control of the
island, such as that which galvanized around Vieques, was another catalyst linking Puerto Ricans across class and background (McAffrey 2002;
Ramos-Zayas 2003). Another factor was agreement on the goal of furthering Puerto Rican empowerment in and beyond El Barrio. These are
the same dynamics feeding into the view that *"El Barrio es de todos,"*
which also provided the basis upon which I gained acceptance among
many of my Puerto Rican informants, despite my being a nonresident of
El Barrio. I was seen—or at least I believe I was generally seen—by El
Barrio's Puerto Ricans and Mexican leadership as someone who would
contribute to El Barrio by documenting their struggles, rather than pro-
ducing one more drug, crime, or poverty exposé.

Still, differences between Puerto Ricans from the island and from El
Barrio are not insignificant. As an island-born Puerto Rican whose work
has long focused on U.S. Latino/a cultural politics, I am well aware that
these differences have implications not only for debates of cultural
authenticity, but also for access to jobs, education, resources, and ultimately upward mobility. Indeed, under the present conditions of gentrification, those with higher educational attainment and money have
greater access to the new middle-income home programs, to establishing
"Puerto Rican" shops, restaurants, galleries in the area, and sometimes
even to achieving leadership positions. And educated Puerto Ricans from
the island enjoy greater advantages here, having been exempted from the
prejudice and discrimination that has long deprived those born and
raised in the United States of opportunities for upward mobility. In fact,
the three most notably recognized Puerto Rican cultural spaces developed in recent years, La Fonda Boricua (a Puerto Rican restaurant), the

Spanish newspaper *Siempre*, and Mixta Gallery (a space for music, poetry and art), were all founded by educated Puerto Ricans from the island who had moved to New York to further their studies or professional endeavors. Being well educated, some with higher professional degrees and possessing some modest capital, they were in relatively good standing to develop these small yet important meeting places de rigueur for Puerto Ricans and Latino/as in El Barrio and beyond. Yet, as Jorge, La Fonda's owner, added after agreeing that his education and middle-class background had contributed to his successful restaurant endeavor in El Barrio: "No es cualquier blanquito de Puerto Rico que cae en El Barrio" (It is not any "little white"—used here to signal wealthy, white, and well to do—Puerto Rican "from the Island" that ends up in El Barrio). But rather, he noted, it is people in the social sciences, artists, and those with a social and political outlook and ability to get in with "their people" that are attracted to El Barrio. Jorge readily attests to a particular type of cultural capital at play among place-makers in El Barrio: this is sometimes alternatively described as having "Boricua" or "community" sensibility, yet another element binding Puerto Ricans of different backgrounds and mediating everyday relationships in the area.

Additionally and perhaps most important, newcomers benefit from their untainted political status; their reputations are unharmed by their participation in previous politics in El Barrio. As one informant put it while referring to those who struggled to open doors in the past but have been bypassed: "There are a lot of people in El Barrio who paid the price, with their mental health and their reputations to open spaces for Puerto Ricans in this community and are now bypassed because they don't look good, and are bitter. Because nowadays you have to have a Ph.D. to be a leader, you have to be a professional." Not insignificantly, there was a greater number of Black and dark-skinned Puerto Ricans among the U.S.–born contingency of *"los mismos de siempre"* vis-à-vis their island-born counterparts, a trend undoubtedly contributing to their unequal experiences of racialization. All of these differences contributed to a general skepticism from old-timers toward educated Puerto Ricans and Latin American artists and activist residents, and the relative ease with which they were seemingly raised to positions of public visibility.

Melissa Mark Viverito, a community activist and new home owner, who is involved in Mujeres del Barrio and the Vieques Solidarity Network, among other issues, represents some of the new Puerto Rican activists who have recharged activism in East Harlem. Educated in private schools in Puerto Rico, raised by parents who were born in the Bronx and who had an activist trajectory of their own, she represents an "anomaly," since she returned to New York after her parents had migrated to the island. Like many Puerto Rican students, she became politically active while attending college, in her case Columbia University, an experience that exposed her to racism and to the fate of Puerto Ricans in New York. She described as a natural progression her move to the nonprofit sector to work for the empowerment of Puerto Ricans with two of the largest and most recognized Puerto Rican organizations in New York: the National Puerto Rican Forum and Aspira. Finding herself "empowering my own but not living in my community"—with "community" here meaning among Puerto Ricans, not a particular spatially bounded "community"—she decided to move into El Barrio in the late 1990s, purchasing a house through one of the first home-ownership programs in East Harlem. Melissa is aware of the frustrations and criticisms that are oftentimes directed to politically connected newcomers like herself and is frustrated that her contributions and activism are overlooked because of conditions that are out of her control. In her view and that of many younger activists, common agendas should prevail. More than the petty resentments of newcomers, however, these attitudes should also be considered in relation to the never spoken, yet ever more evident, "cultural capital" that is increasingly required of Latino/a leaders in a heightened bureaucratic environment. In this context, activism and progressive politics fall short if not complemented by professional and entrepreneurial skills. This is not how some old-timers remember politics in the 1970s, when there were plenty of openings for "community" and "young turks" to join and attain political and economic mobility through activism, community jobs, and local politics.[15]

Awareness of these issues is not to deny the existing collaborations among Puerto Ricans in El Barrio. Rather my purpose is to acknowledge the commonalities that mediate collaborations along the lines of class, education, and a shared vision of El Barrio as a Puerto Rican and Latino/a space while forcing attention on the ensuing exclusions that are always part of alliances. That is to say, not included in these groups are those Anna Morales alluded to when she noted those who didn't want to be at community board meetings, public hearings, electoral debates, or even the voting booth. Those are the truly disenfranchised, and within those circles one will likely find greater gaps with the mostly educated and middle-class Puerto Rican leadership.

Indeed, concerning class and education, the bulk of Puerto Ricans involved in public forums or debating questions of change in El Barrio were college educated, some with professional degrees, and hence represented a relatively select group in a population where only about 56 percent of its residents have received a high school diploma.[16] Service occupations abounded in these networks, such as social work, health, advocacy, or administration with city or nonprofit programs with children, senior citizens, housing, and education. Also present, especially among the younger generation, were entrepreneurs working as cultural promoters in public relations and other private enterprises. Echoing what others repeated in different guises, one noted: "Our leaders in the past were afraid of money. They only operated nonprofits, but now their institutions are lingering, too dependent on public money and elected officials. But we're not mistaken. It's all about money, and you need money to attain self-sufficiency." But they saw themselves as entrepreneurs with conscience and accountability. Erica González, a member of Mujeres, the community board, and the former board of the EZ, who has a background in public relations, described her marketing skills as a medium aimed at promoting Puerto Rican artists, Latino/a poets, and progressive politics: "Our things and our people through economic self-sufficiency." At the same time, civic activism demands disposable time to attend meetings at different times of the day or night, and this too further differentiated them from residents who are rearing children or working double shifts to make ends meet. Thus many were retired, others worked independently or part time, while still many others were young single professionals less burdened by family responsibilities. Moreover, and directly relevant to this work, some of them were homeowners, though in the majority of cases they had purchased and renovated their homes before the tightening of the market. Others had benefited from older state disposition programs favoring tenants and from the state-funded, middle-class home-ownership programs.

Class identities of racialized groupings—whose life trajectories and experiences may stride and transcend variables more closely identified with the "working poor," not "middle class"—are never static and unproblematic, particularly in such a primarily working-class community as East Harlem (Prince 2002a, 2002b; Jackson 2001). People had histories, particularly the U.S.–born contingent of *los mismos de siempre:* more of them straddle class lines, not only by having parents, friends, or relatives living in public housing or on public welfare, but also by having intimate contact with the drugs and poverty long afflicting this community. I'm unable to delve deeper into these differences, other than calling attention to the shared outlook among *los mismos de siempre* despite their heterogeneity of experience, background, and insertion in different sectors of the economy. Briefly then, I am referring to social and cultural workers, activists and self-recognized interlocutors for their community, similarly concerned with the promotion of Puerto Rican and Latino empowerment and of El Barrio's identity of place. As a group, they were generally in a better position to benefit from, rather than be directly threatened by, the gentrification of the area, processes they desperately sought to control.[17]

Finally, and echoing the same processes by which public representations of El Barrio—purposefully or not—often end up referencing its Latino image, El Barrio's Puerto Rican and Latino/a identity is also inadvertently fed by many Puerto Ricans and Latino/as who may in fact not share a direct commitment to this vision. Many Puerto Rican intellectuals involved in cultural networks in El Barrio said to shun ethnic politics strived to create coalitions and alliances. Still, it was the opportunity to participate in vibrant Puerto Rican and Latino networks that first attracted them to El Barrio, they admitted. Even those who came solely because of home-ownership opportunities, as is the case with the Puerto Rican artist/curator Tanya Torres, were active participants in these networks. Her Mixta Gallery, in the storefront of her new home, quickly became a stronghold for Latino/a professionals and artists from throughout the city. Even Puerto Rican and Latino/a visitors who negated or distanced themselves from the ethnic-based politics of space, which they considered "anachronistic" or narrow, found themselves participating in Latino/a cultural, artistic, and political networks, and in so doing directly and indirectly fed into ethnic-based cultural and political networks in the area. Thus the importance of underscoring the different contexts, uses, and purposes of this nexus of culture and place, rather than simply addressing its construction or historical persistence.

EAST HARLEM IS JUMPING

> We want you to come every week and bring a
> friend. Because East Harlem is jumping. Tomor-
> row we have another opening, of Fernando's digi-
> tal work in La Cantina. Fernando, who was part
> of the cultural revolution of Nuyoricans. This rev-
> olution continues today, except now it is digital.
>
> Aurora Flores, speaking to audience at Julia's Jam

Artists represent a particularly important sector among Puerto Rican place-makers, along with intellectuals seeking the sense of community that they believe El Barrio represents over and above other Latin neighborhoods in the city. Many of them saw their move to El Barrio as a political project, one of rescuing and asserting the community before it disappeared. Yet artists have long been recognized as pioneers and catalysts of gentrification. Searching for cheaper rents, they are oftentimes among the first to move to poor and ethnic neighborhoods, infusing them with an artistic and bohemian feel that developers can easily exploit. Loisaida, or the Lower East Side, had already succumbed to this process. There, a cultural renaissance, with its accompanying legacy of exotic and hip alterity, had been easily taken up by the real-estate industry, which reshaped it as consumable difference (Mele 2000). But the arrival of Puerto Rican and Latino artists into a primarily Latino and minority neighborhood, some purposefully committed to the area's identity of place, inspires new questions about the interplay of art and gentrification. Namely, artists and their efforts toward marketing El Barrio provide a good entry point into the stakes of these initiatives; despite contradictions, their marketing efforts represent a crucial response, a confrontation, even if not a direct challenge to the area's gentrification.

East Harlem is certainly "jumping" with a greater number of artists, students, intellectuals, and cultural institutions, which in turn have attracted young professionals from all over the city and beyond to attend poetry readings, openings, and other programming. During the spring 2002 Nubo Expo exhibit, which gathered a group of "multiracial, multi-cultural, multidisciplined artists" and was produced by Aurora Flores and the Taller Boricua Workshop at Julia de Burgos Latino Cultural Center, some attendants proudly raved about the most "Soho-looking" crowds they had seen in El Barrio. A young woman was visibly ecstatic as a local resident proudly told them about the short-lived La Cantina Restaurant, another exhibition venue that could be visited within the radius of a block. The changing composition of visitors to the area is pub-licly visible on the "cultural crossroads" along 106th Street and Lexington Avenue, which one visionary, artist Fernando Salicrup, had described as a "gatekeeper to gentrification" some years earlier and is now marketed as a draw for visitors from the city and beyond.[18]

Someone well acquainted with the pros and cons of marketing El Barrio is Aurora Flores, a cultural activist, artist, and public relations pro-fessional, who is at the forefront of these efforts. From her office in El Barrio, she has worked with many local institutions and produced numerous cultural events in New York and beyond, including Julia's Jam at the Julia de Burgos Latino Cultural Center, a recurring monthly event started in 2002 and frequented by many of *los mismos de siempre*, particu-larly cultural activists, along with Puerto Rican artists and professionals from the area and beyond. Discussing the perils of marketing in regard to the area's gentrification, she reaffirmed her goal of attracting "everyone" to El Barrio. Whenever possible her events in El Barrio are listed in the *Village Voice, New York Post,* and *Daily News,* not solely in the Spanish or local newspapers, while visitors are always welcomed with warm greet-ings and encouragement to bring more friends. But as she quickly and vehemently noted, this general marketing is purposefully intended to attract greater recognition to East Harlem's cultural production, never to mainstream it—as in whitewashing. In her words: "I see these efforts and events as pearls and showpieces of our cultural heritage that should be heralded and spotlighted for 'everyone' to see." With this comment, Aurora underscored the importance of challenging the ghettoization that often hampers recognition of Latino/a culture. Most important, the goal is to wrest control of how this production is defined and presented in sectors as wide and diverse as possible. Not insignificantly, this marketing strategy also helps mark El Barrio as Puerto Rican and Latino/a to potential gentrifiers, as opposed to promoting this vision solely among those that already acknowledge or support it. And most of all, she also insisted, her goal and that of other cultural activists in El Barrio is to attract progressive Puerto Ricans and Latino/a who could serve as buffers to gentrification. As she explained:

> This is a cultural movement and the people who are in the leadership of this movement recognize that artists are in the vanguard of gentrification. But this movement is about attracting the progressive Puerto Rican and Latino/a, who will provide a balance to gentrification. This won't be like the Lower East Side's Nuyorican Poets Café, where the only Latino is Julio at the door, and the rest are young *blanquitos.* Our goal is to market Latino culture without losing or hating our culture.

This is yet another version of Bodega's dream of Puerto Rican empowerment, however this time it is not only the upwardly mobile middle-class Latino/a, but more specifically the progressive one, who is considered a buffer to gentrification. Most significant, her words point to a general concern among cultural activists about the need to promote Puerto Rican and Latino/a culture without losing or "mortgaging it." Indeed, cultural activists had long seen their institutions abandon their Puerto Rican roots in the process of marketing themselves, and were amply aware of the constraints local cultural institutions faced when seeking funds for cultural programming.

The Nuyorican Poets Café in Loisaida is a good example of this predicament. Initially established as an alternative movement, it continues to embrace Nuyorican and Latino/a culture, however some argue that only as a "content"—that is, as a bohemian version of multiculturalism where "Latinidad" is oftentimes more a metaphor of inclusion than a description of the artists and audiences in this gentrified neighborhood (Morales 2002). These experiences underscored the constraints and opportunities that accompanied local efforts, raising questions about the level of openness and inclusiveness conveyed by their marketing crusade. Yet the quandary—that, as crucial as marketing is to its defense as a Latino/a barrio, these efforts could easily further its gentrification—remains. Melissa Mark Viverito addressed questions about how cultural institutions in El Barrio could benefit from Upper Manhattan's current economic and tourist "boom." Her words are evocative of the drive for recognition, while protecting "our space."

> When we think about all the money that some [cultural] institutions are getting versus what the community is saying—that they don't represent them—you begin to see the links. So, if getting recognized means that we as a community need to mainstream ourselves and mainstream our culture, then obviously I don't want that recognition. We need to look and analyze what comes with recognition, and stay true to who we are and what we represent.

Simply put, cultural enthusiasts were asking themselves about the price of recognition from general audiences, fully aware that it could potentially transform and "mainstream" them along with the audiences they serve. The lesson was a simple and straightforward one: a "Puerto Rican" or "Latino/a" content is no buffer to gentrification. Rather the issue is on what basis is Latino/a culture represented, and with what kind of audiences and political agenda. And by this I do not mean to suggest that artists and cultural institutions in El Barrio had no interest in attaining mainstream recognition and visibility for El Barrio. Rather, the pressing concern among many local actors is to maneuver and wrest some control of how such visibility is attained, and for what reasons. Aurora Flores, for instance, was particularly adamant on differentiating between mainstreaming as "inclusion" and mainstreaming as whitewashing; what she sought was visibility and recognition from as many sources possible—that is, recognition sans ghettoization. And moreover, concomitantly and increasingly so, this "cultural renaissance" grows and is directly

informed by previous and ongoing frustrations with dominant requirements for cultural validation long affecting their work and that of their
institutions in the area. This is the context that informs the increased concern with staying true to "who we are," and with the promotion of El
Barrio as an artistically and culturally specific site anchored in the historical struggles for inclusion that had been waged in this community
and are as relevant today as ever. Most significantly, their cultural work
was seen as a deterrent to the area's gentrification, specifically, to the
area's "cultural gentrification." This ambitious statement of assertion is
evident in the quests by many activists for more popular Puerto Rican
and Latino/a spaces, instead of transforming these spaces to the likings of
outsiders. In their efforts to maintain a site as a Puerto Rican or a Latino/a
space, they sell and announce it as such to the outside world.

This nexus of culture and place however, does not invoke a static version of Puertoricanness or Latinidad, but instead projects a Caribbean-
centric, racially diverse, diasporic, and politicized view. Events at the
Julia de Burgos Latino Cultural Center are a good example: the lineup is
frequented by Puerto Rican and Latino/a artists and Afro-Caribbean
music, such as YerbaBuena, a grouping of young Puerto Ricans and
Latino/as playing Puerto Rican "music for the new millennium," and
Pa'Lo Monte, made up of young Dominican, Puerto Rican, Panamanian,
and Haitian musicians. So identified, these groups help mark the space
not solely as Latino, but most specifically as Afro-Caribbean and Nuyorican. At Julia's Jam, Aurora Flores, who serves as both producer and
emcee, always opens and closes the events with the cultural sociopoliti-
cal history that made the space a reality to the community. Occasionally,
she breaks the ice with her own poetry or folkloric songs, embracing and
engaging the audience to participate. A representative lineup reads:

7–8:30 P.M. – Poetry with Tato Laviera, Sandra Garcia Rivera; Open Mic

8:30–9 P.M. – "Cuentos" with Nicholasa Mohr

9–10 P.M. – YerbaBuena (P.R.) & invited Guests, this week: Pálo Monte
(D.R.)

10:30 P.M. – Jam Session, bomba, plena, rumba, palo, musica jibara,
etc. . . . "Julia's Jam is quickly becoming the next Afro-Caribbean

Figure 6.   Bomba and plena at the Julia de Burgos
Latino Cultural Center. Photo by the author.

Cultural Corner!!! There is an Open Mic segment, so those of you who
do poetry, rap, play an instrument, tell jokes, etc. and want to do your
thing . . . it's a good place to do it." Aurora Communications[19]

Along with this primarily Puerto Rican lineup of artists, other Latino/as
perform, and to a lesser extent African Americans, all of whom are presented or self-identified by their nationality—very much à la multicultural
collage—to underscore the different constituencies being showcased and

Figure 7. The renowned Puerto Rican artist Rafael Tufiño, also known as the "painter of the people," at a seminar on Puerto Rican art at the Julia de Burgos Latino Cultural Center. Next to him is Fernando Salicrup, flanked by a digital poster by Salicrup in honor of Tufiño. Tufiño is an important figure of the Nuyorican artistic movement. The audience came to hear recollections of his artistic career spanning New York and Puerto Rico. Photo by the author.

represented. The result is an intergenerational space that is primarily Puerto Rican and Latino/a and projects and aligns itself with El Barrio's past, affirming Latino/as' continuity into the present. To emphasize this point, many of the returning artists are positioned within El Barrio's cultural past and present before the start of their performance. Younger poets such as Mariposa, Stephanie Agosto, and Caridad, or La Bruja, are presented alongside more established authors and poets of the likes of Nicholasa Mohr and Tato Laviera, as well as Pedro Pietri and Papoleto Meléndez. Julia de Burgos, the Puerto Rican poet who lived and died in El Barrio, after whom the center was named, and a symbol of nationalism and struggles for gender equity, is always remembered. The audience is also told that Tato Laviera is "our poet from El Barrio," that Nicholasa Mohr's writings were among the first representations of Puerto Rican reality in New York written in English, and that Fernando's digital artwork is part of the same artistic revolution that he has contributed to since the 1970s. Back then, artists had rejected the high-art outlook of mainstream museums and art galleries, which were divorced from communities, and rallied for inclusion, democratization of art, and cultural equity.[20] The context has certainly changed, but artists' poetry and lyrics about their transnational and transcultural experiences are still as much of a claim for cultural equity today. In this way, they convey a continuous history and linkage between cultural production of the past and present. The resulting narrative presents an unbroken "cultural memory," a collective set of knowledge disseminated outside formal channels of history and vested with cultural meanings; it continues to unfold today, despite changed circumstances.[21] Puerto Rican and Nuyorican culture is a dominant reference, but so are Afro-Caribbean and U.S. Latino/a culture.

Another example of the types of cultural assertions that were emerging in El Barrio, particularly of their reference to a continuous and living past, is the exhibition of Puerto Rican graphic art and posters at La Cantina, held in the spring of 2002. Organizers intended to evoke the early cultural activism of the 1970s, when posters were a primary medium of political communication and exhibitions reached out to "the people." As one of the artist-organizers stated, they wanted a show that evoked a moment: before there were budgets, money, or the New York State Council on the Arts, when it "was not about an individual, it was about a culture, of pride, respect and love." Their aim was to reinstate a different logic than what has since been generalized among Puerto Rican institutions by funding sources and cultural policies, to what many believed were deleterious effects. Similar projects launched by new Latino residents and artists moving to El Barrio include the *New York Latino Journal*, an online magazine that, in the words of publisher Rafa Merino Cortés, will feature the other side of history, current news, and commentary regarding the Latino experience, and is intended "to delve into *la lucha* and everything around *nuestra gente*, for *nuestra gente*."[22] Additionally, after a long search, Judith Escalona was finally able to open a space in El Barrio for PRdream.com, a Web site on the history, culture, and politics of the Puerto Rican diaspora. The press release announcing the opening of an exhibition space for artists working in new media evokes the local and global aspirations at the heart of many new initiatives. Its goal: "To connect El Barrio to all parts of the globe that recognize its long history of music, art, poetry, and dance," reinstating the wish for recognition of El Barrio's productive artistic and cultural history both locally and beyond El Barrio's physical boundaries.

Dreams of cultural empowerment and visibility, however, can't do much to ensure the permanence of cultural spaces in the area. La Cantina closed some months after the exhibit, as did Mixta Gallery, roughly a little more than a year after its opening. A new Puerto Rican restaurant and music space—Edwin's Café—opened, closed, and reopened again. Just as quickly, Carlito's Café and Galeria—a new space of poetry, art, and music, from tango to bomba to Mexican regional music, cofounded by Bolivian Eliana Godoy and other Latin American artists and newcomers to El Barrio—was launched with an exhibit of the work of Puerto Rican artist Diógenes Ballester. Artists hoped the bar and café would strengthen their financial position and ability to stay in El Barrio. All of these closings, openings, and reopenings evoke the excitement of the moment, but also the intermittent and vulnerable nature of many cultural spaces in the area. Revolving around periodic events, such as poetry jams, art openings, and institutions working independently from each other, and relying on the hard work of individuals, the "cultural renaissance" was, for many, more illusion than reality. East Harlem still suffered from lack of public illumination: its streets were dark and sleepy, not the likely sites for any renaissance. Could they pay up their rents? Could they keep their place? Will the politically charged cultural renaissance last, bloom, or subside? Is it all a matter of time? All of these questions were very much on people's mind, lingering as a warning of all that was at stake in each and every one of these initiatives.

Lastly, like other transformations in El Barrio, the cultural renaissance is not experienced uniformly by most residents, or seen as equally accessible to the different constituencies encompassed in the rubric of Puerto Rican and Latino/a cultural enthusiasts; not that it ever could be, given the range of new cultural initiatives emerging throughout the area and the growing diversification of the population. For one, news of cultural events in El Barrio is disseminated through particular media networks and by word of mouth, circulating to, and thereby preselecting, particular constituencies. Recall Tato Torres's point about the different communities that coexist in El Barrio. One such example is the restricted/parallel circulation of two of the Spanish-language newspapers in El Barrio: *Siempre*, with announcements of Puerto Rican events, is primarily found within Puerto Rican stores and hangouts, where one is less likely to find *La Voz de Mexico*, which lists Mexican events and is found primarily in *taquerias* and Mexican commercial establishments. Moreover, some questioned whether other Latino/as were in fact welcomed in "Puerto Rican spaces" (many of them marked by their emphasis on Nuyorican culture and Afro-Caribbean music) or that "Continentales" (recent Latin American immigrants, mostly young and educated) were the most dominant presence in the new cultural spaces. Others feared that downtown hip audiences, or else the Puerto Rican "intelligentsia" from throughout the city—not local residents—were the main target of the new cultural programs. Gentrification is never measurable by the increase in rent prices, but by the level of comfort and openness of "improved" or "reinvigorated" cultural places among different groups who may be recognized as members of the "same group," but for reasons of class, ethnicity, education, or nationality occupy disparate positions.

But undeniably El Barrio is "jumping." Yet the future is difficult to predict. Associations of culture and place, in all of their opportunities and constraints, are directly implicated with the area's transformations. Yet, in light of ongoing pressures presented by gentrification, this insistence on "marketing Latino/a culture without losing it" represents a significant statement of assertion, validation, and pride in cultural production that is actively present and not ready to go. This is particularly the case regarding cultural activists' efforts to market and promote their culture, only to be repeatedly downplayed and challenged by an attending economic logic favoring marketable ethnicity, depoliticized from history and struggle. In other words, people knew full well that culture needed to be marketed, now more than ever, as part of their affirmation to place. This included not only El Barrio, but also the government-backed and -owned cultural institutions they still controlled, on which their cultural projection was still largely predicated. Such is the case with the Julia de Burgos Latino Cultural Center, which, like other Latino/a cultural spaces in the city, could potentially fall into private hands.

In all of its contradictions, the cultural moment is thus part of the same processes that artists, activists, and residents sought to resist, or at least to appropriate, even if their only recourse was promoting a gentrification by and for Puerto Ricans and Latino/as; that is, by making sure El Barrio continues to be "*de todos*." Which is obviously a partial *todos*. This alone renders the political ramifications of East Harlemites' economic empowerment and representation as a largely inconclusive project. But in invoking a different approach toward the marketing of culture in El Barrio, these claims are also especially meaningful. For they reinstate ethnicity to place, upholding diversity in cultural production while fostering a remembrance and connection to the past with the hope that it not be so easily disregarded in the future. But to see this we should turn to the concurrent institutionalized marketing initiatives that are part of El Barrio's gentrification.

THREE

Empowered Culture?

THE EMPOWERMENT ZONE
AND THE SELLING OF EL BARRIO

> It is not a question of getting money just for anybody who needs
> money; there's an aesthetic to the wealth. And Thelma's Lounge
> doesn't represent that. Bobby's Record Shop does not represent
> that. Juan Valdez Cafeteria does not represent that. Starbucks
> does. HMV does.
>
> Felix Leo Campos, director of After Dark,
> speaking about the Empowerment Zone

The marketing of culture, be it through museums, restaurants, or even parades, is central to tourism, one of the most important industries feeding the city's international standing. It was therefore expected that the Upper Manhattan Empowerment Zone (EZ) legislation, introduced in Congress by Charles Rangel in 1994, and still in effect, would launch a Cultural Industry Investment Fund, providing a perfect example of the close alliance between culture and profit in urban centers like New York City. Intended to "stimulate the production of cultural products and services which will attract larger audiences, create jobs, and increase the economic benefits of Heritage Tourism in Upper Manhattan," the initiative explicitly treats culture as a tool for the creation of jobs in amusement, recreation, travel, gifts, and other services.[1] The EZ's stated goal of "preserving the distinct character" of neighborhoods is subordinate to the awarding of grants on the basis of economic impact, increased tourist traffic, and job creation and retention. In short, "heritage" is ancillary to tourism, put in the service of viable tourist districts containing cultural, entertainment, dining, and recreational attractions.

I suggest this initiative has much to teach us about tourism as an urban development strategy, and about the intricate and tense relationship between culture as "industry" and culture as "ethnicity" in the development of such initiatives. Not that the intersection of ethnicity and tourism is new. In global urban centers like New York City, ethnicity in the form of "diverse cuisines" or shopping and entertainment districts has long been touted and sold as a tourist attraction in its own right, and examples abound of ethnic enclaves such as Little Italy and Chinatown as sanitized tourist destinations. Similarly, Latino culture and Latinidad have been the subject of culturally oriented urban development initiatives such as Paseo Boricua in Chicago and Villa Victoria in Boston. These developments have been described as spaces that showcase and celebrate Puertoricanness and as important economic development projects that provide barriers to gentrification (Matos 2001; Florez González 2001; Rinaldo 2002). But Manhattan is too expensive a piece of real estate, and Puerto Ricans too politically vulnerable to establish comparable developments, local tourist proponents would soon learn. The application, or more appropriately, the misapplication of the EZ Cultural Industry Investment Fund therefore presents a keen example of the overt ways in which ethnicity can be easily underplayed in relation to industry, revealing the real objectives and priorities of neoliberal-based tourism development initiatives.

In part, the EZ's stance can be easily explained by the antagonistic demands of tourism for difference, or that which vests places with value as "destinations," and standardization that provides uniformity of services, pleasure, and comfort (Kirshenblatt-Gimblett 1998; MacCannell 1999). In other words, as dependent as current tourism strategies may be on the "uniqueness" of particular places, events, things, or people, they are also required to make these spaces safe, comfortable, and entertaining. Which is to say, for purposes of tourism, ethnicity must always be contained in the right package, "tourist bubble," and cultural industry

(Judd 1999). This business treatment of culture is also explained by its likely use as a deterrent to ethnic and racial debates by making business considerations the primary award variables within the initiative. In so doing, the initiative speaks to contrasting systems of evaluations at play in the economic and cultural realms that have for so long troubled cultural policy writers and their quest to find commensurable, yet uncontested, value between these fields (Throsby 2001).[2] Namely, the EZ business treatment of culture represented a direct challenge to the dominant definitions and uses of culture in East Harlem, where cultural initiatives have been recurrent resources for struggles over rights, representations, and identity, and where most cultural institutions had been funded as part of such struggles.[3] Yet tourism always presupposes the creation of difference, which in El Barrio could only mean heritage and culture. Given this, the EZ approach to culture as primarily a profit-making device did little to exempt it from particular ethnic and identity associations, and was in fact a catalyst for tensions with important racial and cultural implications.

Lacking in cultural industries and entertainment infrastructure, Upper Manhattan communities (comprising Washington Heights and West, Central, and East Harlem) were left with marketing their culture and the ethnic and historical identification of their neighborhoods. But whose culture? What aspects and representations? And on what basis? Upper Manhattan residents are more than 50 percent Latino, yet it is Black cultural institutions in West and Central Harlem that carry a national and international reputation among prospective tourists.[4] By limiting East Harlem's funding eligibility to certain sections and imposing requirements that only institutionalized cultural industries could meet, the EZ virtually guaranteed that cultural institutions in West and Central Harlem would be most prominently featured in EZ-sponsored tourist promotional materials and the ones eligible for the largest amounts of funding.[5] Hence, as of 2001, it was estimated that only 1.5 million out of the twenty-five million-dollar Cultural Industry Investment Fund had been directed to East Harlem (Kreinin Souccar 2003). Coupled with the lack of Puerto Ricans and other Latinos on the EZ board and staff, this disparity led to controversy over inequities in the distribution of grants, funds, and resources, exposing the permanence of old ethnic/racial tensions in East Harlem; ethnicity was as much a basis for distributing resources and entitlements in 2002 as it was in the 1960s. The EZ, after all, was not targeting the raceless poor, but rather Blacks, Dominicans, and Puerto Ricans with particular histories and experiences of struggle, both with state redistributive systems and with one another over similar resources. The program's disavowal of ethnicity brought these and other concerns to the forefront, primarily the difficulty of turning culture into a profit-making device with little regard to the "people" who always author and inform it.

Blatantly tied to the logic of industry and business, this initiative became a catalyst for ethnic and racial contests, and is telling of the close nexus between cultural initiatives and processes of gentrification. The EZ initiative was foremost about educating and governing East Harlemites along neoliberal conventions. It was most effective at confronting the political uses of culture as a recourse of identity and representation by favoring marketable ethnicity.

THE PROBLEMS AND PERILS OF MARKETING EAST HARLEM

The EZ Cultural Industry Investment Fund was not the first government initiative that spurred residents to think about culture in terms of profit making and tourism. Shifts toward self-sufficiency in state and federal government programs for culture and the arts, the expansion of audiences, and the privatization and diversification of funding sources had already pressed local institutions and cultural workers to market themselves if they were to survive in a more competitive environment.[6] Most East Harlem cultural institutions were founded during the peak of civil struggles over representation in the early 1970s. They were sustained by government sources; thus later pressures to privatize their funding were particularly hurtful to their operations and mission. El Museo del Barrio, perhaps the only Puerto Rican cultural institution in East Harlem that has managed to grow and diversify its funding sources, is a good example.

For El Museo, becoming competitive entailed not only opening a gift shop and marketing itself more aggressively, but also shifting its mission from specifically Puerto Rican art to Latin American art, which by the mid-1980s had become far more attractive to private funders. This change worked wonders for El Museo, which since 1996 has attracted a range of private and nonprofit funders and visitors from all over the city. Yet the lack of Puerto Ricans and Latinos on the museum's staff and the steep decline in Puerto Rican exhibitions became an immediate subject of great controversy. The shift marked the loss of an institution initially founded to place Puerto Ricans on the map locally and nationally—a vivid indicator of displacement.

Long before the EZ, marketing concerns were at play during the ten-year planning process of the community board's planning document, *New Directions,* which portrayed East Harlem as a centrally located and accessible neighborhood ripe for outside development, and which thus constituted a marketing document in and of itself. Section 197-A proposed the development of a cultural crossroads along 106th Street and Lexington Avenue at the present site of the Julia de Burgos Latino Cultural Center; it would complement other such crossroads (or core development centers) that emphasized business, education, transportation, and retail, serving as a cultural stronghold for the community. Artist Fernando Salicrup, who spearheaded the crossroads idea, explained that the plan was intended to stop gentrification by developing one sector that would function as the area's Latin stronghold, although like all recommendations in *New Directions,* the crossroads idea was double-edged. For one, the plan's recommendation for a tourism crossroads uniting larger Fifth Avenue institutions (such as the Museum of the City of New York, El Museo del Barrio, and the Central Park Conservancy Garden) and smaller local institutions could easily backfire by submerging the latter to the logics and demands of the larger institutions.[7] Moreover, designing an area as a "cultural stronghold" provided no guarantee that Latino cultural institutions would ensue. Instead, such a designation could be used potentially to justify the development of any type of art and culture institution, which is not what was initially envisioned by proponents of the crossroads. At least for now, however, the "crossroads" area continues to serve as a Puerto Rican and Latino cultural hub. It is the site of the Puerto Rican restaurant La Fonda Boricua, the Julia de Burgos Cultural Center, and the studios of longtime resident Puerto Rican artists such as Diógenes Ballester, José Morales, and James De la Vega. However, as primarily rental tenants in a coveted spot in close proximity to the Upper East Side, many of these artists, their cultural institutions, and the cultural renaissance in the crossroads face an uncertain future.[8]

The EZ and its Cultural Industry Investment Fund, however, marked the first time in East Harlem's history that the community had been directly encouraged to market itself and to think about how best to attract people into the area strictly in business and entrepreneurial ways. This view was communicated sternly by funding criteria that included "broad impact through increased audience and tourist traffic and job creation, leverage of significant additional public or private investments, potential to increase the supply of quality cultural productions, merchandise, goods and services," along with sustainability, fiscal and programmatic feasibility, and leadership qualifications. All of these business prerogatives were listed masterfully on a twelve-page questionnaire, which questions applicants in terms of "products and services" that will be provided to "patrons and consumers."[9]

Obstacles were soon forthcoming. First and foremost was the problem of recognition and evaluation of Upper Manhattan communities. This obstacle is amply evident in the tourism market study commissioned by the EZ to investigate attitudes and spending habits of visitors to Upper Manhattan. The study attests to the general association of the area with "urban decay" and lack of safety. In fact, Upper Manhattan visitors came primarily from outside the city, often from abroad; they tended to be white and frequently visited as tour-bus passengers, a choice of transportation that reveals visitors' negative perception of the area. Most significant, the study shows that East Harlem lags far behind Central and West Harlem in public recognition; tourists come to Upper Manhattan for jazz, gospel, soul food, and Harlem's historical landmarks (Audience Research and Analysis 2000). The most visited cultural sites include the Apollo Theater, Sylvia's Restaurant, and the Abyssinian Baptist Church, which are not solely among the oldest and largest institutions in the area, but are also the ones most targeted by tour-bus lines, indicating the role of the tour-bus industry in shaping Harlem's image to the world. Overall, the study shows conclusively that there are few *recognized* tourist attractions in East Harlem, translating to little cultural recognition of El Barrio, and of its Latino heritage.[10] Only the Museum of the City of New York and El Museo del Barrio were amply recognized by interviewees, but those institutions are located along the upscale Fifth Avenue Museum Mile strip, physically separated from the core of El Barrio. Visitors would first have to cross a public housing project and an unilluminated commuter train underpass, both well recognized, racially marked spaces— scorned by some, celebrated by others, as physical deterrents to touring audiences and gentrifiers—before reaching other sectors of El Barrio.

Indeed, in contrast to Central Harlem, with its housing stock originally created for an affluent class in the nineteenth century and relegated to African Americans after the real-estate market floundered, East Harlem was always one of the poorest communities, a bedrock of immigrants housed in "common tenements."[11] Not only does it lack the pretty brownstones and historic districts that draw visitors to Harlem, but East Harlem's architectural deficit was worsened after it became a target of urban renewal. Add to that the disparity in historical cultural capital between these communities: East Harlem's Latino history is largely undocumented, and thus suffers under the misconception that Latinos are a transient population, not a constituent component of U.S. society. Consequently, their history has never approximated the level of recognition enjoyed by Harlem and its cultural renaissance. Little wonder then that its more sympathetic chroniclers in the past described East Harlem as a "plain Jane" in comparison to Harlem (Sexton 1965). Its cultural institutions, such as those at the cultural crossroads, are also considered too small to constitute a "complete destination" and keep foot traffic in the area, as demanded by contemporary tourist industries. Dolores Hayden's predicaments of representing marginal history are thus amply evident in East Harlem, where that history is embedded not in architectural monuments but rather in "public processes and public memories" throughout the whole urban landscape (1999). Just as a lack of nationally recognized history does not mean that there is no history, a lack of recognized attractions does not mean that there are no places residents value that may be marketed to tourists; rather, tourist sites have yet to be created and valued as such. Tourist attractions are not natural creations, but the outcome of infrastructure, such as museums, trajectories, tour routes, and other memory-holding physical spaces that create a "safe" mode for discovery and pleasure (Kirshenblatt-Gimblett 1998; Desmond 1999). Nor is the "worthiness" or the value of things and places inherent to them, but rather results from their assessment against established systems of value and signification. Within the Western canon, as writers have repeatedly noted, these values prioritize the supposedly universal appeal and applicability of art and culture, over and above their ever-present ethnic, cultural, and social content and significance, constructs that are only achieved through the erasure of heterogeneity and the maintenance and creation of exclusions (Bright and Bakewell 1995; Bourdieu 1993; Marcus and Myers 1995; Deutsche 1998). Leo Campos reiterates this point in the opening epigraph to this chapter when he recalls that there is indeed a sense of "aesthetics" at play in the EZ Tourism Initiative: it favors that which is sanctioned according to "universalist" aesthetic standards or is rightly packaged in "safe" and "efficient" ways.

In fact, my interviewees had no trouble listing numerous tourist-worthy sites, all of which spoke to El Barrio's history and its Puerto Rican and Latino heritage: from festivals and celebrations such as the old-timers' stickball game to the Three Kings Day Parade and the 116th Street Festival, as well as newer events such as Cinco de Mayo, along with mural walls, *casitas*, and community gardens. Ismael Nuñez, a resident and member of the Cultural Affairs Committee of the community board and a freelance journalist, whose writing has appeared in *Harlem Times* among other local publications, came up with numerous possible tourist sights after my initial prompts:

> We can put up plaques where Don Pedro Albizu Campos lived, where Vito Marcantonio lived, where the first stickball game was played, and where Julia de Burgos used to live. People need to know about the Spanish Methodist Church, which was taken over by the Young Lords, and about the Park Palace Ballroom [formerly at Fifth Avenue and 110th Street], where Machito, Tito Puente, and Ismael Rivera and other Latino stars played. All this can make up a trajectory for tourists.

This is exactly the type of tour that tourist entrepreneurs are attempting to develop in El Barrio, so far with little success. Consider the "Spanish Harlem Salsa Walking Tour: A unique visit to New York's most ignored neighborhood," led by José Obando, a salsa musicologist from Guayaquil in Ecuador and formerly involved in El Barrio's Salsa Museum. The tourists' visiting "sites" include the former residences of Tito Puente and Machito, as well as La Marqueta, *botanicas*, former nightclub sites, social clubs, and corner hang-outs of past and present salsa musicians who are still residing in El Barrio. Far from the static image tourist sites oftentimes command, many of these sites are still important to this community. Another good example is the Spanish Methodist Church, also known as the First People's Church, after the Young Lords—the civil rights activist group—took it over in 1969. In March 2003, it was "retaken" by the Poets Opposing War as part of the antiwar demonstrations, which included a program of music and poetry that gathered new generations of poets, of the likes of hip-hop/urban plena activist group the Welfare Poets, and Nuyorican Poetry Movement veterans Papoleto Melendez and Pedro Pietri, the latter present at the first takeover. Again, the past and the present converged in a cultural program asserting El Barrio's cultural memory, while marking the church's significance as a community landmark.[12]

Obviously, then, East Harlem does not lack cultural resources, nor places, nor memories, nor a willingness to market its culture; rather, it lacks the resources to promote its values, which are at odds with dominant aesthetic hierarchies that devalue ethnicity in favor of universally sanctioned culture. Also challenging is the abundance of sites imbricated in a history of opposition and struggle by a minority people, undoubtedly a difficult prospect for tourist purposes, not easily packaged in the "proper infrastructure" where tourists can linger comfortably. Put simply, East Harlemites' memories, events, and cultural appropriations of place, such as murals and *casitas,* or places of remembrance of past and continuing political struggles, are directly at odds with the treatment of culture as a venue of entertainment and consumption located in identifiable structures and places ready to generate profit, employment, and visitors. As discussed earlier, this predicament has led to renewed efforts among Puerto Rican artists to market their culture with a politicized and historically aware agenda as a means of marking culture on to space. But against this admittedly difficult situation many others were disheartened. As if repeating what they had been told by EZ staff about their community, more than one tourist enthusiast believed that East Harlem's lack of visibility to tourists was simply a byproduct of its lack of tourist, cultural, and historical attractions. A member of the East Harlem Chamber of Commerce put it this way: "Harlem has the Apollo, Sylvia's, the Studio Museum, and they have their brownstones and their ethnic vendors on the street. I bet you they won't lose those vendors. But what are you going to do in El Barrio? There are no real museums, not even one restaurant where you could feel comfortable, with AC for the summer or a banquet room." Air-conditioning, a banquet room, and a "real" museum are the keywords here, denoting residents' awareness of the high-scale aesthetics expected from tourist developments in Upper Manhattan.

Thus, in addition to hindering the evaluation of East Harlem's cultural value, as determined by many of its Latino/a residents, the EZ confronted East Harlemites with the question of how to sell culture along EZ stipulations, through organizations, entertainment, or dining venues that would be recognized by outsiders as "worthy" of foot traffic. By emphasizing the need for specific places—"infrastructure," in EZ terms—that can be showcased and sold to visitors, the initiative made El Barrio particularly susceptible to contending interpretations of its history. In this way, the initiative was complicit with processes of gentrification and with Latinos' marginalization. It communicated to tourism enthusiasts that their only available recourse was either to transform their institutions, or embrace the nationally recognized cultural institutions that were threatening to leave (such as the Museum of the City of New York) or that were being proposed as part of new developments (as in the case of the Museum for African Art, which I discuss in the next chapter). Nationally recognized institutions were less vulnerable to doubts about East Harlemites' ability to anchor tourism in the area. But embracing these institutions came at a cost. Not only did they ease the path for new developments in the area, but they also fed into the dominant alternative multicultural history for East Harlem.

EAST HARLEM:
THE REVOLVING DOOR OF IMMIGRANTS

Not all East Harlemites consider the area as a Puerto Rican and Latino stronghold, but as a multicultural community with a revolving door of immigrants, a community that is of and for everyone to claim. Developers are among the most avid advocates of this view, but so are the largest and oldest social service and cultural institutions in the area. These include the Museum of the City of New York and Union Settlement, the first social service organization in the area, which celebrates an annual multicultural festival. The museum, although located in East Harlem, targets the entire city and its different constituencies. It has played a pivotal role in the representation of this revolving-door image through programs such as Celebrate East Harlem, a festival that presents the arts and music of groups with historical connections to the area, and walking tours on multiethnic East Harlem, where visitors are taken through "one of Manhattan's most diverse communities." Indeed, like other poor, ethnic neighborhoods in New York City, East Harlem has a very diverse history that warrants study, celebration, and public dissemination. The why, how, and when of this multicultural vision of East Harlem's history—which was enthusiastically embraced by major institutions while altogether veiling Puerto Ricans' and Latinos' history and presence in the present—is not insignificant. For one, this view is not solely deployed to communicate inclusiveness, but also to justify gentrification as a natural and inevitable process that is intrinsic to the community's history. Indeed, Puerto Rican tourist enthusiasts continually challenged the notion that they were temporary transients, clarifying that they had outnumbered most population segments since the 1950s. They resented the consistent pressure exerted by institutions, politicians, and the media to underplay their identity in ways that hindered their ability to market their culture and El Barrio, particularly as a response to gentrification. The comments of district leader Felix Rosado are evocative here:

> One of the biggest assets we've had in this community—that we've never exploited—is our name. Corporations would pay millions of

dollars to be able to say "Spanish Harlem." And yet we have never marketed ourselves as Spanish Harlem. Instead we have to dance around these issues for fear of offending any other communities or ethnic groups. We have to dance around our ethnic heritage and our culture. We should be able to say, Well look, we have ethnic groups, Irish, Jewish, etcetera, yet we're proud to be Puerto Rican, Dominican, or Cuban, and market that. Aretha Franklin sang about it, Elton John sang about it . . . yet we can't market ourselves as Spanish Harlem to try to get some of that Fifth Avenue crowd over here to say, Hey we are Spanish Harlem!

Rosado used "Spanish Harlem" to imply unity among Latinos, a common strategy to strengthen the validity of Puerto Ricans' claim to space in a context where Puerto Ricans felt they were being asked to "dance" around, rather than promote, their past. Assertions of the area's Latino identity, however, presented their own set of challenges. This identity was also being eagerly embraced by interests intent on advancing the area's transformation in ways that delegitimated criticisms or claims by Puerto Ricans to place and to history. This is why the shift of El Museo del Barrio's mission from representing Puerto Ricans to showcasing all Latinos and Latin American cultures in the mid-1990s remains such a heated topic of community discussion. While motivated primarily by the preeminence of mainstream-sanctioned categories such as "Latin American art" over Puerto Rican and Latino art among art foundations, corporations, and the art establishment, it was presented as a response to the area's changing demographics—an act of inclusiveness toward our "Latin American neighbors." Hidden within this mission were the institution's elitism and desire to distance itself from the area's primarily poor and working-class Latinos.[13] The debate over the museum was then evocative of the threats presented by processes of Latinization, particularly when co-opted to further marketable ethnicity, that is, Latino culture to the liking of corporate interests. This threat was posed to all Latinos, since Latinidad was used to veil exclusions around the axes of class and race along with the museum's Eurocentric designs, a realization that galvanized a few non-Puerto Rican Latinos alongside Puerto Ricans in rallies seeking community representation in El Museo's board of directors. But most of all, the threat was most challenging to Puerto Ricans since the museum's repeated public claims of its desire to become a "world-class institution" were a direct affront to its history. After all, the museum had been established as an outgrowth of Puerto Ricans' struggles for community control of education as a counter to the elitism and racism of U.S. museums.

Tellingly, heightened debate over El Museo del Barrio throughout 2002 was triggered by the discovery of trash bins loaded with art catalogues from the institutions' early exhibitions as well as important archival documentation of its past. Overtly symbolic of the institution's expunging of its Puerto Rican history, this act outraged residents and nonresidents alike, leading to the launching of the "We're Watching You" campaign by the Cultural Affairs Committee of the community board, then headed by Debbie Quiñones. The campaign sought a say in the institution, a reconfiguration of its board, as well as the development of policies, such as catalogue distribution plans, that would ensure the institution remained true to its Puerto Rican past and to its community mission. Incidents like this vividly displayed the unique predicaments hindering acknowledgment of Puerto Rican culture and history, in particular its subordinate, "dispensable" status, making activists ever more vigilant about the uses and misuses of discourses of Latinidad. Gloria Quiñonez described her feelings about El Museo del Barrio:

> I feel as passionately about the roots and history of El Museo del Barrio and anguish over the marginalization of the Puerto Rican participation in El Museo. However, I think it's really wonderful that we have the Mexican community and its art represented at the museum. The Museo is *la casa puertorriqueña,* and it was founded because the Met and the MoMA would not show our artists' work. It was established with a lot of struggle, blood, sweat, and tears of the people of this community. We don't want to lose that. . . . That does not mean that you don't invite another as you do to your own house, but you have them in the living room, you have them in the dining room. But you don't give up your toilet and your kitchen and your bedroom and your bed forever and ever. Right? . . . I don't see going to the Harlem museum and saying, Give up your space for Puerto Rican art and Dominican art and dilute yourself. We would not dare do that.

At the heart of the debate was the mere irreconcilability of a barrio identity and past with El Museo board's desire for a "world-class museum" and the liability that a Puerto Rican past presented to their wish for greater scope and visibility. But there were starkly different stances to this predicament. Puerto Rican activists upheld the intrinsic value of all that is Puerto Rican, alternative, diasporic, grassroots, and community. Yolanda Sánchez, founder and director of PRACA, spoke during the "We're Watching You"–sponsored town hall meeting held in 2002 between El Museo del Barrio's board and concerned residents and artists. Her words are evocative of this position:

> The questions raised in the 1960s about self-identity and about the historical and current status of citizens of non-European descent, folks like me, are questions that are still valid today. When we people of the diaspora, from places other than Europe, continue to be marginalized. This society seeks to impose other values. A hundred percent of cultural institutions that are supported by public funds, by your taxes and by mine, are run by Eurocentric values, their board members are WASPs and their museum holdings and shows project their conviction that quality, for the most part, is a European invention. If you had bought into the notion that Puerto Ricans cannot develop a quality museum and that a focus on Puerto Rican creativity will diminish the museum, it is time for those to renounce and open the way to those of us who are secured in our identity. The development of a Puerto Rican museum only enhances the quality of art in the city, it does not diminish it.

But El Museo's board saw otherwise. A more marketable and tourist-friendly museum entailed a reconfiguration of El Museo's past and of its very identity. In other words, subverting Puerto Ricans' and Latinos' peripheral position in the field of Latin American art demanded the very linkage of Puerto Rico to this category as defined by art historians, collectors, and curators. This is a path that obviously leaves mainstream standards for Latin American art—where Puerto Rican and U.S.-based Latino artists have been historically marginalized—unchallenged.

Not everyone involved in the "We're Watching You" campaign, or who was critical of El Museo's position, held the same views. Nevertheless, there was a general agreement that El Museo's new Latin American mission implied hierarchies of recognition and representation whereby all that is Puerto Rican, Nuyorican, diasporic—paradoxically, in fact, that which was most "global"—would be the most ignored. In other words, there was a general concern to reinstate, not dilute or undermine, an open cultural space that would be true to the institution's original and alternative mission in ways that would invert rather than consolidate hierarchies of representation. Hence, it was not the establishing of connections with mainstream museums or the extension to Latin American art that was at the heart of activists' concerns, but rather how and on what ground this would take place. Hence the recommendation by the "We're Watching You" campaign that El Museo complement their planned exhibition of the Museum of Modern Art Latin American collection—noted for lacking Puerto Rican and U.S. Latino artists—with an exhibition of U.S. Latino artists or with a showcase of El Museo's holdings shown in an equal manner alongside MOMA's collection, all part of the goal of fostering greater parity in their representation. Or in the words of a campaign sympathizer: "This museum was built for my children, so they know and learn to appreciate their history. It was not built so people can advance their careers, socialize, or drink champagne."

What people sought to communicate through the concerns, raised in meetings and public debates on this issue, was hence always more complex, open, and politically charged than what reverberated in the media. The local press in particular was quick to posit the issue around the facile dichotomies of "Puerto Ricans versus Latinos" or else between those who wanted to keep El Museo as a "ghetto or barrio museum" and those who sought its development into a "world-class museum." These dichotomies fail to represent local demands for equitable, mainstream and even global recognition of Puerto Rican culture and of El Barrio's history, on their own terms, not by imposed standards against which they would always be considered "deficient" and flawed. [14]

Simply put, the paradigm of Latin American inclusiveness or of El Barrio's multicultural history presented a similarly dire predicament to Puerto Rican activists: It could be easily put to the service of more marketable versions of ethnicity that would erase what was more politically alternative of El Barrio's Puerto Rican legacy in favor of that which more easily conforms to established evaluative structures of art, tourism, and mainstream society. The eventual outcome, people feared, was the "cul-

Figure 8. Panelists at a town hall meeting seeking community representation in the board of directors of El Museo del Barrio. The meeting was organized by the Cultural Affairs Committee of Community Board 11. Seated from left to right are members of the board of directors: John Carro; Susana Torruella Leval, former director of El Museo; Tony Bechara, chairman of the board; David Gibbens, chairman of Community Board 11; Debbie Quiñones, then chair of the Cultural Affairs Committee; and the panel moderator, Ramona Hernández. Photo by George Lucas V, courtesy of Community Board 11.

tural gentrification" of the area, at the expense of the still largely working-class Puerto Rican, Mexican immigrant, and Latino residents in the present.

The erasure of Puerto Ricans' and Latinos' current presence by El Barrio's multicultural revolving-door image is evident in the one tourist map of East Harlem, distributed by the EZ: the "Rediscovering East Harlem" map.[15] The map was coordinated by the East Harlem Historical Society in conjunction with the Union Settlement Society and intended to show the different immigrant groups that have left an imprint on the area. The map is difficult to read because it is loaded with markings, lines, and other inscriptions for numerous events, trajectories, and legends; it identifies up to eleven ethnicities, in addition to providing a multiethnic category for those places and institutions that played a significant role for more than one group. But its message is sufficiently clear: all groups that have ever lived in East Harlem have their own memory places, and their independent histories and trajectories can be traced through a story of ethnic succession and assimilation. East Harlem is thus presented as "many places at once" and as "one of New York's City's most dynamic and spirited neighborhoods," a relativistic message that is further stressed by the presentation of the memory places of long-gone or declining groups in the area, such as the Finnish, Dutch, Greeks, and Italians, alongside African Americans and Puerto Ricans, the two largest groups in the area since the 1950s. This presentation treats each successive group as but one ethnic group that will eventually disappear—read "assimilate"—leaving only memory places. Not surprisingly, the map's historic approach to East Harlem's heritage leaves no room for contemporary issues, or for memory places still in the making. In the words of artist Fernando Salicrup: "The problem is that they only care about the past, they are interested in folklore, what happened to the community before. Or they want to know about the struggles of the 1960s and 1970s, but they forget we've been struggling since." Indeed, the Young Lords, who were once demonized and persecuted, are now safely mentioned in the map, but they too are melded into a story exalting the political radicalism shared by all working-class immigrants in the past.[16] Given their limited portrayal, Puerto Rican cultural activists have discussed developing a Latino map, modeled after the multicultural map but devoted solely to marking and promoting Puerto Rican and Latino memory places. Lacking the institutional support enjoyed by the makers of the first map, however, this plan has languished.

The map, along with local apprehension about the inability to promote Puerto Rican culture and institutions in El Barrio, presents yet another problem for the evaluation of East Harlem's Puerto Rican and Latino history: a cleansed past, even if ethnically tainted, is always more marketable than an ethnically tainted present. Speaking to these dynamics is the small but growing Harlem tourist industry, one of the most vocal proponents of East Harlem's multicultural vision, where El Barrio/East Harlem is repeatedly subsumed into Harlem, or else bypassed altogether.

A case in point is the reduction of East Harlem to "Little Italy," ignoring Puerto Rican and Latino heritage altogether. A racially loaded ad by Harlem Your Way! Tours promises visitors a lavishly exotic visit to the greater Harlem area:

> Take a syncopated Champagne Jazz Safari to a Harlem cabaret. Feast on a hearty, soulful breakfast at a Harlem church followed by a tour of the Harlem community. Visit our museums, art galleries, churches, schools, stores, restaurants, and for a unique hands-on experience browse in the African Vendor's Market. Bargains galore! Explore the WORLD OF HARLEM BROWNSTONES! Exercise while seeing Harlem. Bike it or walk it! Do Harlem up RIGHT. Go in a grand style limo—with champagne! See "Little Italy" in East Harlem.[17]

This last reference is to the eastern strip of East Harlem, where tourists can buy Italian ice and visit the Church for Our Lady of Mt. Carmel. The inclusion of "Italian" sites, and the exclusion of Puerto Rican and Latino ones, is another reminder that what is less ethnically identified and tainted is more valuable to tourists. Bonnie Urciuoli's (1993) discussion of Italian Americans and Puerto Ricans in relation to the celebration of the Columbus Quincentenary is relevant here. The ability of Italian Americans to commodify aspects of Italian culture, some of which have been successfully tied to high culture in the European past, she notes, is intrinsically connected to the ethnicization of Italian American culture. Conversely, the racialization of Puerto Ricans prevents them from commodifying aspects of their culture. Constructed as such, the latter's culture was deemed to have less "heritage" value, rendering Puerto Ricanness always less marketable than Italian culture. Similar dynamics are at play in the tour brochure, where Italian culture is used as the conduit to cleanse the area's ethnically tainted past. After all, El Barrio, like all of Harlem, is best known as a ghetto and raced community, and as an unlikely tourist destination. Even Central Harlem, despite the tourist renaissance that it is supposedly undergoing, faces this problem. No wonder, then, the tour buses are so popular, and why the regular fare of "authentic Harlem"—the churches, jazz clubs, and restaurants—is always complemented with a visit to the Old Navy, Starbucks, and

Disney Stores, which are obviously intended to challenge negative stereotypes about Harlem as poor, crime-ridden, and underdeveloped.

East Harlem residents have had ample affirmation of this pervasive image problem, which affects the development of any local tourist initiative. Henry Calderón, president of the East Harlem Chamber of Commerce, remembered in great dismay when Discovery Tours announced bus tours in which East Harlem was included as a place to "explore gang territories and their graffiti messages."[18] Many others were well aware of the kind of misinformation that was disseminated by those few tours coming into East Harlem, which are primarily led by non-Latinos (yet another concern). Ismael Nunez was aghast at what he heard during a multicultural tour of the area by the Big Onion Tour Company in conjunction with the Museum of the City of New York: "They said that Puerto Ricans started coming to East Harlem after World War II, which is not true, and they did not know who Muñoz Marín was, after which 116th Street is named, or that Schomburg, the Black intellectual leader, was Puerto Rican. And there was no mention of anything Mexican." Put simply, promoting, and most important, controlling tourism in the area was seen to be extremely significant not only as a deterrent to gentrification, but also to bind culture and history into place—for revaluing El Barrio's past and determining its future.

POLITICS AND THE RACING OF THE EZ

Race and politics were always implicated in discussions of the EZ, and nowhere was this more evident than in one of the informational meetings held by Congressman Rangel to discuss East Harlem affairs with East Harlem's leaders. The meeting was held in the Taino Towers residential complex, whose leadership is primarily Puerto Rican and Latino, during the height of the EZ controversy in the summer of 2001. Neither Senator Olga Méndez nor Adam Clayton Powell IV was present, reducing the meeting—at least in the eyes of the Puerto Ricans present—to a polarized exchange between "Puerto Rican residents" and "Black elected officials." When the floor was finally opened for questions, there was a short but heated debate between Rangel and El Barrio–born-and-raised Puerto Rican district leader Felix Rosado, well known for his pro-Puerto Rican position. Angered and defiant, Rosado wasted no time in accusing the congressman of dismissing and disrespecting his Puerto Rican heritage by favoring Black institutions over Puerto Rican applicants to the EZ. When Rangel claimed to be unaware of such complaints, Rosado insisted that Latinos' lack of representation was common knowledge, well documented in the media. To the obvious surprise of the audience, Rosado ended by openly remarking, "I'm Puerto Rican and proud." In swift support of Rosado, Miriam Falcón López, the Puerto Rican district administrator for Assemblyman Powell, stood up and applauded, quickly earning the admonishment of Rangel, who was suddenly uncomfortable with the ethnically charged situation. But she persisted. In her words to Rangel, "Rosado had the courage to stand and raise the issue of how he feels about Latinos instead of what you'd like to hear." After the meeting, some were angered at the congressman's patronizing tone toward Latinos; he had dismissed their concerns over the EZ and chided them when they openly complained. "A blind man would have seen through it," one stated.

This was not the only meeting, exchange, or interview in which Puerto Rican leaders expressed such heated resentment and frustration over the EZ, or where Harlem's Black leadership was blamed for the lack of success of Puerto Rican projects and proposals in El Barrio. Indeed, the EZ may have tried to underplay race and ethnicity in favor of industry, but ethnic and racial issues were nonetheless an open subject of debate. The most highly charged topics were complaints regarding Central and Black Harlem receiving greater amounts of funding than East Harlem, and the lack of Puerto Ricans in leadership positions at the EZ. Both were regular topics of discussion in the meetings of Boricuas del Barrio, which deliberated about whether to sue EZ for funding disparity. According to their information, among funds given to West and East Harlem, "less than 2 percent [of EZ funding was given] to a Puerto Rican group in El Barrio/East Harlem."[19] Politicians, for their part, pointed to their funding of East Harlem institutions, dismissing the complaints. Indeed, funding for cultural institutions had gone to East Harlem, but mostly to large institutions such as Hope Community, to rebuild its recital hall for art exhibition purposes; El Museo del Barrio; or to new institutions with funding and infrastructure, such as the National Museum of Catholic Art and History, organizations that are already in a position to attract private and governmental monies. Many Puerto Rican activists believed that funds did not go to the most needy and most "Puerto Rican" institutions. In particular, people bemoaned the lack of funding for small and alternative spaces developed in response to gentrification. Many Puerto Rican leaders, seeing this funding pattern as a move to "de-Latinize the area," saw their complaints delegitimated and invalidated as ethnic chauvinism by the EZ's Black leadership, who in turn were seen by Puerto Ricans as presenting Black "interests" as "global interests."

In this way, the EZ reignited a debate that is decades old and strongly connected to policies for ethnic accommodation and containment. Any connection to an initiative popularly dubbed "Charles Rangel's baby" intimated the influence of an elite cadre of Black political contemporaries to Rangel, who have long made their political trajectories in Central and West Harlem. This was the case notwithstanding the fact that, not unlike Puerto Ricans in East Harlem, the political base of Harlem's longtime Black leadership was also dwindling as a result of a variety of factors, not least of which were demographic and political changes in the area.[20] This perception of EZ's Black control, along with preference given to Harlem over East Harlem in the media and tourist promotion materials, not to mention the paucity of Latinos on either the staff or the board, triggered numerous debates with unavoidable racial and ethnic implications. During the two and a half years that I followed this debate, some accommodation to Puerto Rican demands was made: more Latinos were appointed to the staff; and Puerto Rican Irving MacManus, board member of El Museo del Barrio, was appointed to the Upper Manhattan EZ executive staff as head of the Cultural Industry Investment Fund. But Latinos' representation on the EZ board remained unchanged, with only eight out of approximately twenty-four members. Questions were still being raised about the representation of East Harlem board appointees with regards to ethnicity, race, place of residence, and background and associations with important area institutions such as Mt. Sinai Hospital—one of the largest private employers in East Harlem—exposing the fragility of these actions toward appeasing deeply held qualms about the initiative.[21] People were fully aware that EZ's corporate-centric stand was unaffected by such appointments. In fact, Irving MacManus was the first to explain to me that East Harlemites suffered from a legacy of entitlement, that they lacked "entrepreneurial spirit" to produce "competitive" proposals.

Undoubtedly, against the exacting business prerogatives for culture, the submission of "incompetent" proposals is not at all surprising, while *"chanchulleros"* (opportunists) are never lacking whenever money and resources are at stake. During the course of my research I heard much gossip and hearsay implicating many Puerto Rican cultural institutions in El Barrio in economic self-interest, clientelism, mismanagement, and opportunism. I surmise that exploring these charges would be less revealing than examining the very premises and operations of the EZ initiative. For one, in each case, the EZ's business prerogatives and preference for marketable culture remained largely unchallenged as the standard against which local demands and proposals were swiftly dismissed and invalidated. Most important, these premises not only affected Latinos in East Harlem, but also most small businesses and residents in Central and West Harlem. After all, the largest economic loans and incentives were given to large corporations and developers, who were in turn displacing local merchants who were being pushed out by high rents and stiff competition from chain stores such as HMV and Old Navy.[22]

Expressing the sentiment of smaller cultural organizations in West and Central Harlem, Voza Rivers, chair of the Harlem Arts Alliance, a group of 160 organizations and individual artists, churches, and tavern owners, evoked similar criticisms from East Harlemites when he noted: "The only voices at the board are from the big giants like Schomburg and the Studio Museum, but they do not represent the broader community. The institutions that have been doing good work with little money, and have a local constituency and have been consistent with their work in this community, are not getting the money. And there are a number of us that feel disenfranchised." Even the debate over the EZ board and staff was basically flawed, given the little decision-making power vested in board members. One of the new Puerto Rican board appointees in 2001 admitted being baffled about the board's activities. Folders are provided at the last minute, with undecipherable information, he explained, and one could ask few questions before being asked to vote. In this way, the debate over EZ funding pitted one group against another in a conflict whose resolution was out of reach, and where the greatest beneficiaries were large developers.[23] This was also a struggle in which the terms of debate became twisted and muddled, always in favor of development. Consider the fact that debates over the paucity of funding for El Barrio were turning Latino community activists and former foes of gentrification into advocates of development. The ethnically charged environment also left little room for awareness of the common problems affecting both East Harlem and Harlem residents and merchants. Such problems were not reducible to faulting "Black politicians," the EZ bureaucracy, or politics and contacts, but were far more insidious and concerned the penetration of capital into these communities.

Both Blacks and Latinos were adversely affected by the EZ's lack of outreach and by impossible guidelines, excessive bureaucracy, and applications that, as I repeatedly heard, "everyone except the pope had to sign." They were also affected by a policy that required applicants to develop detailed business plans. It is noteworthy that, while the EZ was intended to foster privatization and a business ethic among Upper Manhattan communities, it was ultimately a federally backed program, requiring a greater amount of paperwork and bureaucracy than would be involved, for instance, in the already taxing process of obtaining a commercial bank loan. This inherently favored larger institutions with the staff and infrastructure to comply with the grant writing requirements of the EZ. In addition, applicants had to explain how they will generate jobs, a particularly difficult proposition for smaller cultural institutions that are predominantly understaffed and underfunded. East Harlemites were also hurt by the lack of an EZ location in the area. Furthermore, the EZ staff lacked East Harlem residents as well as Latinos, who could have served as local envoys to the initiative; nor were there any materials in Spanish. Erica González, who in 2002 represented East Harlem on the EZ board, noted: "They say that they've done outreach, but outreach is not about leaving flyers for a seminar outside an ATM. That's far from outreach to our community." Latino residents also felt that they were more likely to be sent to technical assistance, that is, to training or learning workshops—or "camp," in local lingo—to learn how to prepare budgets and restructure their organization. This added to the perception that the EZ was demeaning and patronizing to Latinos. Debbie Quiñones, who was also a former member of the EZ board, explained her frustrations at realizing that applications from East Harlem did not qualify for the funding requirements as set up by the EZ; they lacked annual reports, books, and business plans. Yet sending thirty-year-old institutions to technical assistance communicated to them that they were inept. The tensions were hence unavoidable. In her words, "They are telling us that our culture is colorful, and all, but not ready for economic assistance."

The staff in charge of the Cultural Industry Investment Fund was frustrated with the criticisms from Latino institutions, but insisted that they had done the outreach. Nonetheless, applications from East Harlem were not forthcoming, while many of those that were submitted were inappropriate for the funding requirements. Yet, for the EZ staff, outreach translated into more preparatory workshops, which delayed the funding process and undoubtedly led to more resentment. A particularly telling example is the impasse involving the exchange between Candy Jackson, a staff member at the EZ nonprofit division, and José Carrero, a local Puerto Rican entrepreneur, then manager of La Marqueta. Ms. Jackson was speaking at a meeting to address people's complaints about the EZ. She had been at the EZ for less than a year and had been asked to announce a workshop purposely designed to address the lack of proposals from the community. The workshop was designed to help "institutions get the funding and ultimately create infrastructures that led to sustainability," a description that repeated the charged issues of quality and sustainability that East Harlemites had been hearing over and over. Ms. Jackson obviously could do little more than public relations to assuage the community. In the solemn and patronizing tone of someone "who's been there and done that," Carrero noted:

> You've been there for less than a year, but we've been going back and forth with this for almost five years. Your staff turnover is faster than McDonald's, okay, and we get less service than we do at McDonald's.

With all due respect, I know you're doing a good job and you're trying to reach out; we have gone to workshops time and time and time again. If somebody in the community has a restaurant and can convince a bank, which is the most conservative group of human beings, of institutions, that I have ever met besides some Orthodox churches, and he can turn his business into a viable business and get money from them, why can't we convince the EZ of the same things? What's the difference? . . . I'm wondering now, we started out with twenty-six million dollars, what's left?

By then, eleven million dollars had already been earmarked, the representative explained, while another young woman from the EZ stressed what everyone else knew very well already: that if they had complaints, they needed to see their elected officials, underscoring the importance of contacts and politics in the funding process. Yet East Harlemites lacked influential politicians that could advocate and vouch for them or their proposals as suggested by the speaker.

But most heavily charged were the issues of quality and the business demands of any culture initiative. For one, a rejection was seen to imply that one's cultural institution, and by default, one's culture, was faulty and of low quality. On closer inspection, however, it is evident that EZ requests for business plans and for placing a monetary value on all cultural "products" presented a trap to Latino cultural institutions whose work and offerings, largely undocumented, lacked an undisputed reference for estimating their value in cultural, much less in monetary, ways. Consider the case of Raices, a Latin music collection and research center founded in 1981, and one of the few local organizations to be funded by the initiative. As director Ramón Rodríguez conceded, it got funding thanks to its parent organization, Boys and Girls Harbor, a large nonprofit children's organization with an entire development staff at its disposal. Still, lacking a business plan, it received funds for a feasibility study but had serious problems appraising its collection. As Rodríguez noted, "There was no bag of reference for this collection. A Hispanic record had never been appraised. To us this collection is worth gold, but to society it's unworthy." The director was annoyed and bewildered. When Machito and Tito Puente died, he had been interviewed by all the major television networks: People had come to Raices for information on these famous musicians. Staff for the movie *Mambo Kings* had spent four months doing research in his collection, without paying a fee or even giving a contribution. Yet proving the value of his collection had been a struggle. The final appraisal came at the hands of Colombian ethnomusicologist Jorge Arévalo, who gave it a market-replacement value of about one hundred thousand dollars, far from what could be considered a "valuable" collection. As Arévalo explained, there is no market for Latin American musical material and the collection was not object based, two important criteria hindering its evaluation. Sensitive to the collection's historical, educational, cultural, and documentational value from the perspective of Latino history, however, Arévalo added another value—that is, its cultural value—which he described as priceless.

Another example of the clash between EZ standards and local projects is provided by the Made in Puerto Rico Store and the affiliated International Salsa Museum, a small institution with big aspirations, as suggestive by its self-designation as the "ONLY salsa museum on the planet." The store was founded in 1996 by Efraín Suárez, a local Puerto Rican businessman spurred by the lack of bodegas selling Puerto Rican products in the area. Two years later, the museum opened in a small room behind the store to document, according to the founder, the unknown history of musicians who developed this New York–based rhythm. The involvement of José Obando, along with the help of a marketing and communication expert, soon led to an educational program and a Web site.[24] The museum is not big enough to hold even four visitors at once, yet through its Web site, a weekly cable channel, and an innovative, unlabeled, makeshift collection of salsa paraphernalia collected from locals, it has received a lot of local and even international attention since its founding. On a Saturday, visitors included a local youth looking for a Puerto Rican flag sticker for his boom box, a family from the Bronx, a couple of students, and some tourists, among them a salsa enthusiast from Germany who had heard about the museum on the Internet and proceeded to interview the owner about salsa, much to the owner's delight.

As a new project then lacking an official museum charter, the museum was undoubtedly an unlikely candidate for EZ funding. However, it was not the rejection that most irked museum proponents, but rather the skepticism they encountered at the EZ over the value of their institution and their ability to carry out their plans. These and other doubts were communicated in a rejection letter that Suárez was quick to share with me and others as proof of EZ's patronizing assessment of their work, which they vehemently challenged. The letter stated that the institution lacked a "stable formal structure necessary to implement operations that will sustain a museum of the magnitude [they proposed]"; it also questioned the appropriateness of its staff and even the attractiveness of salsa music to international visitors. "The current staff consists of salsa 'icons' but does not include staff with museum management or curatorial expertise. Management should be familiar with museum industry best practices and strategic models to ensure development of the most efficient and appropriate strategies. . . . The proposal also lacks analysis that demonstrates an understanding of the audience demographics and demand for salsa music from domestic and international visitors."[25] Suárez was astounded by these words, which he felt disregarded not only his ability to carry out the project to completion, but most significantly raised questions about the value of salsa by asking him to prove that it could be a potential draw for national and international visitors.

In this way, the EZ business stance provided no recognition for community needs that were not closely aligned with outward requirements and the demands of tourists, developers, and visitors. One last vivid example is the case of St. Cecilia Church, a Roman Catholic church with primarily Latino parishioners. Its proposal to the EZ for a handicapped entry ramp was initially denied, but the church was then encouraged to apply for the tourist initiative for the repair of the roof and steps—that is, the more "visible" areas. Father Skelly, the parish priest, noted in disbelief how he had been encouraged to apply under a tourism initiative when his church is rarely visited by tourists and when there are no plans for bringing tourists to his church. Last we spoke he was thinking of applying, reasoning that "the stoops are used by locals."

Evidently, there were a variety of responses toward a policy that found many critics and few converts in East Harlem. Many simply ignored the initiative altogether, not caring to apply to its educational workshops— one of the reasons there were few proposals originating from East Harlem. Others decided to reapply after being rejected, purposefully adopting the business requirements and lingo of the EZ, though most often reluctantly, nonchalantly, and with considerable skepticism toward the initiative. Not that these type of accommodations are new; local institutions have long been subject to similar pressures from funding sources, always with costs involved. The difference is the heightened pressure exerted by the EZ and its neoliberal cultural policies on institutions, not only in their programs, but on their outlook and structure. Debbie Quiñones put it in succinct terms when she shared her concerns: "I worry that East Harlem residents will suffer. Who will provide services? What you have now is an educational facility becoming a theater, a housing group becoming an arts group, while an arts group becomes a housing one. It's all opportunism and a fad." Indeed, for those who sought support, accommodations were unavoidable. But people were far from silent. Condemning the initiative and exposing EZ's rejection of proposals as examples of discriminatory trends by the EZ were important devices for resistance and struggle. Moreover, as in other instances documented in this work, the ethnic claims by Puerto Ricans, so undermined by local politicians and EZ officials, had larger repercussions for East Harlem. Indeed, imputations of EZ's ill-treatment of East Harlem were initially voiced by and on behalf of Puerto Ricans, but many of the same actors strategically presented it as an "East Harlem" issue, not solely a Puerto Rican problem, whenever it was politically appropriate. The community board was important in this regard, leading to an official letter from this body to the U.S. Department of Housing and Urban Development (HUD), which oversees EZ legislation, requesting an in-depth investigation into its failures in East Harlem. When HUD's secretary dismissed its criticisms, claiming that monies had been allotted to East Harlem, community activists were adamant. In a letter responding to the secretary, the board once more reiterated the specific nature of their criticisms:

> We ask that your report exclude projects and programs that are not exclusively East Harlem projects and programs. . . . Furthermore, of the projects claimed to benefit East Harlem, we are interested in knowing how many are owned or operated by individuals reflective of the demographics of East Harlem, which is largely Puerto Rican, African American and Mexican. Moreover, we also want the data on how many projects are owned or operated by East Harlem residents."[26]

In other words, the race and ethnicity card was not abandoned as contrasting definitions about who should receive monies, and on what basis, were never entirely reconciled.

In fact, despite all the public disavowing of ethnicity, it was ethnic demands that did the most to bring about changes in the EZ. In the June 2003 meeting of the Board of Directors, Kenneth Knuckles, the newly appointed president and CEO of the EZ, affirmed that East Harlem would be one of his priorities, describing a new policy of transparency, community outreach, and accountability. In a subsequent interview, he confirmed that criticisms from East Harlemites had been heard and conceded there was a "structural nonalignment" between the requirements of the EZ and the community. Tied by the regulations of EZ legislation, however, the problem could only be addressed through education and more technical assistance. This alone ensures that community debates over the EZ won't be so easily abated.

TOURISM — OPPORTUNITY AND PERIL

The EZ initiative may have tried to erase racial and ethnic tensions by treating culture as a profit-making device, but this neither freed it from its racial and ethnic ties in the area nor erased the spatial identification of different groups with particular neighborhoods. Residents of East Harlem were amply aware that the selling of Upper Manhattan had implications for their future, including the possibility of their displacement. Blacks and Latinos would be once again pitted against each other for a piece of the pie, in a struggle now waged around national and international recognition in arts, culture, and tourism. But this is a contest that ultimately has no winners. It was not "culture," but culture industries that were the object of economic interest; the largest beneficiaries were developers and outside visitors, not local residents. Namely, it was marketable ethnicity that was favored, not the kind of cultural strategies and programs of self-assertion proposed by local economic and tourist enthusiasts, such as those spurred by gentrification.

In effect, what the EZ Cultural Industry Investment Fund told East Harlemites is that the future of tourism in the area is not likely to depend

on its Puerto Rican and Latino roots, but on the existence and development of nationally recognized institutions whose value could never be
doubted. The EZ generalized a discourse of quality and efficiency, requiring that cultural institutions transform themselves along the lines of standardized art and nonprofit museums, in a context where the threat of
gentrification had made everyone fearful and defensive of their heritage.
People were repeatedly told that popular sites, events, and cultural institutions will always be eclipsed by "high art" and corporate projects as
anchors for tourist and cultural initiatives. Their legacy was not good
enough; "official" and "efficient" institutions needed to generate tourism
and create jobs, income, and consumers.

Thus in hindsight, the EZ initiative is better seen as a disciplining
force: it did not promote culture as a tool of economic development, but
rather disseminated a particular way of dealing with culture. Evidence of
this is the fact that local institutions obtained funding for studies, business plans, technical support, and other instruments of instruction rather
than for the development or expansion of their institutions. Knuckles's
comments above suggest this will continue to be the case. Perhaps this is
a prelude to effective growth and expansion, but then one might ask,
Expansion on what basis, to benefit whom, what audiences, what types
of cultural expression, and what kinds of producers and consumers?
Considering that canons of quality are never universal, but always
socially constructed and implicated with social hierarchies and exclusions, these questions beg another: Who are the ultimate beneficiaries of
transformations in the name of quality and efficiency?

The Cultural Industry Investment Fund was not meant to increase
openness or opportunities for residents to market or define their culture
or community, but rather to secure El Barrio for private development. For
one, despite numerous challenges to the mantra that only institutionalized cultural institutions can lead the way toward tourism, there was only
so much local institutions could accomplish with limited resources. If they
wanted tourism, they necessarily had to develop "marketable" and "sustainable" proposals.

This is a demand that self-selects those with the right capital and political contacts to prepare "bullet-proof" proposals. Coincidently, at the
time of this writing, development proposals from politically connected

stakeholders like artist-administrator Fernando Salicrup and Eddie Baca, a former chairman of the community board—both planning to accommodate affordable housing, artists' housing, and cultural and community space—were circulating in the community board and local political forums. Critics felt that community demands for more Latino-generated development would only benefit the most politically connected. Others quickly dismissed these concerns. The proposals at least come from inside the community, I was told; they were not generated by outsiders, evidencing again the contradictory corollaries to the linkage of culture and space. Predictably in the current fiscal climate, both projects face insurmountable challenges. In this context, support for the more marketable and efficient cultural institutions in the area, including those that had previously disparaged their location in El Barrio, or that were proposed as bait for new developments, remains the surest path for tourism in East Harlem. As a result, willingly or not, tourist enthusiasts found themselves supporting projects implicated in the area's gentrification. Indeed, beyond controversy over EZ funds, the reports that the Museum of the City of New York would leave the area in favor of a downtown location, that El Museo del Barrio would revamp its Barrio origins, and that there were proposals to build a new location for the Museum for African Art dominated the cultural news and discussions in the community board and among local activists. The proposal by the Museum of the City of New York featured a move to a downtown location touted as "A New Site for a New Century" and a "world-class museum" for the "capital of the world." It cited the poor location in East Harlem as a reason for insufficient attendance, confirming the community's fears that El Barrio was far from a coveted location. Furthermore, El Museo del Barrio's plan to wean itself from El Barrio was met with substantive criticisms of the institution's disdain of its past. Such criticisms were naturally met with requests that the two museums remain in El Barrio to help anchor tourism and attract name recognition and visitors to the area. This is the context that framed discussions about the Edison project and the Museum for African Art.

FOUR

The Edison Project

ON CORPORATE HEADQUARTERS, MUSEUMS,
AND THE EDUCATION OF EL BARRIO

What do Disney, Starbucks, Old Navy, Magic Johnson and
Bill Clinton have in common? Each has helped ignite the
new Harlem renaissance by setting up shop uptown. Unfor-
tunately, petty politicians are trying to block Edison Schools,
the nation's largest school-management company, from
following in those trailblazing footsteps. Obstructionists
do hate visionaries.

Daily News, editorial, August 18, 2001

Amid the Museum of the City of New York's impending move out of
East Harlem, another museum was aggressively negotiating to move in.
Promising to bring the "first national headquarters to relocate north of
Ninety-sixth Street," as well as jobs, increased tourism, and world-class
architecture, among other benefits, the Edison Project (involving a charter school and Edison's corporate headquarters), along with the Museum
for African Art, proposed a move to Fifth Avenue and 110th Street, a coveted and long-contentious location.[1] Bordering East and West Harlem,
this location holds an important historic and symbolic position among
both Puerto Ricans and African Americans who have placed it at the center of numerous struggles over race and turf. A few years before the proposed project, for instance, the placement of a statue of Duke Ellington in
this location caused controversy among Latinos who felt a famous Latino

musician was more appropriate. Soon after the death of Puerto Rican bandleader Tito Puente in 2000, community activists mobilized and successfully rallied to have the city rename a five-block stretch of 110th Street as Tito Puente Way, as if reclaiming the area's Latin heritage. Plans to erect a statue of Tito next to Ellington and to relocate the Salsa Museum to the spot were in the works. The corner was also the site of the Nueva Esperanza (New Hope) community garden, which would soon be bulldozed to make way for the Edison Project, an action underscoring the vulnerability of many publicly owned spaces in the area. Thus, initial reactions to the establishment of the Museum for African Art on the spot were loaded with race and turf issues.

Yet, in an unexpected political twist, the appropriateness of an African art museum in a "Latin area" was soon the least pressing community concern about the project. In fact, during the two years I followed the debate, some of the most ardent proponents of Puerto Rican culture in El Barrio emerged as the museum's most vocal supporters. Suddenly African culture was everyone's common heritage. To deflect Latino criticisms, Edison mounted a carefully orchestrated campaign before the local community board. Their goal was to re-signify the Museum for African Art as a celebration of the global African diaspora, including, of course, Latin America and the Caribbean, that is, a museum about "everyone's common heritage." As supporters repeatedly told residents and organizations in East Harlem, the project would educate residents about their own common heritage while creating a global tourist and entertainment destination that would provide jobs and place the neighborhood on the map. But as residents would soon realize, the museum came with a stiff price. Culture was the bait for a larger project for privatizing social services and further commodifying place in El Barrio. The move of the nationally recognized cultural institution from trendy Soho to unknown East Harlem would require approval of the entirety of the Edison Project, including the charter school and the Edison corporate headquarters, one of the largest and most controversial for-profit educational management groups in the country. In addition, the project required a rezoning of the area from residential to commercial use to accommodate Edison's corporate headquarters. When originally included as part of the Milbank Frawley

Circle–East Harlem Urban Renewal Area in the 1960s, the location was zoned for housing and residential development. But housing was never built there, and housing of any kind would soon be a fading memory once the rezoning was approved.

Given the area's history, debates about the project both united and polarized residents. Public hearings on the proposal were among the most widely attended gatherings since the late 1990s, when debates over the Pathmark supermarket divided the community over the first large-scale commercial development that East Harlem had seen in decades. In similar fashion, opinions for and against the Edison Project ranged widely. Issues as varied as the fate of children, the state of public education, the relative value of public space, privatization, pollution, asthma, and gentrification permeated the positions of critics and advocates alike, making this a complex issue with repercussions baffling to many involved in the debate.

Ultimately, the project was abandoned in the fall of 2002, after Edison's stock shares plummeted and the company faced charges of fraudulent reporting practices and criticisms of its educational strategy in Philadelphia. Supporters were left longing for Edison's promises for economic development, while opponents had to find consolation in the fact that it was the company's decision and ailing finances, not their opposition, that had scrapped the project. The project had actually been unanimously approved by the city council in December 2001, after East Harlem's community board had rejected it and after the borough president had made recommendations to deny the zoning change.[2] The events of September 11, 2001, helped pave the way for this decision, as private investments were suddenly deemed a scarce commodity to be attracted at any cost, particularly in minority communities where investors had seldom shown any interest.

Within the Edison Project, "culture"—as represented by a nationally recognized museum and the promise of an educational institution that would improve education for East Harlem children—served both as an inducement to the approval of a business initiative and zoning change, and as a business end in itself. After all, the museum and the charter school would be important economic ventures; their inclusion in the same plan with the construction of a corporate headquarters was not only a ploy to assure support for the entire project, but it also exemplified the strategic role of culture as an object of and medium for profit. These new corporate combinations find fertile territories in entertainment- and service-lacking neighborhoods like East Harlem, where years of neglect have rendered them vulnerable to the view that privatization is the only way to obtain social services and entitlements. But the Edison Project reveals the limits and fallacies of these cultural entrepreneurial strategies. Culture may increasingly function as a medium and object of profit, but it is never fully expunged from particularized racial and ethnic identifications. In fact, as in the EZ, these identifications were strategically mobilized and activated within debates of the Edison Project, exposing the racial and ethnic dynamics on which development proposals were always predicated.

GENTRIFICATION WITH KENTE CLOTH COVER

No one could deny that Edison had done its homework. After a much-publicized defeat in 2001, when New York City parents voted against Edison and its bid to manage five public schools in Brooklyn, Manhattan, and the Bronx, Edison could not afford to lose the battle in East Harlem. In the months prior to the hearings during the summer of 2001, Edison engaged in aggressive public relations operations with strong advocacy and many presentations to community groups. First they hired Tonio Burgos, a nationally recognized lobbyist with deep political roots in East Harlem, where he served on the school board and the community board, and was well connected with longstanding Puerto Rican political leaders in the area. Burgos in turn hired Francisco Díaz, a current resident and former state assemblyman and member of the school board and community board as community consultant for the project.[3] Both had similar trajectories in the civic sector before moving to the private sector, although Díaz's newcomer status in the world of lobbying added to his image as a community-concerned and neutral insider, not solely an advocate for Edison.[4] Guided by Díaz's local knowledge, Edison engaged in a massive grassroots effort including multiple presentations to sell the project among influential prodevelopment organizations in the area, from Hope Community to East Harlem Council for Community Improvement to the Community Board 11 Committees on Economic Development, Zoning, Public Safety, Transportation, Parks and Recreation, and Cultural Affairs. In each forum, they spoke seductively about their proposed contributions to East Harlem, although many issues were left unanswered. During a presentation at the Cultural Affairs Committee, for instance, they described their curatorial vision for the museum as a diasporic one encompassing Afro-Caribbean culture and heritage, signaling here Puerto Rican and Dominican culture, a highly effective move for neutralizing concerns about the museum's cultural alignment with El Barrio. But the museum has in fact never cultivated this vision. As of 2002, among more than forty exhibitions since 1984, only one evoked directly the African legacy in the Americas: "Face of the Gods: Art and Altars of Africa and the African Americas." Far from evidence of a diasporic vision, this exhibition represents an exception from a primarily continent-centered African approach that leaves little room for African diasporic arts and culture, much less for Hispanic Caribbean or Afro-Latino cultural expressions, as residents had been promised.[5]

Through these presentations, the Edison Project accumulated friends and preliminary endorsements, which they quickly publicized in order to recruit additional supporters. The Edison team made so many visits to the different community board committees that an African American member assured me that she supported the project but had become "sick of the Edison people." In preparation for the public hearing, "the Edison people" had also called upon teachers and African-garbed volunteers, some coming from Boston and Washington, D.C., to testify about the wonders of Edison Schools, replete with African greetings and exhortations of "our common African ancestry." One supporter summoned "the ancestors," linking community approval of the project with the appeasement of those absent yet "watching us from above." They even provided snacks and refreshments for special attendees before one of the hearings, creating a festive ambiance for participants. To further assure themselves of support at the second hearing, Edison supporters mobilized members of

Figure 9. View of audience during public hearing organized by Community Board 11 to debate the Edison Project, 2001. Photo by the author.

Positive Workforce, an East Harlem–based local minority construction advocacy organization that hires Black and Latino men from throughout the city in construction trades. These men had apparently been promised construction jobs on the Edison Project, making them immediate and vehement supporters. To the visible delight of the Edison team, and to the annoyance of locals who resented their overt presence, Positive Workforce loudly cheered supporters of the project and hissed and booed opponents just as loudly. Meanwhile, some of the residents who would be most affected by the move, such as those living in the immediate project area, complained that they had neither been informed of the hearing, nor consulted by the project's proponents. Opponents of the project therefore faced many challenges in making their case. Among them were members of the school board and teachers since most charter schools are not bound to union bargaining agreements. Also opposed were parents speaking against "the sale of our children"; the founders and frequent visitors of the Nueva Esperanza garden, scheduled to be destroyed by the development; and local residents in the immediacy of the project. Nearby residents in particular feared an increase in pollution and traffic and growing rates of asthma, a concern that had attracted much publicity and attention from local politicians, but in reality carried little weight against proposed developments. Protests had not deterred the construction of a bus depot despite community complaints of environmental racism—all except one depot in the city are located above Ninety-sixth Street. Incidents of asthma would be just as useless in stalling this new construction.[6]

Primary among their criticisms was the furtiveness of the move, which made the public hearings more spectacles than real debates. Indeed, Edison had already purchased the lot from Mayor Giuliani before residents had a say in the matter. Even the activists of the Association of Community Organizations for Reform Now (ACORN), which was then at the forefront of organizing parents against the Edison takeover of schools in New York and Philadelphia, were unaware of the purchase in East Harlem until the project was publicly debated in the news. In a phone conversation, Bertha Lewis, of ACORN, explained:

> The horse had been out of the barn for two years. We were so surprised to learn that all the while we were fighting them in these five schools, they were dealing to build their headquarters in East Harlem. That's when we realized that the five schools were connected. It was all part of a larger ploy that we could not envision and could not take on. Politicians and local leaders had been spoken for. So we focused our struggle in the schools.

Given that Edison had long since purchased the land, residents were left with few options. On the other hand, the tie with the museum had gained favor for the project among tourism-hungry East Harlemites. Exhausted by the debates over tourism and threatened by the impending move of the Museum of the City of New York, many East Harlemites were ready to approve the project, along with the charter schools and the zoning changes, just to have an "internationally recognized museum" in their midst. As a young local resident explained after one of the public hearings for the project, "Why should people of El Barrio travel downtown to see a decent museum? Our community was not good enough for the Museum of the City of New York. Are we going to say no to the only entertainment in this community?" Once again, empowerment was equated with development, and ethnic pride with access and choice, this time to internationally recognized museums. This was the case even though many speakers in the hearings gave little evidence that they understood the full implications of this tripartite project.

Diverting attention from the full implications of the project in terms of rezoning or the fate of public education was obviously part of Edison's marketing strategy. It consistently presented the project as being all about choice in education, entertainment, jobs, and the coming of an internationally recognized museum, never about a corporate headquarters requiring a zoning change or about the anchoring of Edison in New York City. As a result, the debate turned into one about culture and education, while the project's potential effects in terms of gentrification and the privatization of space and services were left unquestioned. The void of information on the project's commercial component was evident in the statements of many of its supporters. Most of these focused on the museum, favoring its move to East Harlem, making little or no mention of the school and the corporate headquarters. Other museum supporters plainly admitted to having little knowledge about the different components of the project. Residents seemed to be particularly confused about the implications of the zoning change in terms of traffic, housing costs, and, perhaps most importantly, the nature of the proposed school. It was not uncommon for supporters of the museum to state publicly that they knew little about the concept, nature, and functioning of charter schools. In other words, there was much diversion but not enough information to help residents understand the full ramifications of the project.

But not everyone was oblivious to Edison's strategy. Well aware that the project involved three separate businesses and that its cultural aspects had been used to endear residents to the venture, one objector accused Edison of promoting "gentrification with kente cloth cover." Other opponents made a point of embracing the museum while rejecting the school and its corporate headquarters. Yet the project was connected for a reason. In Díaz's words, "It was the perfect marriage." Edison needed the museum to acquire the zoning permit while the museum needed the backing of a major corporation to fund its building. Residents were told they had to approve or oppose the totality of the project, not its pieces.

Long disillusioned with the many outsiders—from clergymen to government workers to volunteers and corporate interests—seeking to profit from the "needs of the community," residents also resented a mostly white team bringing teachers and volunteers from outside El Barrio to tell them how to improve their schools or the value of their community. Older residents recalled the era of white social workers and wondered if the 1960s, and the move toward local empowerment, had ever happened. Consider the comments of a female resident voiced during one of the hearings. In the solemn tone with which everyone announced their linkages to East Harlem and their legitimacy to speak on the issue, she described being born and raised in East Harlem, in addition to being the product of a community public school, now also attended by her children. Though in favor of the museum, she rejected the project, favoring instead investment in existing schools and promoting residents' control of "their community":

> Outsiders come in and they make promises. They overlook their promises. How are we going to be guaranteed all these jobs? One school, okay, that's wonderful. What's gonna happen to all the children in District 4 schools who can't go to that one school? We already have budget cuts to the educational program. We don't need to lose any more funding from struggling schools, and frankly speaking, I think that as a community, we need to be more united and do this kind of thing for ourselves. We don't need people from Boston or elsewhere coming in here to try to tell us how to do what we need to be doing for ourselves [applause from the audience]. You know, the deficits in this community are because we are not getting the funding that we need to do these things ourselves.

With these words, she challenged the underlying assumption made by the Edison team, that their proposal provided the best solution to the plight of minority children. Instead, she focused attention to the reality that faulty schools are the result of a lack of funding, and that they—"the community"—could produce perfectly good schools if given appropriate funding. The concept of "community" was repeatedly deployed during the hearings by both opponents and proponents of the project, be they Black, white, or Latino, although this time to imply commonalities across ethnicity and race. In this instance, "East Harlem" was more commonly used as the primary designation for the area, presented as a victimized, poor, and exploited community, conditions that were seen as due mostly to a lack of funds and of outsiders who exploit both its assets and its deficits. In doing so, residents challenged the implicit and primarily negative claims about the value of East Harlem and of its residents that underlaid the appeals by the Edison people. Here it is important to recognize that "needs" and "lacks" are not value-neutral conditions but are always manipulated for a variety of purposes to advance policies as well as to pathologize and racialize populations, particularly when tied to "cultural" and ethnically defined groups (Chin 2001; Kelly 1998). Consider the comments of Anthony Baldwin, the president of the Nueva Esperanza garden, who was made invisible during the Edison team's presentations of their project. His statement was a clear attempt to reverse the dominant discourse that East Harlem was "faulty" and "needy" (of jobs, entertainment, or museums) as promoted by Edison's presentation; he described El Barrio as valuable, famous in and for itself. Because only proponents of the project had been given time to present their positions to the audience in the hearings, the statement is also a challenge to the inequality that predicated the discussion.

> Madam president, community leaders, corporate developers for Edison Schools, and the Museum for African Art, and a warm welcome to my neighbors in the most famous neighborhood in the world. My name is Anthony Baldwin. I give you my name because I am the president of the unnamed vacant lot in the special part of the improvement district located at 2E–4E 110th Street, block 1615 [applause]. The name of the vacant lot is Nueva Esperanza garden, I call it the garden of hope. When my neighbors decided to nurture, clean, and enhance this part of our community over a decade ago, it was an abandoned dump, much like this famous neighborhood was portrayed by the media to the world. We did not ask for a corporate handout. We offered a helping hand to create a safe city and safe streets. We are more than successful. Witness [pointing to the procedure]. I have had visits from the attorney general's office, calls from the mayor's corporate council, e-mails, certified letters, hand-delivered certified packages, and every other type of communication known to man, except respect for what my neighbors have created. I also understand that Edison came here, and the Museum for African Art came here, and they were allotted fifteen minutes. Nobody offered

my garden any block of time to come here and make our point. I know
that what's going to happen is that everybody's gonna come here because Edison puts on a good show. But it's not about a show. It's about
taking control of your community.

Baldwin evoked a common view among opponents of the project, who
feared that developers sought to benefit from the fruit of residents' work,
reminding the audience that it is they who had made the location attractive in the first place by building a beautiful garden. This garden was a
tourist attraction, too; outsiders are coming when they are not needed.
The garden advocate's argument in defense of public space, however,
had little support among the audience, having been repeatedly delegitimated in public debates. As documented by Miranda Martínez (2001),
community gardens had been seriously undermined by former mayor
Giuliani's auctioning of city properties to the private sector. Describing
them as empty lots in need of development, the administration repeatedly denied the value of gardens as social spaces, invalidating in the
process gardeners' and residents' claims to these spaces as cultural, community, and hence "public" sites. Central to this strategy was to pit gardens against housing, schools, and other services that were presented as
truly representative of the "community's needs and interests," forcing
community gardeners to prove their "worthiness" as public space vis-à-
vis housing. Little was said of the fact that, as shown in chapter 2, these
spaces are sold for upscale developments and housing that would be out
of the reach of the housing needy.

Residents were also highly skeptical of Edison's overt interest in setting up shop in East Harlem now that the neighborhood was "coming of
age." Rumors that the Museum for African Art had earlier rejected a
Harlem location and never wanted to be located in the ghetto, choosing
instead Soho as their initial location, fed people's skepticism about
Edison's interests in El Barrio. Such rumors brought to the fore the fact
that East Harlem was far from a "global location," but a compromised
one, and that if it was just now "coming of age," it would be for others—
outsiders—to profit. Opponents also pointed out that it was a failing, not
a thriving, corporation that was coming to El Barrio. A local resident and

public education advocate noted that Edison had lost two hundred million dollars since it was founded in 1992, almost foretelling the deal's demise some months later. Its coming to East Harlem was an experiment, a survival strategy that provided little guarantee of permanence and stability, as residents would soon discover. Many questioned if residents would ultimately be left with an empty building better used for the housing needy.

THE HISTORY AND POLITICS OF LACKS AND NEEDS

The most taxing challenge facing opponents of the project, however, preceded Edison's corporate muscle-flexing and showmanship. The conditions of poverty have long been used by locals and outsiders alike to advance a variety of public sector projects targeting poverty and social ills, and were now being usurped for commercial and profit-making enterprises. Accordingly, the project was presented as a remedy to the community's lacks, including good schools, economic development, entertainment, and other needs that the government and public sector had repeatedly failed to deliver. As discussed earlier, residents were highly resentful of this discourse of "lacks" and of the ways in which it had been deployed in the hearings to debase and discredit El Barrio. Yet, the paucity of services in the area could not be addressed with reminders of the structural factors that have hurt El Barrio. Nor could reminders of the merits, strengths, and capacity of East Harlem residents do much for the educational ills of East Harlem's children.

As a result, the existence of real needs in the community rallied many in support of a project promising a unique tourist, business, and educational asset to the neighborhood. Community leaders and development enthusiasts, from old-timers such as Roberto Anazagasti, Bill Del Toro, and Fernando Salicrup to new ones such as John Rivera, then president of the district's school board, and Mike Lugo, from Hope Community, as well as many community board members, publicly defended the project as an opportunity to put East Harlem on the map, make our children "citizens of the world," and bring tourists, businesses, and jobs. They defended the project as a global opportunity that promised choices and alternatives in the form of community events, adult programs, an alternative to public school, and entertainment, among other offerings. In other words, the museum and charter school project were linked with business opportunities, jobs, global culture, entertainment, and choice, and hence with the attending "discourse of globalization" that dominate public debates about development not only within El Barrio but throughout the city and beyond (Gregory 1998). As neatly expressed by Francisco Díaz, lobbyist for the project,

> You don't know what an honor it is for me to be part of something like this, in the neighborhood that I grew up. There are forces behind this. And you'll see that I'll be in the board of the school, and I'll be buying into the stocks for the school. Because I'm a technocrat and a technician, I understand the role of private and nonprofit sector, and that's what we need in this community—more technicians that can protect this community.

Like him, others were convinced of the inevitability of private developments, and hence the need for local technocrats to wrest control over it. The promise of acquiring control of schools and services through private ownership (in this case through the purchase of stocks in the school) was contrasted to the ephemeral empowerment provided by publicly funded projects, obviously a direct critique of East Harlem's continued disenfranchisement, despite numerous "empowering" policies.

In a similar manner, the subject of unemployment was repeatedly raised to deflect criticism of the project. Opposition to the project was presented not only as being against "our children," but against progress and jobs. Residents continually repeated the "20 percent unemployment rate" throughout the forum. As such, Edison's business-educational-cultural complex had been made indistinguishable from "Disney, Starbucks, Old Navy, Magic Johnson, and Bill Clinton," and thus from notions of progress and "vision" sweeping through Harlem. Timing was crucial in forging these sentiments. The EZ, the corporate-centric Giuliani and Bloomberg administrations, and local policies, particularly post–September 11, had shaped an indiscriminate preference for business and a terrain in which communities could struggle for mere fragments of control over the privatization-driven developments enveloping El Barrio. This context explains why the agenda of groups such as Boricuas del Barrio and Mujeres del Barrio is directed at making sure Puerto Ricans have a say in El Barrio's economic developments. Dr. Giorgina Falú, a member of the community board, and of Mujeres del Barrio and Boricuas del Barrio, who had been a critical voice against EZ's treatment of Puerto Ricans, put it this way:

> Our position is not against development. Our gripe is about them [the EZ] giving significant grants and loans to outsiders and almost nothing to local residents, especially Puerto Ricans and Latinos of El Barrio. It is a crime that outsiders get millions and we, who know our community and how to serve it, and who have been working so energetically for years, get rejected. See, our framework has to be different than just challenging any corporation coming to El Barrio. Now you have the EZ.

Aware of Edison's plans, Dr. Falú was planning her own charter school, one that she claimed would be truly informed by the needs of East Harlem's children. As she noted: "Here come outsiders, but there is no charter school led by Latinos. Why can't we do it? Education is now a business enterprise, but my priority as a Puerto Rican is, as it has been for years, to provide the best and most relevant education for our children. Schools don't work because of the lack of money. They don't work because the people in charge don't truly understand our children." This sentiment was echoed by many Black and Puerto Rican activists who saw the schools as a medium for purposefully keeping their children down. In a district servicing a population that is 96 percent minority, primarily Latino and African American, the lack of Black and Latino teachers and role models was a pressing concern among parents, illustrating that race and cultural sensitivity—fundamental during past educational struggles—continue to be just as decisive today. Many exerted themselves in finding alternatives to public schools, even if they had to pay more money. But this alternative is not open to all residents.

Dr. Falú is a business woman involved in education—she is founder and president of the Universal Business and Media School in East

Harlem—and her views are not necessarily representative of other community activists, who were generally more skeptical about charter schools and their impact on the privatization of schools. Her comments, however, bring another dimension to this already complex issue. Namely, at its core, the concept of charter schools—schools that are autonomous, free of bureaucracy, and under community control—was aligned with El Barrio's history of struggle for educational equity. It thus found receptive ears among residents who were long invested in such efforts. Indeed, supporters of the project included parents and many education advocates in the community who did not identify themselves as enthusiasts of private corporations. They were after meaningful change for "our children." In this manner, and similar to Gregory's (1998) discussion of how past civil rights struggles were always strategically deployed for immediate objectives by Black middle-class activists in Corona, reaction to the Edison Project was shaped by the many educational struggles residents had waged in El Barrio over the years.

And there was a lot of history to draw from in East Harlem. In the late 1960s and early 1970s, East Harlem was at the center of community protests that led to the decentralization of control of New York's public schools. The struggle was part of larger demands for educational equity, mainly in Latino and other minority communities (Ravitch 2000; Roderick 2001).[7] In East Harlem, the fight was primarily about cultural empowerment for Black and Latino children who were considered faulty and ignorant by virtue of their race, class, or language. These struggles led to the hiring of Black and Latino teachers and administrative staff to bilingual and culturally tailored programs as well as to parent involvement and community control in school administration, which in turn led to the creation of the local school boards.[8] In the mid-1970s, East Harlem even saw the election of the first Puerto Rican–dominated school board and, under educator Anthony Alvarado as superintendent, the creation of the first bilingual school district in the city (Pedraza 1997).

In hindsight Puerto Rican educators have acknowledged that the movement became highly bureaucratized, dominated by professionals and distanced from community input. The educational concerns of the local community, particularly in regards to issues of language and culture, were soon ignored, becoming peripheral to subsequent school reforms (Pedraza 1997). This partly explains why few cries were heard when the structures that brought about many of these gains were swiftly dismantled in 2002, when less than a year after the Edison hearings Mayor Bloomberg launched a corporate-centric educational reform based on centralization and standardization. The mayor signed the bill into law in East Harlem surrounded by Black and Latino children, purposely tapping into the district's significance in educational reform. It gave him control of city schools and the curriculum (Steinhauer 2003). Most contentiously, he disbanded the local school boards, publicly blamed as inefficient breeding grounds for clientelism and patronage and for all that is wrong with public education. Opponents to the move defended the boards as important resources for local representation, but to little avail.

My aim is not to debate decentralization or to delve into an assessment of the local school board in East Harlem, except to concur with Dreier et al. (2001) that decentralization policies aimed at empowering local communities are never able to address economic segregation and patterns of economic inequality. This is particularly true when public resources and opportunities, such as public education, which are intrinsically connected to place, are concerned. In these cases, economic and spatial segregation necessarily impacts the meaning of decentralization or the "local" power that poor communities can ably attain from such policies. What is certain is that without local schools boards, there will be fewer forums to assure local accountability of the mayor's recent and swift takeover of the public school system. Following a pattern at play elsewhere, as in Philadelphia, this takeover greatly facilitates the handing out of the school system to private interests. After all, local arrangements with state legislators and mayors, rather than parents and unions, provide more agreeable and "efficient" contexts for such moves. However, East Harlemites were most concerned that centralization would greatly reduce the spaces to voice their views and demand accountability of gubernatorial decisions concerning education. Marion Bell and Bob De Leon, members of the community board, confirmed this point. During an informal chat at La Fonda, they shared their deep consternation at the mayor's decision to move the local school board office downtown, far away from the community, supposedly to open up more classroom space. Yes, they wanted more space to ease schools' overcrowding, but not at the cost of losing the local administrative envoy most accessible to East Harlem parents. In De Leon's words: "We've come full circle. Where will parents go? We are losing everything we fought for in the 1960s. This is centralization all over." Especially hurt by the elimination of the local boards are undocumented immigrants, who under the previous system were eligible to vote in school board elections, one venue of local political participation, as long as they had children enrolled in the system.

Expectedly, there were some important exceptions in the mayor's plan. Schools selected for their performance (primarily located in white and upscale school districts), along with charter and specialized schools, were exempted from his plan, safeguarding their access to alternatives. This in turn brings up yet another key issue that was relevant for discussions of the Edison Project: choice. East Harlem had not only fought for decentralization but also for educational alternatives. In fact, East Harlem had been at the center of previous debates over the development of the concept of choice in public education. East Harlem is home to one of the first choice schools, opened in 1974, which allowed parents to choose schools outside their neighborhood and which led to the development of an alternative curriculum and pedagogy. This was almost twenty years before the development of a citywide school choice program in 1992. The celebrated success of choice schools, such as Central Park East, drew national attention to the area, making it a model for education reform in the 1970s. Building the momentum were books such as *Miracle in East Harlem* (1993) by Sly Fliegel and James MacGuire, and *The Power of Their Ideas* (1995) by Deborah Meier, in which educators recounted the excitement generated by East Harlem choice schools. The program was said to have miraculously transformed the most downtrodden district "underclass" into a national example for school reform. The percentage of District 4 students reading at grade level jumped from 16 in 1973 to 63 in 1987. Choice schools were celebrated as a model for what can be done, even in the "poorest and most culturally deprived neighborhoods in the city" (Fliegel and MacGuire 1993, 11–12). One of the educators involved in East Harlem's first choice schools, Deborah Meier, was even awarded a MacArthur Foundation Fellowship, popularly known as a "genius grant," in recognition of her "extraordinary innovations" in the field of education, bolstering East Harlem's significance in discussions of educational reform.

Appeals to the struggles and gains of the past were thus pivotal for conjuring support for Edison's proposal. In fact, many drew parallels between the choice schools and the charter schools, notwithstanding the dissimilar histories of these schools; one connected to a social movement, the other to a corporate initiative. Consider the passionate comments of an African American mother of two, born and raised in East Harlem, and educated in District 4—information that people commonly volunteered to assert the authority of their views. She drew on past struggles to embrace the Edison School while simultaneously expressing the widespread frustrations many felt with the public school system:

> I stand in support of the museum and the Edison School. . . . One of the things I loved about East Harlem, and one of the reasons I came back here to raise my children, is because . . . in the 1970s alternative schools and education was developed here in East Harlem. So I don't understand what the problem is. . . . Our children in the public schools are failing and I don't understand how you can continue to support something that continues to fail us generation after generation. Education is important. Our children have to compete in a global level. We need jobs, we need education!

For this speaker and others like her, as in the 1970s, it was time to struggle, but this time for the programs that would best equip children for the global economy. Edison addressed this kind of concern by underscoring the choice and improved education that parents so desperately wanted, foremost by promising that East Harlem's children would be provided with the kind of education that would facilitate their successful entrance into the global economy. Presenters for the Edison Project emphasized this message by highlighting the school's technology-rich program in which teachers, students, and parents would all learn together, connected by computers and technology.

The legacy of District 4's choice schools continues to be the subject of debate among policy makers and educators. Many attribute their "success" to the large amount of private and foundation monies that poured into the district, attracted by the hype over choice and experimental education. The highly skilled educators attracted by the freedom to try new educational models are also credited with the district's success. Puerto Rican activists for their part have bemoaned the fact that a few "famed educators" and schools are credited with the district's gains, eclipsing the contributions of Puerto Rican parents to New York City public education (Pedraza 1997). Others underplayed the schools' performance. Some explained it as a matter of selection; that is, they argued that choice schools admitted the students most likely to succeed rather than the neediest, implying the limited "choice" exercised by parents relative to school administrators.[9] Another important criticism is that choice schools have done little to improve the fate of most students in the districts, furthering the already existing hierarchy of schools and resources in which most students remain unaffected by improvements. Similar criticisms are echoed in the "2003 Statement of District Needs," drafted by Community Board 11, which decries the limited scope of East Harlem's "choice programs" (Manhattan Community Board 11 2002). Children are pushed to compete with students citywide for entrance into choice and special programs, the report states, only to be displaced by students from outside the neighborhood. East Harlem students do not even have a high school in the community. The three existing high schools are also alternative or specialized schools requiring a qualifying exam, and like the choice programs do not address East Harlem's neediest.[10] The tale of the flooded auditorium of PS 57, unfinished and unfunded for more than a decade, and the subject of protests in 2001 against years of official neglect of East Harlem children, stands as a stark reminder of the many inequities within District 4 schools.

These inequalities were also corroborated by a report drafted by a coalition of parents and education advocates organized as the East Harlem Coalition to Improve Our Public Schools, whose mission "to guarantee that all, not just some, of East Harlem's students get a good education" is directly informed by awareness of such inequities (2001, 2).[11] The report, written after visits and interviews with principals and administrators in East Harlem public schools, details the need for more space, documenting as examples "closets converted to a math lab, an occupational therapist seeing children in the hallway, a reading-recovery class being held in a stairwell, an empty auditorium unusable for years, to cite just a few" (1). Moreover, in contrast to alternative schools like the Young Women's Leadership School—praised by Oprah Winfrey and featured for the near-perfect rate of college enrollment of its graduates—which have art rooms, ample computer facilities, and strict class size limits, regular public schools are overcrowded and more likely to lack certified teachers and resources. "Two-thirds of the students in the district did not attain reading scores appropriate to their grade," the report goes on to note (7).

The judgment on Edison is yet to be determined. Charter schools are new (stemming from 1998 when the New York State Charter School Act was passed by the state legislature), and much remains uncertain about their performance vis-à-vis public schools. Many interests, both public and private, have a stake in the venture of for-profit education, making it difficult to assess their work neutrally. Without engaging in a debate about their benefits and evils, however, it is important to call attention to two potential outcomes of privatization already evident in East Harlem's experience with choice schools and other alterative models. First and foremost is the issue of educational equity. Some parents with the "right" cultural capital to maneuver through the system stand to benefit, as do some children without educational or special needs. But the majority of the children do not. Moreover, because charter schools are contracted out to a number of entities and given greater flexibility and autonomy in exchange for "results," their systems of accountability within such an autonomous system will likely hinder their appropriate evaluation. And the ability of parents, educators, nonprofits, and community groups to establish their own educational mission, curriculum and administrative structure is likely to be limited with the entrance of large private educational management companies like Edison, who have greater power, contacts, and resources. That is, initiatives directed at local empowerment, such as those that may be planned by local individuals and groups, are likely to find less room to maneuver in the craft and business of education.

Edison's ability to obtain approval for this project is particularly impressive, especially given its lack of an established record, having never managed a school in the city or proved its accountability and "sustainability." Built as it was on thin air and much fanfare, Edison would have therefore received much for very little. Not only did East Harlem promise Edison a great real-estate opportunity, but also a history in the limelight of educational reform, which was potentially invaluable toward its long-term for-profit educational aspirations. A critic explained: "By coming to East Harlem, Edison can show that it is friendly to inner cities. They can show brown kids with computers. And if they succeed in Harlem USA, they'll have the legitimacy to go to other neighborhoods and take over their system." Namely, having a model school readily operating in the global city of New York, with the largest public educational system, and succeeding with "minority" children would have undoubtedly been central to their legitimating goals, not to mention to advancing the attending view that privatization is the only recourse to obtain social services and entitlements, especially for minority children.

BUT IT'S NOT ABOUT RACE!

As seen, many issues came to bear in debates over the Edison Project, and once again race and turf issues were not without significance in this failed yet decisive project. Supporters and opponents of the Edison Project came from all backgrounds, but from early on, it was El Barrio's Puerto Rican leadership, particularly its established leaders, heads of social service units, and politicians, who showed greater public support for this project relative to East Harlem's Black elected officials. In fact, aware of the contested history of the proposed location, Councilman Phil Reed was the first to express concerns about placing the museum in this location. On the other hand, Senator Olga Méndez immediately embraced the idea as a move that would bring progress to El Barrio (Wyatt 2000). In the final public hearing held in 2001, Méndez continued to express her support through a written statement read in her absence, in which she urged East Harlemites to welcome "these two private institutions with open arms and to celebrate the opportunities they will bring to our neighborhood." She reminded them that Edison would ensure that "our kids will sit with teachers and computers, and that they are not left behind in the twenty-first century," even suggesting that the proposal by these renowned institutions provided a "vote of confidence to our people," a testament of the neighborhood's coming of age. She went on to exalt the proposal as one that, in her words, "will put our neighborhood on the map as a place of progressive solution making, rather than of inner-city despair. These are changes that will make our streets safer, our children smarter, our citizens more optimistic." In contrast, during the same hearing, Councilman Phil Reed, then seeking reelection, became silent on the issue. Borough President Virginia Fields, for her part, approved of the museum and the school, but rejected the rezoning request, a move that added to the perception that Black politicians were in outright opposition to the project.

The extent to which this issue had become racially charged was evident during the already racially and nationalistically charged 2001 council district race, in which Felipe Luciano, "the homegrown Puerto Rican candidate," an Afro-Boricua media personality and former Young Lord with no electoral track record, challenged and lost to the "outsider" and incumbent Phil Reed. During a candidates' debate, the Edison Project was the last and most loaded issue raised.[12] Candidates were first told of East Harlem's 20 percent unemployment, of the need for jobs, and of the promises of a project offering one thousand jobs and a $125 million investment in East Harlem before being asked if they supported the museum and the Edison Project. Phil Reed averted the question, stating that he supported the concept, but not necessarily the project. Felipe Luciano first attempted to do the same, but when pressed, assertively stated his support for the project. Exchanges such as this only helped feed the view that it was Black, not Puerto Rican, leaders and politicians who were opposing the project. Indeed, the project's most vociferous opponent was councilman Bill Perkins, from Central and West Harlem. Residing in the immediate vicinity of the proposed project, Perkins vehemently complained about the impending traffic flow and condemned Edison for ignoring the community board's stated needs for housing.

Interestingly, neither Perkins nor any other politician rejected the project on account of its potential impact on education. As noted earlier, housing, regardless of the type or level of affordability, was always a preordained and preponderant concern to promote or counter projects in East Harlem, as, in effect, it was elsewhere in the city.

Because of the seemingly open split between Black and Puerto Rican politicians on this issue, some Puerto Rican and Latino leaders raised concerns over the commitment of Black politicians to furthering the "progress" of El Barrio. Resentful about their treatment by the EZ, they felt it was time for East Harlem to receive its first corporate headquarters, and Edison addressed their longings. The local newspaper *Siempre*, which is generally conspicuous in its support of development, evoked this sentiment in an editorial entitled "Whose Neighborhood Is It Anyway?" The article was written by Eddie Baca, the sole Mexican American resident at the time to have a history of involvement with local Latino politics, first as chair of the community board, then as candidate for district leader. It documented what others expressed covertly in less diplomatic ways. He questioned the opposition of Virginia Fields to a project that had been supported by Senator Olga Méndez and Assemblyman Adam Clayton Powell IV, in what appeared "as overplay by Central Harlem elected officials into our neighborhood." And while warning that his statements were not about race—"Make no mistake, this development is not and should never become about race"—it actually was all about race. As he went on to say, "Is it being unreasonable to have a community board that is reflective of the 54 percent Latino population in East Harlem?" (Baca 2001, 8). The suggestion was clear: Whatever the motive for rejecting a particular development project, an East Harlem Black politician could never be truly representative of Latinos.

This logic delegitimated Perkins's public rejection of the project as racially suspect, even though it had been framed as a defense of East Harlem's need for housing rather than corporate headquarters, as "stated by the community board itself in its 197-A plan." Others confirmed that Edison had indeed been "culturally competent" in aligning the project with the progress of Puerto Ricans in El Barrio. A Puerto Rican director of a social services organization, for instance, even noted that it was not

Edison that "he and his buddies" had supported, but their Puerto Rican barrio friend who had been contracted as consultant for the project. "This is old news, developers come in and work up the race issue to their advantage. They know who to talk to and what to say," a member of the community board noted, attesting to the kind of dynamics that made the project's approval and support for Edison conveniently aligned with support for Puerto Ricans in El Barrio.

When all was said and done, however, Puerto Ricans and African Americans were both as equally responsible and irrelevant to the project's approval. The unanimous vote in favor of the project in the city council (including Bill Perkins, who after much criticism of the project voted in its favor) was a conclusive sign that opposition to the project, on whatever grounds, had done little to deter its passing. Rumors abounded that politicians had been bribed and were pressured to favor the project. Though I could not substantiate these claims, everyone had a theory about which Black or Puerto Rican politician had received money, or "had been spoken for," and for what reasons. Supporters, in contrast, believed that the constituents had led the way.

Ironically, and to the chagrin of Puerto Rican development enthusiasts, the project was publicly presented as an example of Harlem's—not El Barrio's or East Harlem's—cultural renaissance. It was even co-opted by some as an example of the EZ's success in maintaining the area's cultural heritage.[13] "This is the kind of project that makes me proud of the work of the EZ," Congressman Charles Rangel exclaimed during the EZ's open board meeting in February 2002, which included debate of the Museum for African Art's proposal for two million dollars in aid from the Cultural Industry Investment Fund. This time, however, the connection with Edison was strategically avoided as the museum emphasized its status as a purely nonprofit institution in search of help. Aware of Puerto Ricans' and Latinos' criticisms against the EZ, Rangel expressed his regret "that similar proposals were not emerging from Washington Heights and El Barrio," and that "many professional Puerto Ricans have gone, that we need to bring them back, so they can give us the kind of proposal we can fund." To consider the Museum for African Art a "Harlem project" was already troublesome to East Harlem audience members—it was a Soho-based institution and a for-profit educational company coming to, *not originating from*, local entrepreneurs. But it was Rangel's statement about the "lack of fundable projects in East Harlem" that echoed most strongly among development enthusiasts. For it asserted that, notwithstanding the museum's appeals to everyone's African heritage, new developments would always be "Harlem's," never East Harlem's, projects. Added to the implication that East Harlem had no local cultural program of its own, that its projects were not "fundable," and that it lacked "professionals to carry them out," this provided confirmation that it would be projects like Edison that would receive funding. The economic gains of one group would symbolically come at the expense of another. Obviously, then, "culture" had been successfully appropriated by Edison, but never expunged from racial and ethnic complications. Such identifications were always centrally involved in the project.

FIVE The Mexican Barrio

MEXICANS, PUERTO RICANS, AND THE TERRAIN OF LATINIDAD

With headlines such as "El Barrio, menos bacalao y mas chile" (El Barrio, less codfish and more chile) and "Mapa latino con acento mexicano" (Latin map with a Mexican accent), local news on the 2000 census stressed what was obvious to anyone familiar with El Barrio: Mexicans are the fastest growing Latino group and they are actively reshaping the city's landscape.[1] In the past decade, Mexicans have formed vibrant communities in Corona, Sunset Park, and Jackson Heights, but because of its location in Manhattan, El Barrio's Mexican community has surfaced as one of the most visible and well known. El Barrio is home to one of the largest concentration of Mexican populations in Manhattan; it is a stronghold of merchants and community organizations, not to mention the site of some of the earliest and largest annual festivities celebrating and asserting Mexican culture in the city.

Yet Mexicans were almost entirely absent from local development debates, such as community board meetings, public hearings, and electoral debates, an absence explained not solely by the exclusive bases of these forums, but also by the transnational politics that at least for now are dominant among this largely first-generation immigrant community. Like other East Harlemites, some Mexican residents were optimistic about increases in housing and that they would benefit from new construction while others feared their future displacement. But even more than African American and Puerto Rican residents, Mexicans were bypassed by developments that were neither directed nor marketed at them or else were entirely out of their financial reach. The few present in forums over housing inquired about housing for immigrants, but their questions remained unanswered. A statement by a part-time worker at a social/housing service organization, who had learned about a new housing development through her Puerto Rican boss, evoked the exclusion but asserted the importance of speaking up: "Yes, I placed an application for one of the homes. I knew I would not be selected, but I put down my name anyway. I want them to notice that we are also here."

Bring up the topic of gentrification, however, and Mexicans would always surface. Within the culturalist frameworks dominant in such debates—seen largely as a matter of one ethnic/racial group displacing another, instead of a matter of class—Mexicans were in fact generally seen as agents of gentrification. Never mind that they, along with other immigrants, many of whom are undocumented and hence ineligible for public housing subsidies, were the most vulnerable to rising rents. An African American resident, echoing comments not dissimilar to those voiced by Puerto Ricans, put this in succinct terms: "The whites and the young people are not the gentrifiers, they come and go. But the Mexicans are here to stay." This explains why many Puerto Rican residents said they were delighted about the coming of Mexicans: their flags, stores, and mere presence was a deterrent to white in-flight to East Harlem, a real hindrance to gentrification. Still, Mexicans were consistently described by Puerto Rican residents as a self-contained group, with whom they lived *"juntos pero no revueltos"* (together but not mixed). Mexicans and Puerto Ricans live side by side in El Barrio, yet Mexicans are nowhere to be found in Julia's Jam, or in La Palma Nightclub, or in the pages of *Siempre,* whereas Puerto Ricans were entirely absent from Salon Cinco Dancing Lounge, or the pages of *La Voz de Mexico.*

Its representation notwithstanding, this community was actively engaged in a variety of local and transnational politics in and beyond El Barrio. And despite the physical segregation between Puerto Rican and Mexican spaces in El Barrio, encounters and exchanges between these groups were not so uncommon.[2] Culture and identity were prominent in Mexicans' staking of claims to rights, visibility, and political recognition. Not unlike their Puerto Rican counterparts, these efforts simultaneously implicate Mexican activists and organizations with neoliberal politics and policies, though in their case, it is the politics of two nation states, the United States and Mexico, and their particular concerns about immigrants as resource and peril. These strategies in turn involve negotiations with, but also require a distancing from, Puerto Ricans and other Latinos, particularly evident in exchanges between El Barrio's Mexican and Puerto Rican civic leadership. Indeed, despite their contrasting histories, positions, legal statuses, and other differences, Mexicans and Puerto Ricans are jointly invested in El Barrio as a "Latino space," although their cultural politics sometimes directly confront one another. As the newest Latino group carving a place through nationalist discourses and appeals to cultural citizenship, Mexicans help reinvigorate politically charged definitions of ethnicity, at a moment when these are being most contested, though not without a cost. While their claims confront challenges to ethnic-driven demands for rights and entitlements, they also distance themselves from other Latinos, mostly Puerto Ricans, while tying themselves to the needs and demands of politicians, marketers, and other interests for marketable ethnicity. Ultimately, not unlike Puerto Ricans, Mexicans face particular challenges when they adhere to ethnic-specific demands, but also difficulties when they tread the difficult terrain of Latinidad. The cultural politics of this growing community thus demonstrate some of the opportunities and predicaments of ethnic-centered agendas and of Latino-centered coalitions in the neoliberal city.

LOCAL AND TRANSNATIONAL POLITICS

Although there is evidence of Mexican immigration to New York City as early as the 1940s, it was only from the 1980s onward that immigration peaked, making Mexicans a relatively large chapter in the new Latino immigration to the city.[3] Immigrants derive primarily from the Mixteca Baja region (including the southernmost part of the state of Puebla, the northern part of Oaxaca, and the eastern part of Guerrero). This area provided 64 percent of Mexican immigrants, out of which 47 percent came from Puebla at the peak of Mexican migration to the city, which has since grown more diversified (Robert Smith 1997, 2003b). Their settlement in the city, however, is far from concentrated. Mexicans have settled in most sectors where there is a high concentration of Latinos, particularly in the aforementioned neighborhoods of Corona, Sunset Park, Jackson Heights, and El Barrio. However, with few important exceptions, little is known about Mexican immigrants, who have only recently attracted the attention of scholars and writers.[4] The media and public discourse, however, has lost no time in filling this void with a dominant picture of Mexican immigrants as a relatively homogenous community of vulnerable workers, striving to maintain their identity as "good immigrants" by working hard, keeping their cultural traditions, and maintaining their transnational connections back home. This dominant picture echoes the discourses through which Mexican leaders have maneuvered anti-immigrant sentiments by presenting themselves as worthy and hard-working immigrants.

Yet New York's Mexican population is not homogeneous. A little prodding in El Barrio reveals a high concentration of undocumented workers, but also a variety of merchants, artists, students, union leaders, and community members organizing around religion, Zapatismo, and Mexico's culture and traditions, as well as Mexicans who would more likely define themselves as Chicano or by particular indigenous identities. As with Puerto Ricans, however, the most visible and politically influential component in Mexican politics in and beyond El Barrio is a select network of Mexican brokers, or "spokespeople," organized around community groups providing services and representation to this community. Jocelyn Solis (2001) has noted that Mexican community organizations have surfaced as key resources, presenting a public front for a largely undocumented population. Organizations and their leaders in El Barrio were critical bridges between this community and the greater political and social service infrastructures in the city.

Although most of these groups are relatively new, dating to the mid-1990s, Mexican community organizations in El Barrio have gained a great degree of visibility beyond El Barrio. Among them are Mexicanos Unidos en Neuva York (UNIMEX); Mexican Community Center, or Centro Comunal Mexicano en Nueva York (CECOMEX); a local chapter of Tepeyac, a citywide social advocacy organization; and Mexican American Workers' Association, or Asociación de Trabajadores Mexico Americanos (AMAT), part of Casa Mexico and one of the few institutions to have a physical space in East Harlem. These groups differ in mission and objective: some are more directly involved in commercial venues such as festivals, or else in education and workers' rights; others are more secular or identified with Guadalupismo, or fervor to the Virgin of Guadalupe, one of the most important Mexican cultural and religious icons in and beyond Mexico. Predictably, these differences have informed multiple debates over legitimacy, leadership, and ability to represent the larger Mexican community among these groups.[5] At the same time, leaders and members of each group had been mutually involved in organizational meetings and activities of the others. They participated in similar meetings when the Mexican community was summoned for citywide and national events regarding Mexican politics, and they have even forged coalitions with each other. In fact, they shared more similarities than differences.

Foremost, with some exceptions, these groups are founded and led by people who identified themselves as part of Mexico's working and middle classes; they were employed, had prior education in Mexico, and had not immigrated primarily out of economic need, as have many of their counterparts in the city. They thus provided a counterpart to Puerto Rican brokers in El Barrio, with whom some of them have established collaborative relationships. Juan Cáceres, the founder of CECOMEX, the organization behind the Cinco de Mayo Festival in El Barrio, and the first and only Mexican member of the community board, described himself as someone who enjoyed a relatively well-paid job in Guerrero, and who had

Figure 10.   Flag vendors during the Cinco de Mayo Festival in El Barrio. Photo by the author.

come illegally, angered at the government's bureaucracy and denial of a visiting visa. Those associated with CECOMEX share similar backgrounds, including former workers from the Mexican Consulate, recognized to be drawn from Mexico's government-connected middle classes. Ada Omaña, a leading member of UNIMEX, for her part, first came to New York as a tourist and to visit family; she ended up staying after becoming politicized about the needs of the Mexican community in New York. Jerry Domínguez, the director of Casa Mexico and cofounder of AMAT, migrated as a farmworker but was also from a similar middle-class background. He had been educated in Mexico, was enrolled in college in the United States, and worked full time for a union, all activities that put him on an upwardly mobile track. In other words, members of these local organizations identified with and advocated for—but were not part of—the indigenous Mexican workers drawn from the bottom of Mexico's racial/class ladder, who constituted the most vulnerable segment of Mexican immigrants in the city.

Another commonality shared by these groups is a dual orientation: they are both local and transnational organizations.[6] Affected as it is by the policies of two nation states, the Mexican community is never restricted to a local or spatially marked context. Mexican brokers described being especially concerned with addressing everyday issues affecting Mexican immigrants, such as housing, health, and work conditions. A founding member of UNIMEX explained: "The issues of our people are very particular and so basic. It's about getting services, having access to housing on their own, getting documentation, enrolling in school, and many more basic things." Yet to respond to these needs is to get out of El Barrio and to engage in a variety of national and transnational issues. Mexican leaders and organizations in El Barrio are thus predictably engaged with local and transnational politics, all part of their quest for citizenship and a sense of belonging across space and territorial boundaries (Cordero et al. 2001; Jones-Correa 1998; Smith and Guarnizo 1998; Smith 2003a). They all present themselves as grassroots Mexican social service organizations, but foremost as Mexican groups, organized by and for the totality of the Mexican population in El Barrio and beyond. The same applies to their activities on behalf of this local yet expansive Mexican community. As one noted, it is all about securing power and representation, or in the words of a member of Casa Mexico, *"que nos den nuestro lugar"* (that they give us our own place in society), demands voiced on account of and for the totality of the Mexican community from two nation states. As stated by Manuel, an immigrant union organizer, in a comment that demonstrated how much Mexico figured and permeated everyday politics: "We are working at different fronts. We can't move ahead in the states if the conditions of Mexicans back home are not addressed, if we continue being slaves, not citizens, of Mexico and the U.S." Another Mexican worker I met at Casa Mexico stated his awareness of the interdependence of Mexico and the United States, but by underscoring a repeated claim, namely that Mexicans are entitled to rights by both countries on account of their active economic contributions: "The United States depends a lot on Mexico, and Mexico on the United States. And we are central to this relationship. Because we come to work and we produce a lot for both countries. And they have to give us our place, even if they don't want to." Not surprisingly, such emphatic demands were voiced not only at the level of production, that is, in terms of what Mexicans contribute with their work, but also at the level of consumption, as explained by a panelist during an educational forum by Casa Mexico: "We pay taxes even when we buy a Coca Cola!" In other words, equity and representation are not ancillary objects but rather should be the rightful outcome of Mexicans' multiple and daily, yet uncounted and invisible, economic contributions.

Centrally relevant for understanding these dual demands is the critical role Mexican immigrants increasingly play in Mexico's domestic and foreign policies. Mexican activists in El Barrio had been active in political campaigns for Mexico's political transition that ended the political reign of PRI (Partido Revolucionario Institucional, or Institutional Revolutionary Party) in 2000. They favored the election of Vicente Fox and saw themselves as direct actors in Mexican politics. A successful demonstration in favor of the political change in El Barrio was repeatedly mentioned by many as a sign of the power and organization of New York's Mexican community. As Jerry Domínguez proudly stated, "People in Mexico are used to hearing about the Mexican community in Chicago and Los Angeles, but never to hear about us in New York. Who would have expected to hear that Mexicans in El Barrio were at the forefront of Mexican advocacy for change?" This political coming of age was corroborated by a momentous meeting with Vicente Fox in La Hacienda Restaurant in El Barrio, and continues to be reinforced by periodic visits by Puebla delegates and government officials. According to Domínguez, "They have to seek us. We are in New York, the center of it all."

Indeed, Mexico's interest in its immigrant communities is not new, but no president before Fox had placed such importance on immigrants or had actively tried to reshape their image publicly or draw them into his internal and foreign policies.[7] Immigrants were touted by Fox as an "opportunity" for increasing Mexico's economic standing, while contributing to his own legitimacy both in the United States and at home (Romney 2001). Fueling this stance is the dependency of Mexico's internal affairs and that of its immigrants on U.S. policies; in affecting such policies, U.S. Mexicans and Latinos play a potentially vital role in the realm of U.S. public opinion and electoral politics. Latinos were a crucial political force in the last presidential election and, as the largest Latino immigrant group in the states, Mexican immigrants represent important Latino-wide concerns, particularly in regard to such important issues as immigration policy and immigrant rights.[8] Mexican immigrants were therefore seen, and consequently saw themselves, as a pivotal resource for Mexico in its dealings with the U.S. government. Juan Cáceres perceptively explained the potential of Mexican immigrants during a meeting at La Hacienda Restaurant, which displayed photographs of Vicente Fox and Mexican leaders, himself included, taken during his visit to El Barrio in 2000:

> It took us ten years to be heard, but now all politicians are after us.
> If they want to further the length and breadth of their career, they
> are going to seek us. We can help them gain national notoriety because
> they can say that they have worked with Mexicans here and then build
> national coalitions with other Latinos. For Mexico, we are the most
> direct line to the U.S., we are better than Mexico's own office of Foreign
> Relations.

Notwithstanding their apparent political coming of age, it is impossible to lose sight of the constraints and multiple logics that affect their practices as they maneuver with and through U.S. and Mexican neoliberal policies toward immigrants. I am also referring here to the numerous agents operating from the realm of Mexico and the United States, with vested interests in Mexican immigrants as a political, social, and economic resource. The close alignment of the concerns of community groups with Mexico's economic policies of liberalization and U.S. immigration policies demonstrates the interdependence of these three entities. Indeed, the primary areas of concern and advocacy among Mexican groups in El Barrio include amnesty (or legalization), political representation of immigrants both in the United States and Mexico (such as through the *voto en el exterior*, or the right to vote from the United States in Mexican elections), and easier and cheaper transfer of remittances. Demands for amnesty, however, do little to challenge the legal/illegal divide that plagues the fate of immigrants in this country, while accommodations to ease the transfer of wages does little to combat the exploitation of Mexican workers or their low wages. Most important, Mexicans' assertions of hard work and economic value contribute to the view that immigrants are only valuable for their economic contributions as producers and consumers. Additionally, as Bonnie Honig has described for discourses around the category of "foreigner," this type of representation helps to reinstate popular and always contradictory ideals of democracy and meritocracy, while antagonizing groups in benefit of the status quo. Accordingly, alongside anti-immigrant sentiments, immigrants function as models of good citizenship—the reference against which other marginalized groups are measured—and their claims can become easily delegitimated or marginalized (Honig 2001).

Another important trend is the discursive use of immigrants to further policies aimed at opening borders and markets. The Fox administration's efforts to encourage U.S.-based *padrinos* (sponsors) to invest in rural communities as a means of stalling immigration is one example of these policies. These programs include Partnership for Prosperity and Adopt a Microregion, which in the Spanish media are lauded as evidence of the entrepreneurship of Mexican immigrants. Jaime Lucero, the New York–based entrepreneur and the first investor, or *padrino*, who opened a *sucursal* (branch) of his Gold and Silver garment factory in Puebla at an investment of 21.5 million dollars, is perhaps the champion of this initiative. Featured in Telemundo, *Hoy*, and *Noticias del Mundo*, Lucero is oftentimes associated and photographed with President Fox and upheld as the example for *paisanos* (countrymen). In this way, immigrants become the moral cornerstone for furthering the same policies that are making rural regions and immigrant-sending communities in Mexico into "rural enterprise zones" for foreign and domestic investment.

Such is also the case with policies toward remittances, which are Mexico's third greatest source of foreign revenue, surpassed only by the oil industry and tourism. *Paisanos* are thus a leading economic force (Tim Weiner 2001). Intended to direct profits away from companies such as Western Union or Money Gram, or even local ventures such as El Barrio's Delgado Travel, efforts by the Mexican government to ease the flow of money were met with great praise and optimism. Measures include decreased remittance rates, mutual bank accounts, and ATM cards shared by immigrants and families in Mexico, all of which will undoubtedly benefit immigrant families. Also benefiting, however, is the Mexican government, now able to tap into taxes through bank transactions, not to mention foreign investors, who are always keen on more open financial borders. The merger of Banamex (a well-known Mexican bank) with Citigroup in 2001 is particularly relevant here. Citigroup can now expand its markets in the United States by facilitating the opening of bank accounts to immigrants. The launching of "La Red de la gente" or the People's Network, by Bansefi (Banco del Ahorro Nacional Servicieros, a government-backed bank) quickly followed. These immigrant-friendly economic policies need to be situated as part of greater neoliberal trends fostering market-based economic reforms that ease the pathway to private investments. Or in Appadurai's (1996) terms, they represent one of the many disjunctions of the global political economy whereby flows of exchange are open for money while they are simultaneously restricted for people.

Mexican community leaders in El Barrio seemed well aware of the contradictions involved in their shrinking political playing field, although some were more critical or hopeful than others. The result is a mutually conflicting and hopeful position between immigrant advocates and the Mexican government and its policies toward immigrants. Perhaps the best example is provided by the contradictory entanglements of these groups with the Mexican Consulate. When I initially met them, most Mexican activists in El Barrio described themselves as local alternatives to the Mexican Consulate, who they felt had not met the expectations and needs of this rapidly growing population; in particular, they saw themselves as correctives to its elitist orientation. As Ada Omaña noted, "Our organization emerged from the communities' needs, while the consulate has all of these phantom organizations that don't provide for our people." They were also particularly critical of the lack of Mexican American staff knowledgeable of the special needs of New York's Mexican community. At the same time, in reclaiming their place and striving for better services and representation from the consulate, these groups found themselves engaging with the consulate, receiving support in cash and funds for festivities; they maintained open communication with the consulate even if this relationship was one ridden with suspicion and demands for openness. Moreover, despite their critical stance toward the consulate and Mexico's "government machinery," they found themselves courting them for recognition of their events, festivals, and activities. It was at the consulate, for instance, that meetings, demonstrations, and protests were held to debate who could rightfully control the Mexican Independence Day Parade (Desfile Mexicano de Nueva York).

The fate of these local and transnational politics is just unfolding. What is clearly apparent, however, is the widespread recognition by Mexican activists that the United States—from El Barrio to greater New York to the greater United States—constitutes the politically important terrain in which to debate U.S. and Mexican policies that affect them. In this context, it is the contested terrain of Latinization and Latino cultural politics that they must tread. In this regard, I consider two visible and closely related trends: the saliency of nationalism and of cultural politics involving the celebration of Mexican spectacles, festivals, and events. Such strategies became particularly relevant means for acquiring visibility and legitimation and for maneuvering resources from corporations and government sources—this the result of the rapidly shrinking political terrain in which immigrants could seek rights, particularly after the halt in policy solutions to the fate of undocumented immigrants post–September 11.[9] These dynamics are nowhere more evident than in struggles over the 2002 Mexican Independence Day Parade.

PARADE POLITICS

> La Patria no se Vende [The home country is not
> for sale].
>> Poster at a rally to boycott the "fake"
>> Mexican Independence Day Parade, 2003

> To live in the United States is to have the right to
> do business with whomever you want.
>> Carlos Velázquez, GALOS Corporation,
>> interviewed by *Hoy* newspaper

What independence? We work in factories, we
clean gardens and kitchens. Many don't receive
the pay they deserve and are exposed to harmful
chemicals.

Miguel Ramírez, interviewed by *Hoy* newspaper

Use of Fifth Avenue, as in the Irish and Puerto Rican parades, and the
involvement of "foreigners" in Mexican events were recurrent subjects of
debate surrounding the celebration of the first citywide Mexican Independence Day Parade in Manhattan.[10] These discussions galvanized the
Mexican community throughout the five boroughs in 2001 and 2002; the
central location of Manhattan would attest to Mexicans' coming of age.
But the idea that a relatively new immigrant group could rob Fifth
Avenue merchants of a day of business was inconceivable to many as
well as a cause of amusement to many non-Mexican observers. Most significantly, Mexican groups struggled to achieve control of the parade,
which had been organized in recent years by a professional promoter, as
are other ethnic festivities in New York. The debate demonstrated the rising nationalism that accompanies the consolidation of the Mexican community, the widespread recognition of festivals as a resource of cultural
politics, and the opportunities and caveats for Mexican assertions presented by the city's Latinization, where numerous political, economic,
and marketing interests are inevitably involved.

The festival under contention was originally conceived by Patricia
Hernández of the Comité Cívico Mexicano. A seamstress, babysitter,
tamale maker, Puebla native, and Queens resident, Ms. Hernández
described being inspired into organizing a Mexican community event by
an apparition of the Virgin of Guadalupe during a trip to Mexico. She
started to celebrate masses in honor of the Virgin, which, given their
enormous attendance by Mexican constituents, quickly attracted the
attention of local Latino leaders in Queens. Soon she was in contact with
the Hispanic affairs representative for Queens borough president Claire
Schulman and other Latino leaders who helped celebrate and incorporate the Parade in the mid-1990s.

Different stories circulated about the involvement of Puerto Ricans and other Latinos in the event. Some saw it as a generous gesture from another ethnic group with contacts and resources, while for others it was a top-down development by other Latinos to capitalize on Mexicans for political purposes. What no one denied is that the parade had since ended up in the hands of a professional multicultural events marketing company, the GALOS Corporation, directed by a Puerto Rican marketer, Carlos Velázquez, working alongside Ms. Hernández. This is the same promoter who was also involved in numerous Latino events, parades, and festivals for different Latino groups (Ecuadoran, Dominican, Cuban) throughout the city, which earned him the name, among his critics, as *"un señor sin nacionalidad"* (a man without nationality). Drawing on his marketing contacts, the promoter had made the small celebration similar to other ethnic/commercial blockbuster events, giving rise to criticisms that the event had become "Puertoricanized." This loaded reference cries for unpacking—the Puerto Rican Day Parade is the only event on Fifth Avenue in which merchants board up their windows—an outcome of the racialization of Puerto Ricans and their association with criminal activity. Undoubtedly these associations informed the quest to distance the Mexican Independence Day Parade from the Puerto Rican parade. But most of all, the charge was about the authenticity of the event. Organizers were said to have featured Caribbean food instead of Mexican food, and there were rumors that they had even selected a non-Mexican as a beauty queen.

Throughout the summer of 2001, community groups citywide, organized by Tepeyac, the umbrella social-service organization, charged that the Hernández committee was dominated by entrepreneurial interests, not by the "community," and that having non-Mexicans in the organization made it an illegitimate representation of the Mexican community. At a press conference held at the Mexican Consulate in August 2001, community spokespeople repeatedly claimed that a Mexican parade should be organized by Mexicans and for Mexicans, not by people from other nationalities, or by entrepreneurs, variables that were loosely equated with each other. Additionally, activists felt that the parade should be held in Manhattan, specifically on Fifth Avenue, to prove the value of this growing community. Ultimately, the parade was canceled because of the events of September 11, but the debate, highly covered in the Spanish-language newspapers throughout the summer of 2001, was a loud expression of the nationalist claims accompanying these communities' ongoing consolidation and visibility, and of the ensuing contradictions of these claims. In this case, assertions that only Mexicans could rightfully organize Mexican events were meant as a challenge to the dominance of corporate interests and individual entrepreneurs that increasingly profit from ethnic markets. It was not the involvement of corporate interests that they bemoaned, but rather who profits from Mexican-centered events. The "Mexican community," not promoters, should profit from them. This important demand asserted ethnicity over industry—cultural events are not marketing spectacles that any marketer can celebrate without consideration of ethnicity—and challenged the inequities in the production and consumption of ethnic events. These demands provided a daring challenge to corporate, or marketable, Latinidad. The city had awarded a permit to Ms. Hernández, the original organizer, and to professional promoters from GALOS. But opponents succinctly rejected the representation of an event controlled by a single person and committee— as opposed to a larger citywide coalition. Most of all, they disparaged the use of Latinidad (in this case, appeals for Latino unity in the organization of ethnic events) to exclude wider community participation in an event that was poised to become the premier and most public Mexican celebration in the city. But this claim was also a risky one. Not unlike Puerto Ricans' demands over El Museo del Barrio, such demands could also be easily misconstrued as antiquated ethnic politics that had no place in multiethnic "Latino" New York. In particular, they evoked intolerance toward the cross-fertilization among Latino groups, particularly vis-à-vis Puerto Ricans, embodied here by the Puerto Rican promoter. Most daringly, these claims challenged conventional business practices in New York, the global capital of culture industry, where it is a marketer's experience, not his or her nationality, that is supposed to be the determinant factor in the awarding of a marketing contract. To be a New Yorker is to do business with anyone you want, readily countered Velázquez. To complicate matters, charges that the event's founder, Ms. Patricia Hernández, a woman of humble origins, was a "puppet" manipulated by GALOS intimated sexism and chagrin that she, rather than the mostly male leadership that dominates Mexican organizations, would be heading the event hand in hand with the city's mayor and other major politicians.

Mexican activists in El Barrio were also involved in the debate over the festival, and in general agreement that Mexicans should control their events. But with a longer history of collaboration with Puerto Ricans and other groups in El Barrio, they were not immediately identified with the exclusive tone of Tepeyac's message, although this would change throughout the two years that I followed the debate. It is important to consider that, unlike Mexican groups in El Barrio, Tepeyac was not the sole product of Mexican immigrants' struggles and coalitions to seek rights and visibility in the United States. Instead, it is the product of the New York Archdiocese, prompted by requests by local pastors and Mexican parishioners to meet the needs of the growing Mexican community. The archdiocese brought in Joel Magallán, a Jesuit brother from Mexico, and soon thereafter Tepeyac was founded in 1997. Structured around a general assembly, a council, and different Guadalupe committees—organized in honor of La Virgen de Guadalupe in many parishes throughout the city—Tepeyac has grown to be the largest and most influential Mexican organization in New York. It appeals to Mexicans' popular devotion to the Virgin of Guadalupe, and the organization's nationalist objectives have allowed it to tap into the many Guadalupe Committees spread throughout the city, successfully mobilizing them for a variety of struggles in the areas of health, education, and labor, always reinforcing Mexicanness in the process (Rivera-Sánchez 2002; Galvez 2003).[11] Their demands that the festival be an authentic Mexican celebration were embedded in larger nationalist premises where the strength and "integrity" of Mexican culture is seen as a precondition for the mobilization of the community, before and prior to the forging of alliances. In the words of an East Harlem Tepeyac member: "At some point we will be fostering more alliances with other groups, but we now have a sick community that needs fixing, and it is to this community that our efforts should be directed."

In contrast, Mexican organizations in El Barrio such as CECOMEX or Casa Mexico were the outcome of intraethnic associations, or associations with area organizations such as labor unions and social service organizations. Indeed, much is known about tensions between these communities. Particularly well known are stories of Mexicans being victimized by Blacks and Puerto Ricans who saw them as easy prey and as strangers on their turf. Yet stories of assistance and cooperation also exist, suggesting that there have always been more points of encounter among these groups than have been publicly reported. In fact, Mexican–Puerto Rican relations in El Barrio are somewhat analogous to those between Puerto Ricans and African Americans. Just as African Americans have long served as political examples to Puerto Rican organizations in New York, Puerto Ricans and increasingly Dominicans function in similar ways relative to Mexicans. Thus, upon my asking Mexican leaders in El Barrio to recall their evolution into civic leaders active in community affairs, all of them recalled the assistance of Puerto Ricans as having been central to their own organizational efforts and activities. Well-known Puerto Rican civic leaders in El Barrio, such as Gloria Quiñonez, Walter Torres, and Francisco Díaz, were independently and repeatedly mentioned by leaders such as Juan Cáceres from CECOMEX, Ada Omaña from UNIMEX, Jerry Domínguez from Casa Mexico, and Javier Guzmán of Tepeyac, who recognized them as key contacts that afforded them with access to elected officials, district leaders, the community board as well as services, community resources, and even local spaces for community organizing. As recalled by Juan Cáceres:

> I was advised in my organizational efforts by local politicians from El Barrio. Federico Colón opened the door to Adam Clayton Powell IV, and they helped me find a place to work on the organization. From them I learned the importance of social service organizations and political advocacy, as well about the importance of community events and festivals, because everyone had events in this community.

Cáceres went on to acknowledge the help of Dominican Horacio Pérez from the Manhattan Neighborhood Network in the establishment of the short-lived cable show *"Mexico Lindo,"* and of El Barrio/Puerto Rican entrepreneur Nick Lugo, who introduced him to the world of festival organizing. The first Mexican festival in El Barrio originated on a Mexican music stage organized by Cáceres within Lugo's blockbuster

Hispanic commercial feast that is celebrated annually along 116th street. Cáceres now organizes a Cinco de Mayo event and a Mexican Independence festival in El Barrio under the auspices of CECOMEX. Both events now constitute blockbuster events in their own right, new traditions, attracting thousands of Mexican and Latino visitors from throughout the city.

Exchanges between Mexicans and other Latinos are also evident in the founding of AMAT, the workers' advocacy organization based in El Barrio. Its director, Jerry Domínguez, acknowledged the importance of the gradual opening of labor unions to immigrant workers and the help of the Centro de Trabajadores Latinos, headed by Dominican Mónica Santana, an organization that had engaged in previous advocacy over immigrant rights. Working with Local 169 Union of Needletrades, Industrial and Textile Employees (UNITE), Mexican workers made headlines throughout 2000 by winning the first worker contracts for immigrants after waging a major campaign against green grocers on behalf of undocumented Mexican immigrants.

Yet acknowledgments of cooperation in the past and continued collaboration across groups do not imply a lack of conflict or competition between Mexicans and Puerto Ricans. A Latino identity does not pervade the scope or identity of Mexican groups in El Barrio. After all, the context in which they operate is one of assertion and self-definition, processes that parallel and even work against the everyday exchanges and personal relationships across and among El Barrio's ethnic and racial groupings. I have in mind here Rua's (2001) discussion of the PortoMex and MexiRican identities in Chicago formed in relation to everyday practice and personal relationships, or Smith's (2003) description of second-generation youth's engagements and greater identification with Puerto Ricans, identities and identifications that find little space in more institutionalized contexts. In fact, Puerto Ricans and Dominicans regard their roles as facilitators and mediators of services among newer immigrants as examples of their generosity and disinterest, which are used by these groups to establish their greater knowledge, history, and claim to the city. Not surprisingly then, this discourse is also resented by Mexican and other Latino groupings seeking to establish their own stakes in the city,

insofar as it undermines their own agency and ability to become politicized and visible on their own. The still-evident dominance of Puerto
Rican culture within the New York Latino construct is also perceived as
a threat to the cultural memory and needs of other Latino subgroups.
This impasse was expressed movingly by Adela, the daughter of a
Mexican immigrant who described passing as Puerto Rican while growing up because her Mexican identity had been ridiculed. For her, Puerto
Ricans had opened some doors by increasing the visibility of Latino culture in the city, but they had also closed others, including the door to her
Mexican identity as a youth. Conversely, tales of cooperation in the past
were also recalled by newer immigrants as a testament to how much
their community has achieved since they received the helping hand of
their fellow Puerto Ricans. That is, this recollection can also be deployed
to establish the relative value, achievement, and hard work of Mexicans
and other recent immigrants when compared to the "privileges" of citizenship afforded to Puerto Ricans. I am reminded here of a successful
restaurateur from El Barrio, who, after recalling the help of a Puerto
Rican neighbor, noted that unlike his Puerto Rican friend, he had since
moved up because of his work ethic and efforts.

Mexicans, Puerto Ricans, and other Latinos in El Barrio are not operating in a vacuum. Their relations are mediated by existing racial and
ethnic hierarchies that are shaped by racialist processes in the United
States and in Latin America and also have particular manifestations that
are historically and regionally situated. In New York City's hierarchy of
Latinidad, for instance, to distance oneself from the lowest ranked
racial/ethnic groups in the city is to estrange oneself from Puerto Ricans
and, increasingly, Dominicans. These groups are considered to be lazy,
uneducated, loud, and less "cultured" as compared to the more cultured,
hard working, and ethical Mexicans, a discourse positioning them as the
premier "good immigrant" and prospective model citizens (Bourgois
1995; Grosfoguel and Georas 2001; Smith 2003; Dávila 2001a).[12] An
excerpt from El Diario's editorial, "Voz del Pueblo," demonstrates how
Dominicans are increasingly assigned the same traits that have long been
attributed to Puerto Ricans. "We Mexicans are hard workers and don't
depend on welfare as do Dominicans . . . many Mexicans are deported

because they are illegal. Each month, Dominicans are deported because they've been jailed for selling drugs, committing robberies, crimes and fraud. We are humble and respectful of our neighborhoods, Dominicans play radio out loud without caring about their neighborhood" (Infante 2001). Recall here my earlier point of how immigrants' role as "good citizens" can be used against others, particularly against subordinated groups, who on account of their race, history, colonial past, and second-rate "citizenship" are deemed to be forever suspect. Here the implication is that Dominicans are deported because they are criminals, unlike other "good" immigrants who are unfairly deported. Indeed, it is not uncommon for Mexicans with upwardly mobile aspirations in El Barrio to exalt their friendship with a Puerto Rican while simultaneously scorning them their "faulty" culture, speech, and manners. These assessments are obviously linked to Puerto Ricans' and Dominicans' positions at the bottom ranks in the city's Latino racial/ethnic hierarchy, making them the irrefutable reference against which other Latino immigrants define themselves as more culturally wholesome and upwardly mobile. This is the same type of rationale fueling a growing desire among Puerto Ricans and Dominicans to be recognized as the real pioneers in the city, for it is "they" who opened the paths to Mexicans' success.

Ironically, the same dynamics used to distinguish Puerto Ricans and Mexicans affect the prospects for Mexican leaders and the first generation to reach out to different segments of their community, such as the second generation and the youth. For instance, Mexican attempts to distinguish themselves from Puerto Ricans and other Latinos through interpretations of Mexican traditions and culture around the church (the Virgin of Guadalupe) can be easily at odds with the experiences of the second generation, which increasingly identifies itself as Chicano, and even Latino, not to mention political radicals, gays, and atheists. A young artist, who identifies himself as a Zapatista, spoke to this when he shared his disregard for "religious" groups and the disdain he felt when he attended a meeting dressed like a *rockero*. Culturalistic appeals are obviously both effective and risky, always potentially excluding groups within the "Mexican" community.

At stake is whether the second generation develops a more racialized identification with Puerto Ricans and other minorities, or instead maintains its present "model Latino immigrant status." Sociologist Robert Smith posits that these positions depend on a variety of factors, including generation, age, location in the labor market, the context of their interaction, or even gender roles. He has nevertheless found that even those among the youth and second generation who adopt a "racialized Mexicanness" position avoid identifying wholeheartedly with Puerto Ricans and other minorities, a trend he connects to their more uncertain position as new arrivals into already established hierarchies of ethnicity and race formed primarily around Blacks and Puerto Ricans (Smith 2001).

Puerto Ricans, for their part, are not unfamiliar with stereotyping. The comments made in 1999 by Herman Badillo—chairman of the board of trustees at the City University of New York and unsuccessful candidate for mayor in 2001—about the supposed problems that Mexican and recent immigrant children present to the public school system come to mind. According to Mr. Badillo, Mexicans and recent immigrants presented insurmountable challenges to city schools because they "came from the hills," from countries with little tradition of education, and were mostly short and straight haired Indians. These racist comments exposed stereotypes of Mexicans as less educated or unsophisticated "newcomers," as opposed to the "urban saviness" of Puerto Ricans. In this case, it is the "seniority" of one Latino group over another that is deployed to maintain the "traditional/modern binary," although this binary is also maintained by the politics of citizenship that permeate relations between Mexicans and Puerto Ricans. As noted by De Genova and Ramos-Zayas in their work in Chicago, it is Mexicans' "illegality" that provides the defining element for their racialization as forever foreign, just as Puerto Ricans' "legality" renders them closer to African Americans (2003).

The 2001 Mexican Independence Day Parade was canceled after September 11, but in 2002 the struggle continued. This time, some community leaders from El Barrio united to challenge control of the event by the original organizers, the marketing firm, and Tepeyac; they formed La Alianza, yet another conglomerate group of Mexican organizations with Juan Cáceres elected as its leader. Others supported the original organizers, among other reasons, as a means of challenging what were seen as

Figure 11.   Special guests of the 2002 Mexican Independence Day Parade. Among them are, second from the left, Juan Cáceres; Salvador Beltrán del Río, Consul General of Mexico in New York; Senator Olga Méndez; Pedro Matar, from the Mexican Trade Center; and Norberto Terrazas, Consul of Human Rights and Legal Affairs. Photo by the author.

the encompassing power aspirations of Tepeyac relative to the other Mexican organizations in the city. After all, the struggle over the parade was not solely about the authenticity of the event, or the involvement of "foreigners," but rather part of larger debates over which group, coalition, or interests truly represents the greater Mexican community. After all was said and done, La Alianza was unable to take full control of the event as it had intended; the promoter had signed a multiyear contract with the original organizer. However, while the permit for Fifth Avenue was denied, the use of Madison Avenue was awarded instead. The goal of a centrally located event within the heart of Manhattan was achieved. Most important, for the first time, the struggle over the parade united a range of Mexican groups in a common cause, as they all paraded on an equal basis down Madison Avenue in a massive display that for the first time attracted media coverage and major politicians, including Governor Pataki himself. In the view of one of the organizers, the "Desfile Mexicano Internacional" had been a truly "international" show of force, "international" for gathering Mexican groups from throughout the different boroughs to march in the global capital of the world. But some months later, the struggle over the parade resumed, which brings me to the sign poster held by Alianza members at a rally to boycott the "fake" parade in 2003. Alianza groups had participated in the 2002 parade, hoping that in 2003 the parade would be transferred from GALOS to this larger committee, but to no avail. Larger and more determined, Alianza ran an aggressive public relations campaign: charges of inauthenticity and accusations of GALOS's lack of financial accountability to the Mexican community covered Spanish-language headlines, while chants of "La Raza no se Vende" (Mexicans are not for sale) disrupted those of "Viva Mexico" by parade participants. At the time of this writing, the "independence" of the Mexican Independence Day Parade is up for grabs, and the issue is not likely to subside in the future. But in the meantime, public claims for a Mexican Independence Day Parade that is organized by and for Mexican communities will continue to speak to the growing consolidation of a Mexican-centered agenda as the means to unite different groups, contest one another's legitimacy, and maneuver for rights and visibility in the neoliberal city. For at stake is not solely control of the parade, but rather quests for space in the Latinized and neoliberal city. This task demands constant negotiations of the terms of collaborations with corporations, marketers, and even with other Latinos.

THE SPECTER OF NATIONALIST POLITICS

Not unlike the nationalist appeals of Puerto Ricans, Mexican-centered politics respond to a variety of forces. Among them are the particular needs of this community, the centrality of cultural politics as a terrain for claiming rights and visibility, and the existing racial/ethnic hierarchies that frame these cultural politics. As discussed above, Puerto Ricans and

Dominicans, the most established Latino groups in the city, constitute the defining reference for Mexicans' quest to establish themselves and their programs, just as Puerto Ricans have long measured and defined their gains vis-à-vis African Americans.

But this emphasis on Mexican-centered politics among local groups and its implications for Mexican–Puerto Rican relations can not be fully understood without considering the impact of local politicians, marketers, and other interests that are also fueling and channeling ethnic-specific politics for particular ends. In fact, some of these actors seemed to rejoice gleefully about the advent and growth of Mexicans. A case in point are Hispanic marketers, who see Mexicans, particularly recent and first generation, as representing the revitalization of the New York Spanish-language market, long considered a more "acculturated" market because of the great number of Nuyorican and older generations of English-dominant Latinos. Aggressively targeting this new marketing segment, the Spanish-language network Telemundo had an exclusively Mexican artistic program during its 2001 "community relations" programming in El Barrio.[13] Likewise, with the help of marketers, the Cinco de Mayo celebrations have quickly become one of the largest citywide events in terms of the number of funders and attention from corporate sponsors.

Meanwhile, while not yet a strong voting bloc, Mexicans were being actively courted by numerous local, city, and state politicians, who have in turn facilitated their involvement in electoral politics as advocates and political insiders. Jerry Domínguez, for instance, was involved in the reelection of Adam Clayton Powell IV, Puerto Rican councilwoman Margarita López, and Senator Eric Schneiderman, while most local groups had been courted by or had met with political figures, including Olga Méndez, Dominican Guillermo Linares, and Charles Rangel. Such interest in a group estimated to be from 50 to 90 percent undocumented attests to the considerable value of the Mexican constituency for local politicians, especially on account of its nationwide political rentability.[14] In 2002, while President Bush was celebrating Cinco de Mayo, locally, Governor Pataki and Senator Méndez courted Mexicans by attending the Mexican Independence Day Parade. Even the Catholic Church finds in

Mexican migrants a resource with which to cope with the irreversible loss of Puerto Ricans and other Latinos to Protestant denominations. (Witness the role of the Catholic Church in the creation of Tepeyac.) Mexican leaders are amply aware of their appeal to politicians and marketers; they capitalize on their popularity whenever possible to obtain economic and political support for their events and activities, invariably reinvigorating ethnic-centered politics by and for Mexicans to stake their claims. Not that these appeals ever result in much financial support or resources. As one noted realistically: "Yes, they all love us. They seek us constantly. But we get nothing. No resources, just words." The skeptical words of Miguel Ramírez spoke to this realization when he underplayed the hype about the Mexican Independence Day Parade when Mexican workers enjoy so few rights and so little "independence." Indeed, a common aspiration among many of my informants was that they no longer be treated as everyone's new constituency and be given the resources to become agents in change in the organizations that now serve and court them. This view invariably informed the controversy over the parade.

Still, the Mexican population was seen as a sleeping giant with whom everyone will have to reckon, many times over and beyond other "dwindling" Latino groups. This stance added to the contest between Mexicans and Puerto Ricans in El Barrio, which was both featured and fueled by the local press, not unlike the rivalry, both real and imagined, between Blacks and Latinos that was often exploited by the mainstream media.[15] Appealing to Mexicans, for instance, was emerging as a common strategy to neutralize Puerto Rican claims in El Barrio, not unlike citywide trends where catering to one Latino group is met by ignoring another. The appointment of Mexican Julián Zugazagoitia as director of El Museo del Barrio amid protests by Puerto Ricans for community representation on the museum's board is a case in point. While requests for grassroots community representation on the board were in fact directed to the primarily Puerto Rican board of directors, these appeals were publicly constructed as "anti-Mexican," a position that had no place in the "Latinized city." Never mind that claims were specifically directed to the Puerto Rican board, or that they long predated the director's appointment. The class dimension of the issue and the community participatory ideals of campaign participants were thus effectively muted. In a similar manner, Mexicans' appeals for community control of the Mexican Independence Day Parade were also taken as examples of their anti-Puerto Rican and anti-Latino position and of their "lack of urban civic-mindedness" about the ways of business in the Latinized city. As the newest and fastest growing group, touted as the future of El Barrio, it was Mexicans, not Puerto Ricans, however, that were most publicly touted and who benefited most from this strategy, even if they did so in mostly "rhetorical ways."

Indeed, ethnicity is never free of larger interests, keen as they often are on generalizing how it is articulated and for what ends. That Puerto Ricans were more likely to embrace Latinidad, even if strategically, while my Mexican informants were more reticent on their nationalist claims is relevant here. Undoubtedly, these different stances to Latinidad reflect these groups' contrasting histories and lengths of time in the city, thus the varied ease with which they engage with a panethnic identity. But they also suggest that as a political resource, ethnic claims never imply the same challenge to dominant ideologies of ethnic incorporation—in this case to Latinidad—and that their potential for expression is also a matter of how they intersect with greater interests at play in the Latinized city. In a similar manner, these different stances to Latinidad suggest that ethnic claims and politics can indeed be highly effective, but situationally so—such as for festivals, at least for their celebration, if not for their financial control—and for certain groups and in particular moments more than others. Arguably, as a mostly undocumented and thus vulnerable group, Mexicans are yet to present real threats to local power structures in the city. Their nationalist and cultural citizenship strategies have not yet been associated with oppositional politics—as has long been the case with discourses of Puertorriqueñidad—at least not locally, making them more publicly palatable. The prevalent discourse framing Mexicans as hard-working "model immigrants," a step above racialized minorities such as Blacks, Puerto Ricans, and Dominicans, provides a likely buffer to their ethnic politics and cultural claims. That claims for social rights are at least for now vested and veiled in the idioms of Guadalupismo and religion or festivals—that are relatively safer than outright nationalist or

political demands—may also be at play.[16] There may not be a single variable responsible for these dynamics, though it is crucial to recognize the
various factors and conditions that may have an impact on the space in
which to voice ethnic claims.

Overall, and in light of the diminishing space for voicing ethnic-
specific claims in the Latinized city, where the panethnic term of Latino/a
increasingly prevails, Mexicans' ethnic demands are insurmountably
important. Mexican activists' demands for equality—that they be given
the same place as other ethnic groups in the city—challenge the dominant canon that rights come with citizenship, and/or that seniority dic-
tates legitimacy. In so doing, they confront the dominant discourse of
accommodation, that is, of Latinization, which empowers through the
strength of numbers but dilutes the particular needs and specificities of
different groups. The fate of immigrants and of the undocumented are
for once brought into the template of New York Latinidad, where immigrant needs have been largely subsumed. Most important, the bases on
which groups are supposed to accept and harmoniously incorporate
themselves, many times by subordinating themselves, within established
hierarchies of race, class, and space, are disturbed and challenged. And in
the case of the Mexican Independence Day Parade, nationalist claims
constitute an important challenge to corporate Latinidad and marketable
ethnicity, spurring ongoing struggles over community control of this significant and profitable event. Even if calls for larger community control
have yet to be effective, these demands are not less significant in upholding that an alternative logic of accountability should prevail.

Finally, it is important to recognize that the consolidation of Mexicans
in New York City also parallels a growing exchange with Puerto Ricans
and other Latinos. Some Puerto Ricans bemoan Mexicans for their losses
in El Barrio, yet I could not find one Puerto Rican leader involved in electoral politics or advocacy who did not try to reach out to Mexicans as part
of their strategies to maintain El Barrio as a Latinized neighborhood. The
statement of a Puerto Rican school teacher evokes this common sentiment: "Everyone says that Puerto Ricans are leaving El Barrio, but no one
denies that Mexicans are growing and are here to stay. So they can't say
this won't be a Latino neighborhood ten years from now. Let politicians

forget about Mexicans because they can't vote, but in five years, maybe ten, El Barrio will continue to be Latino, because of the Mexicans." Even Felipe Luciano's 2001 campaign for a council seat in El Barrio, which revolved around overt nationalist appeals to Puerto Rican empowerment in their "community," was never limited to Puerto Ricans, but made a distinct effort to be inclusive of all Latinos. An Ecuadorian real-estate broker was among his campaign managing group mobilizing around "Latinos Unidos," and Luciano was commonly seen at the Mexican restaurant La Hacienda reaching out to its owner and patrons. This tactic was evident again in the 2002 elections when most Puerto Rican political candidates or incumbents had Mexican leaders among their advocacy team. Similarly, and concomitant with debates over the parade, Puerto Rican politicians were also courted and invited to other Mexican programs, such as the Cinco de Mayo celebrations, where appeals to our *"hermanos Latinos"* were also voiced from the podium.

Whether these exchanges translate into a common political or economic agenda among these groups is another matter yet to be seen. The extent to which Mexican community leaders get real resources, not just expressions of interest and good will, is also up for grabs. For now, it is evident that both Mexicans' and Puerto Ricans' claims of visibility run in tandem and parallel ways in El Barrio and that the forging of intra-Latino alliances is not antagonistic to either group's political strategies. And perhaps most important, as central as nationalism may be to Mexican cultural politics, these local groups both echo and depart from Mexico's cultural politics. Increasingly, Mexicans' powers of assembly and work do not stem solely from long-established discourses—that is, from legitimacies long gained by their use of nationalist, religious, or cultural appeals, or obtained through mediation of the church or the Mexican government. Instead these gains increasingly stem from the struggles, trajectories, experiences, and alliances in specific spaces and contexts, like those that are now actively waged in El Barrio.

SIX

The Marketable Neighborhood

OUTDOOR ADS MEET STREET ART

The best way to reach Hispanic consumers is through the
use of eight-sheets [six feet by twelve feet posters] right in
their own communities. The Hispanic market is America's
fastest growing consumer segment, expanding faster than
the general population. . . . It makes sense to be visible in
their communities.

> Vista Media on "Hispanic American Marketing,"
> http://www.vistamediagroup.com/hisp_am.html

Commissions are hard to come by. People have to appreciate
the artistry, the care of a customized oil-paint mural. Because
it is easy to do a poster, duplicate it hundreds of times and post
all over.

> Edgar Medina, East Harlem resident and artist

Outdoor ads are yet another entry point into the cultural politics of
space in El Barrio and of trends toward marketable ethnicity. These
ubiquitous signs inscribe meaning onto space, especially as El Barrio's
landscape becomes more uniform. Advertised products, intended audiences, and the language and cultural references contained in the ads are
all signs that communicate meaning alongside that expressed by
murals, flags, chain stores, and other markings of space. They indicate
the kind of neighborhood one is entering, the people that inhabit it,

their potential likes, tastes, and ethnic backgrounds. More poignantly, outdoor ads are illustrative of the identities that the market vests in particular neighborhoods, summoning viewers to inquire how they may be affecting or becoming intertwined with current transformations in El Barrio.

The high concentration of outdoor advertisements in El Barrio is not a new or uncontested development. El Barrio has long been targeted by the alcohol and tobacco industries, thus these ads have in fact been a common subject of contention among residents and critics alike. On the one hand, they represent an overt commercialization of ethnic neighborhoods, a commodification of space, travel, and movement—in ways similar to other types of site-specific advertising, such as ambient television—that cannibalize activities like waiting or lounging (McCarthy 2001). Conversely, because of their public nature, outdoor ads constitute a relatively more open medium for interaction and resistance by consumers (Jackson and Thrift 1995). Unlike television or print ads, outdoor ads can be defaced, written over, and transformed in ways that are publicly visible to others beyond the confines of the viewing moment. Therefore, advertising and commercialization have complex and contradictory meanings and effects that are evidently at play in El Barrio.

An interesting trend is East Harlem's continued commercial treatment as a Latino space by advertisers at the same time that gentrification threatens to render it less distinct by displacing Latino shops, restaurants, street vendors, and public architecture, such as *casitas.* Advertising, after all, operates in the realm of images, symbols, and ideas, with audiences constructed on the basis of the need for niched consumers more so than on the particular characteristics of specific constituencies. The placement of ads in El Barrio is also tied to the growing popularity of targeted and segmented marketing as part of advertisers' struggle for eyeballs, which has taken them out to the streets, and to the targeting of more specific constituencies. Encouraged by cheaper rates for advertising in Black and Latino neighborhoods, companies have posted ethnic-specific ads anywhere from storefronts to walls, publicly marking viewer's entrance to an ethnically marked urban space. The number of outdoor ads in Spanish, full of putatively Latino/a themes, is quickly noticeable along

Ninety-sixth Street and Lexington Avenue, at the edge of East Harlem, openly declaring that one is entering El Barrio. This is in direct contrast to the new cafés and renovated buildings that could easily pass as any other strip in the city.

Yet it is not simply the commercialization of urban space in East Harlem that I seek to problematize, but rather its effects and relationships with other visual forms and modes of signification through which residents have built community and inscribed meaning into their neighborhood. In particular, I am concerned with advertising in relation to street art, mainly murals and graffiti (also known as writing).[1] Both of these street-art forms have long served as visual markers of Latinidad, functioning as mediums of remembrance, protest, celebration, in addition to providing an important income-generating activity for some local residents; but they are now increasingly affected by the commercial competition over space. The marketing and commercialization of urban space in El Barrio is not a contest over the signification of outdoor surfaces, or of East Harlem's public identity as a Latino neighborhood, as much as it is a confrontation over who is involved in El Barrio's definition, and for what ends. Examining these processes requires an exploration of different uses and meanings vested in outdoor surfaces by residents, shopkeepers, muralists, and marketers, among others, in relation to larger struggles over the neighborhood's identity and meaning. Despite their different approaches to the neighborhood, marketers, shopkeepers, and street artists share a similar interest in publicly asserting Latinos' permanence and existence in the face of the ongoing forces of gentrification. Sometimes they even work in tandem, blurring the lines between street art and commercial art; but they always lead to the ethnicization and commercialization of East Harlem, processes that run in parallel ways. The important differences between these systems of signification, however, are the objects and treatments of culture, and the different ends to which such identity is being deployed. Against outdoor marketing promotion of marketable ethnicity, street artists vie for validation and public space; their works are an important economic resource for local artists in addition to being important conduits for debates over the area's transformation.

SPACE VENDORS: MARKETERS, SPECULATORS, AND SHOPKEEPERS

Marketers have traditionally coveted ethnic neighborhoods for outdoor ads.[2] In them, they find cheaper placement rates for their ads, as well as an aggregate of highly concentrated populations who, presumed to be ethnically and linguistically homogeneous, provide them with a supposedly large and accessible base of consumers. Today, however, ethnic neighborhoods are even more coveted by marketers due to their growing interest in highly targeted outdoor advertising, represented largely by the work of specialized outdoor marketing companies such as TDI/ Infinity and Vista. In recent years these companies have grown increasingly standardized along advertising industry conventions, segmenting and measuring their markets in ways that have afforded them greater visibility as a legitimate and effective advertising alternative. According to the Outdoor Advertising Association of America, outdoor advertising expenditures reached $5.2 billion in 2001, growing about 10 percent a year for the last decade, a faster pace than other sectors of the industry (http://www.OAAA.org). Outdoor advertisers now use syndicated measurements of their reach and new means for tracking and mapping neighborhoods for target marketing. Most important, outdoor advertisers have developed innovative tactics to secure the exclusive right to sell any imaginable outdoor space through the establishments of contracts with landlords, private companies, and the government, granting them the exclusive sale and commercial use of a variety of private and public venues in the city. In yet another example of the ubiquity of "privately owned public space" (Kayden et al. 2000), advertisements can now cover entire subways and buses, and when no space is seemingly available these companies can now readily adapt the urban landscape to their benefit, installing the needed "street furniture"—such as telephone booths and bus shelters—to put up their ads.[3]

Developments such as these have greatly facilitated outdoor marketers' objective and promise of providing maximum exposure to every imaginable product, or in industry lingo, neighborhood "penetration" at a fraction of the rate charged by broadcast media.[4] These companies' promise of maximum coverage is demonstrated by the slogan for TDI/Infinity, one of the largest outdoor companies targeting Latinos. Presenting itself as the only medium able to overcome differences in language, style, and taste among Latinos, it touts that "No matter which radio stations they tune into, whether they watch Spanish- or English-language television, or what newspapers they read . . . [an outdoor ad] meets 6 out of 10 Hispanics face to face in their neighborhoods each month!"[5] This coverage is further expanded through the simultaneous sponsorship of public festivals and events. A company ad representative calculated that their Latino promotion during the 2000 Puerto Rican Day Parade had reached an excess of two million people through ads strategically placed on subway exteriors, phone kiosks, and street walls all over the heart of El Barrio.

Notwithstanding these companies' claims, urban space is not easily controllable. Many potentially saleable outdoor spaces remain out of reach, and are sold instead by budding local entrepreneurs through a range of "illegal" (without the pertinent permits) and "one-man" operations, heightening the number of interests staking a commercial claim to neighborhood space.[6] As explained by the same outdoor ad representative, "Neighborhoods like this are free reins for advertisers . . . and it's very difficult to detect what ads are illegal and which ones are not. A person can sell a wall for up to ten thousand dollars a month; it may take three months before someone notices it's illegal, and when they do, the penalty is a mere one thousand dollars. Meanwhile, that person has pocketed thirty thousand dollars." Not all "illegal" outdoor locations are as profitable as this example suggests. According to the same informant, such walls are sold for two hundred to seven thousand dollars, depending primarily on location and visibility. The important point here is this vendor's view that ethnic neighborhoods are "free rein" for the sale of ad space, and that large companies are not alone when staking commercial claim to East Harlem but are joined by a number of vendors profiting from a fickle yet vibrant segment of the informal economy. But not everyone profits. The biggest winners are outdoor advertisers rather than the many local shopkeepers on whose walls the ads are posted. A longtime merchant, and owner of one of the *"farmacias Latinas"* that are known as such for the numerous services they provide their customers, from fax service, to copies, money orders, lottery tickets, phone cards, religious paraphernalia, and medical advice, told me that he had been selling his walls to outdoor advertisers for ten years for only fifty dollars every six months. When I told him how much more money he could charge for his walls, the old man did not flinch or show surprise and quickly dismissed me by insisting that "a wall is a wall, people want to make a penny for everything. I don't care." His statement once again confronts us with alternative values to those of marketers. It would not surprise me to learn that other vendors are equally as lackadaisical about their buildings' walls. The launching of a TDI/Infinity Outdoor Latino is a response to this kind of opportunity. With this new unit, this global outdoor advertising company can stake a stronger claim to neighborhoods like East Harlem and other Latino/a strongholds in the city by acquiring "Latino walls" through the establishment of exclusive contracts with the owners of the most visible and profitable neighborhood spaces.

Not surprisingly, the unit is spearheaded by two Latinos. A common trend in global marketing is to achieve immediate expertise in selling to culturally different constituencies by hiring "expert" personnel from such constituencies. It is headed by Joel, a Cuban-American from New Jersey, and Mike, a young Ecuadoran marketer from Queens, both of whom stated their determination to increase their company's control and exclusive sale of Latino/a outdoor space. True to their role as representatives of "their" Latino/a community, they described their work as one of representing Latino/a culture through popular representations turned into ethnic knowledges, as well as through ethnic assertion. Indeed, as with other culturally targeted ads, outdoor ads can also be seen as public statements and a gauge to measure advertisers' recognition of minority consumers, a long-neglected population. In this tenor, covering Latino/a neighborhoods with "the right kind of advertising" was a gauge of "empowerment and recognition." Joel and Mike were especially concerned with placing ethnically sensitive ads and, foremost, "elegant" (more costly) ads that would supplant the stereotypical cigarette and beer ads that have long dominated minority spaces.

These claims are obviously tenuous at best when considering that such "measures of empowerment" are most beneficial to corporations, not Latinos. Latinos may have come a long way in the eyes of advertising executives, yet, as I note elsewhere, Latinos and Latino neighborhoods are coveted insofar as they promise a contained and cheaper venue for ads (Dávila 2001a). Their commercial treatment is concomitant to their consideration as second-class consumers, undeserving of the kind of advertising investments that other population segments receive; thus the dominance of cheaper outdoor ad formats for addressing this constituency. The two Latino outdoor marketers were well aware of these dynamics, insisting that it is not advertising density but *advertising quality* that provides a measurement for advertising spending parity.

The result of this targeted marketing effort is the Latinization of El Barrio's landscape through advertisements in Spanish, including "ethnic"-sensitive maxims and images. Johnny Walker touts *"con el buen gusto se nace"* (one is born with good taste) and *"se ve que sabes"* (it shows you know), associating the taste for whisky with that for one's roots, while Tecate reminds Latinos that Spanish is better than English with *"Cerveza es mejor que beer"* (Cerveza is better than beer). Milk advertisers appeal to Latinas' supposedly greater maternal instinct through grandmothers that prompt us with *"Y usted, les dio suficiente leche hoy?"* (Did you give your loved ones enough milk today?) And when Latinidad is not directly marketed through language, it is indexed through "urban-style" ads, synonymous with Black and Latino urban culture: Air Jordans, Converse, Newport cigarettes, and hip hop. Indeed, East Harlem, along with the South Bronx and Sunset Park are marked as "Latino" in outdoor advertising maps. El Barrio is routinely included in Hispanic marketing tours, where residents and their environs are "shown" to prospective outdoor marketing clients, and, depending on their needs, sold as undifferentiated spaces whose value and commonality reside in their aggregates of Latino residents, or else as hubs for particular Latino/a subnationalities. Through arbitrary assignments, the same neighborhood may therefore be described as a perfect target for reaching Mexicans, Puerto Ricans, or Dominicans in ways that have little to do with the ethnic makeup of particular neighborhoods, and a lot with the needs of particular advertisers. It was most likely in this spirit that a young Latino market tour leader, who led me through Brooklyn's Sunset Park during the summer of 1999, stated confidently that he was able to distinguish between these neighborhoods by the colors displayed in their storefronts: green for Mexicans, blue for Dominicans, and red for Puerto Ricans. This arbitrary assessment was based, he explained, on the incorrect assumption of which colors predominate on the flags of these countries. The content and meaning of "Latino" and "Latinness" can shift according to the needs of particular advertisers. The effects of these strategies are amply evident in El Barrio, where it is common to see ads that either dramatize national distinctions, or else appeal to unity among different Latino groups. Ads for Pronto Envio and Tecate beer are more likely posted in the storefronts of Mexican *taquerias* along Lexington Avenue, instead of in Puerto Rican establishments. Local shopkeepers themselves are also engaged in these dynamics. Covering their storefronts with ads is an important medium for making strategic linkages to particular constituencies; they are communicating that they specialize in this or that product or service, or that they are equipped to serve the tastes of particular groups. As a local shopkeeper noted: "I have Black, Mexican, and Puerto Rican customers. The cigarette and beer ads work for all, but for the Mexicans I put up the ads from Pronto Envio and the phone cards."

But the principal boundaries enacted by outdoor ads are those between El Barrio as a Latino/a neighborhood, its contiguous neighborhoods, and the rest of the city. This is communicated not solely through the language or ethnic specificity of a given ad, but also by the types of ads, the products they advertise, and, most directly, by their location and ubiquity. A Latino/a neighborhood, according to two ad reps, is one that has many Latinos and is cheaper to cover with ads. "To me it's all very clear," one stated. "From Ninety-sixth Street up there's no problem. It's Hispanic. All the way from First to Park, and from there on, they are all Afro-Americans. And from 135th upwards, they are all Dominicans." Notwithstanding his confidence over these boundaries, these areas are not as uncontested as he describes. As noted earlier, the border of Ninety-sixth and 100th streets is, in fact, one of El Barrio's most gentrified areas. One can even trace the process of gentrification by following the type of advertisements that are springing up versus those that are fading. Some high-traffic areas like Lexington Avenue are filled with advertisements, but other avenues look clean and demure like the Upper East Side to the south. In the upper 100s however, ads are far more common. But the rep's point about these neighborhoods being "free rein" to advertisers is still accurate. These much poorer communities are believed to be more passive and less likely to challenge the commercial inundation of their space. The number of ads thus functions as an index of poverty and marginality: the poorer you are the more likely you will be surrounded by ads. Particularly apparent in these neighborhoods is the type of ad the industry calls "eight-sheets" (six feet high by twelve feet wide), which have long been the cheapest and most common format in ethnic neighborhoods. Sold in bulk packages for as little as $150 each a month (as of 2000), they are placed primarily outside "points of sale," on the windows and walls of grocery and convenience stores in the area. These ads are nowhere to be seen in upscale neighborhoods in the city, where residents, according to Joel, would be bothered by their "ubiquity" and "ordinariness."

The type of products advertised and the placement of the ads are additional markers of El Barrio's physical and spatial boundaries. Above Ninety-sixth Street, ads address a "community" of basic-goods consumers, for products such as coffee, food, milk, beer, and cigarettes, or for money transfer companies, or else social services, a choice of products that forcefully inscribes the marginality of the neighborhood and its residents/consumers. The contrast with the demure ads of the Upper East Side or the flashy ones on Times Square could not be more stark. This status is also communicated by the placement of eight-sheets in the less prestigious venues, such as corner walls, rather than in the expensive, glossy, illuminated, and protected phone and transportation booths, which are common advertising venues in midtown and upscale neighborhoods in the city. Never illuminated and more susceptible to damage and writing than these other venues, eight-sheets are also more likely to be deemed as cheapening and debasing to the neighborhood. Or in Joel's succinct terms, "They have a bad rep."

Indeed, many eight-sheet advertisements in East Harlem are either damaged, faded, or covered with writing. Unlike ads placed in phone booths and bus stops, which are protected by glass, eight-sheets ads require the constant supervision of a concerned seller in order to prevent damage to them and, by association, to the product's image. But El Barrio is no Times Square. Once installed, many ads are often forgotten, sometimes for long after the advertising contract has expired. Many are left hanging until the space is sold to another advertiser. Such faded ads are a stark reminder that ads may be commonplace in ethnic neighborhoods, but they do not necessarily imply profitability or advertising value of this community. Advertisers may have been attracted to El Barrio's cheaper rates, or to the possibility of reaching a "homogenous" and "easy" target, or in some cases the advertiser could have been offered space for free or at below-market rates as an add-on to a larger campaign in mid-Manhattan or trendy Soho—ethnic neighborhoods are never their top priority. Although not an eight-sheet, a faded giant mural ad for Channel 47 stayed up for almost two years on 106th Street before the space was sold to HBO Latino in the spring of 2001. Such ads pervade the neighborhood with a sense of decay while the advertiser is provided with free and continuous, albeit faded, exposure.

Outdoor advertisements constantly communicate for, and on behalf of, El Barrio, and always at multiple levels. In their content, they assert Latino/a culture through the use of language and images or themes that showcase differences among various Latino subgroups. Additionally, through the use of medium, location, or even advertisers' care of their ads, ads can also reinscribe and thus mark the neighborhood's marginal identity vis-à-vis the rest of the city. After all, El Barrio is no advertising hub. Notwithstanding signs of affluent consumers entering the area, it still remains an advertising-unworthy neighborhood, where advertisers have to be lured and attracted.

CONVERSATIONS AND ENGAGEMENTS

Once posted, street ads become part of larger webs of street communication, where public signs, be they ads, murals, or street paintings, seldom remain untouched, becoming a gauge of public opinion. Assessing the spatial and communicative impact of outdoor ads thus requires examining them in relation to the various other signs, images, and messages that may subdue, challenge, or transform their commercial meaning, even when the intention of these expressions may be difficult or impossible to establish. For instance, the vandalization of the first mural of Mexican icons in East Harlem—painted by local artist James De la Vega as a welcome to the Mexican community—gave El Barrio residents much to talk about concerning the ethnic tensions between Puerto Rican "long-timers" and the Mexican "newcomers" (Cardalda-Sánchez and Tirado-Avilés 2001). But how does one interpret the writing painted over an outdoor ad, or the mural harmoniously painted next to another? Is the first instance an oppositional statement to the commercial message, or perhaps a more general claim to space chosen for its value and visibility? Is the second evidence of accommodation between street art and advertisements? Moreover, how is street art and its messages affected by the commercial sale of, and competition over, space?

Before considering these questions, it is necessary to acknowledge the intimate relationship between street art and commerce. Street art sustains not only the artistic, but also the economic aspirations of local artists. This is the case even though some forms of street art are generally seen as more or less culturally or economically driven. Such is the case with murals and graffiti. Much has been said about the differences of these forms of street art. An obvious difference is that murals are generally considered to be more time consuming than graffiti, which by definition is always quick and spontaneous and often done covertly, without wall permits; it is thus considered illegal, even if the designs may have been more carefully planned than a mural. Because of this, writing or graffiti has generally been defined in terms of its "illegality," the very quality that makes it so conducive to unrestrained communication (Philips 1999). This quality, in turn, is one that graffiti artists often embrace. Lady Pink, a famed graffiti artist and one of the first women to paint in El Barrio's Wall/Hall of Fame—an internationally famed graffiti wall among the graffiti and hip-hop world—affirmed, "We're art pirates." This stance is

Figure 12.   Mural of Puerto Rican revolutionary Lolita Lebrón by the Puerto Rican Collective; located on 109th Street. Photo by the author.

in sharp contrast to the insistence by artist James De la Vega, who calls himself a street artist and is visibly annoyed when people call him a graffiti artist. As he made explicit to me, he always gets permits for his work, which is intended to uplift the neighborhood, rather than "debase" it, as people generally believe is the case with graffiti. This is not how all graffiti artists see themselves or define their work, and this dominant association should not be interpreted as evidence of strict boundaries between graffiti and mural artists, or between their work. The point here is the greater status awarded to murals and mural painting relative to writing within established Puerto Rican and Latino dictums for what constitutes "authentic" artistic and cultural expressions.

The politicized identity of murals stems from the history of Latino grassroots politics, particularly in the social movements of Chicanos and Puerto Ricans in the late 1960s and 1970s, when they were pivotal visual expressions of social demands and activism. This role—evident today to

Figure 13. "Zapatista" mural by Ricardo Franco. Photo by the author.

a lesser degree—has afforded murals an uncontested status and wide public recognition as important places of memory, vesting their authors with the role of "cultural workers" and community artists.[7] This aspect was most recently represented by the murals of the Puerto Rican Collective, a group that has since been disbanded but whose members are still cultural activists in El Barrio. The group was formed initially in 1996 as a committee of the National Congress for Puerto Rican Rights, in preparation for the one hundredth anniversary of the U.S. occupation and colonization of Puerto Rico. The initiative produced murals that were heavily influenced by nationalist imagery, such as that of Puerto Rican revolutionary Lolita Lebrón, which touts, "If men don't work for our independence, we women will do it." Similar iconography is also evident in the murals of Mexican artists, who are increasingly stamping El Barrio with populist, political, and nationalist images. Ricardo Franco, the author of the Zapatista mural painted outside a local *taqueria*, described his work as a statement of assertion and solidarity with the indigenous people of Mexico and the suffering of Mexicans here and everywhere. The Mexican flag, the Virgin of Guadalupe, and Aztec symbolism adorn the face of Comandante Marcos and his claim for "*Un mundo donde quepan muchos mundos*" (A world where many worlds can coexist), a message of tolerance and coexistence that he saw as needed by indigenous peoples in Chiapas as it is by Mexicans immigrants in the U.S., undoubtedly also referring to current struggles over space in El Barrio.

In contrast, graffiti has been a consistently derided and misunderstood expressive form. While a multiethnic and multiracial phenomenon from the start, it has been generally associated with "Black cultural products" of hip-hop culture, as are break dancing and rap, as opposed to rightful expressions of Puerto Rican and Latino culture where Hispano-centric definitions dominate (Rivera 2003).[8] Tied as it is to hip hop, graffiti is also seen as more commercialized by record companies and by advertisers whenever there is a need for urban packaging to provide "street credibility." Ezo is a painter and resident of El Barrio, who recently moved his studio/gallery from the Bronx to El Barrio because of this area's greater appeal and accessibility to dealers. In his words, "You can't get a dealer from Soho to come to the Bronx, they'd be horrified." He has a long history as a graffiti artist, which he explains as follows: "Murals have a history that spans Rome and da Vinci and the Mexican murals, but the roots of graffiti was with gangs, trains, and illegality. It's taken a while, over twenty years, but graffiti has begun to get worldwide status as art, and mural status." In fact, writing has commanded considerable more "artistic" status relative to murals, particularly in the early 1980s, when it became the rave of New York City galleries (Ivor Miller 2002). El Barrio's Hall of Fame is a good example of this transformation. An outcome of the illegal appropriation of a school-yard wall, it is now organized with the school's permission, and has grown into an important forum for artists to gain wide recognition and exposure, including postings on graffiti Web sites and dissemination by tourists and enthusiasts. In other words, not only do graffiti artists have as many artistic aspirations as mural artists, but both are important genres of Puerto Rican,

Latino, and urban-generated expression and are connected to particular social struggles, quests for empowerment, and representation.[9] Moreover, both mural and graffiti artists have long enjoyed commissions by commercial and nonprofit entities, rendering both groups likely candidates for co-optation and engagements with multiple commercial interests. Fears of co-optation and concerns over their image—and control of their work, its content, and authenticity—are thus equally common among all street artists, notwithstanding the hierarchies and distinctions made between different forms of street art (Ivor Miller 2002). This is the case even for commissioned commercial murals, favored by some merchants for their decoration and community relations potential and their ability to reflect the makeup and flavor of particular constituencies. While obviously a source of income, these commissions are regarded by artists as an opportunity to show their artistry, that is, as a form of advertising of their work. Artists earn as little as three hundred to five hundred dollars, or in the thousands for more recognized artists, a price I was told was always dependent on numerous considerations. These earnings are obviously hardly commensurable to those of outdoor marketers. Nevertheless, it is not solely large corporations that have stakes in the commercial use of urban space. In fact, as indicated by Edgar Medina's statement in this chapter's opening epigraph, outdoor advertising represents a direct challenge to many local artists. After all, eight-sheets and posters are always cheaper alternatives to hand-painted street art.

Differences drawn between forms of street art, around what is more or less commercial, cultural, or Puerto Rican, veil the fact that, in its variety, street art actively disturbs marketable ethnicity by providing alternative or oppositional statements to the purely commercial dominion of space provided by ads. This is done through spontaneous commentary or sabotage, as in the case of writing over ads, or through the display of national heroes and the commemoration of historical events that do not revolve around objectified images of commercial Latinidad. Additionally, all genres provide artists with a way to gain exposure and income, always with the hope that their art would lead to income-producing commissions, not to mention self-expression, communication, and enjoyment. All of this is predicated on the circulation of a particular ethos for accessing walls and space, namely in prioritizing cultural motivations while disavowing purely economic ones, not an uncommon reference to artistic claims. But most important, this cultural economy of signs depends on the ability to access wall space, a task that becomes more difficult as a result of the area's gentrification. Walls are becoming scarcer, not solely because of new developments and the growth of outdoor advertising, but most insidiously because of stiffer antigraffiti legislation. As said, graffiti has long been criminalized and subject to legislation. Since the mid-1990s, however, antigraffiti efforts have been the cornerstone of New York City's new anticrime and quality-of-life initiatives. The idea, tellingly described as the "broken window theory—that unaddressed disorder is a sign that no one cares and actually invites further disorder," is that street art creates "urban blight," and that it needs to be policed. And local artists are feeling the crunch.[10] The result is the heightened criminalization and persecution, not only of the already persecuted graffiti artists, but of any street artist lacking the appropriate permits for the use of any surface, public or private. Against this context, the negotiation through street art of multiple issues of space, identity, meanings, and money becomes especially contested.

MURALS, ADS, AND THE GENTRIFIED NEIGHBORHOOD

Perhaps the best example of the heightened stakes involving public space in this context is provided by the content and reception of the artwork by James De la Vega. Born and raised in El Barrio, De la Vega has become one of its most well-known street artists. He is author of multiple murals containing Puerto Rican heroes alongside nationally recognized heroes of liberation struggles (from Marcos to Malcolm X to José Martí); he depicts self-help, spiritual, and nationalist messages, and functions as a public intellectual and community spokesperson from his storefront art shop. There he receives requests for tours of his murals from students and visitors, as well as commissions from Hope, Banco Popular, Old Navy Stores, and others. He is arguably the most visible and controversial artist in the area.

This notoriety came relatively quickly for De la Vega after earning a Bachelor of Arts from Cornell in 1996 and returning to El Barrio. As on other university campuses, Latino students at Cornell were then enmeshed in struggles to establish Latino studies programs. This fueled a great deal of cultural activism, which precipitated De la Vega's artistic inspirations. As he noted, it was time away from El Barrio that confronted him with the area's deterioration and inspired him to paint, primarily empty walls and abandoned buildings, areas that needed "beautifying" and uplifting through murals of assertion and cultural renewal. One of these is the "salsa heroes mural," which he painted in 1996 without pay, outside a pawnshop at the corner of 104th Street and Third Avenue; it featured past and present New York–based Puerto Rican salsa heroes such as Ismael Rivera, Hector Lavoe, Tito Puente, and Marc Anthony.

Yet the days of free murals are long gone for De la Vega, whose notoriety has placed him at the center of debates over his role in the area's gentrification. As noted earlier, artists are recognized agents of gentrification, many times to their own regret. But no one has been as aggressive as De la Vega in seeking new audiences by advertising throughout the city (mostly through chalk messages on sidewalks), hosting open workshops, selling "I Love Spanish Harlem" T-shirts, and holding neighborhood tours for high school and college students, even creating the artwork for the Latino-themed show *Luis*. And centrally located at the "heart" of the crossroads, De la Vega is matched by few artists in attracting so much attention and criticism. Some uphold him as an example to follow, while others resent him for turning their neighborhood into a ghetto "show and tell." Still others feel he has distanced himself from his roots, commercializing his art and embracing and expediting the area's gentrification.

The fact is that De la Vega is doing nothing new; he is just more aggressive than his predecessors. Still, he does not buy into the marketing furor, as he is often accused. Not unlike other street artists, he also cultivates a "noncommercial" identity by drawing the fluid though rhetorically important distinction between what he described as "artists who fight against the machine and those that paint for the sake of money." He has refused to repaint the salsa heroes mural to accommodate some advertising. Another local painter was quick to take the opportunity to accommodate the store owner who wanted to depict the acclaimed landmark in advertising for his store. Repainted, the mural now features chains, bracelets, watches, wedding rings, electric pianos, guitars, DVD players, and other products sold in the EZ-Pawn Store inside, flanking the famous musicians along with an oversized sign of "WE BUY."

What De la Vega increasingly favors are the kind of commercial proposals that give him greater notoriety but allow him to maintain his "noncommercial," greater "artistic" image. When Old Navy opened its store on Thirty-fourth Street, he agreed to provide the event with an "urban feel" by painting on the sidewalk. During one of my first visits to his studio, I encountered a Madison Avenue gallery owner who had learned about De la Vega through the artist's postings of his name throughout the city as a form of advertising. There was also a fashionably clothed visitor proposing that he paint the background for a fashion show by Oscar de la Renta. This sparked the immediate interest of the artist because "de la Renta is Dominican," and because their matching names would make this "not just marketing" but "a nice fit." Though it never materialized, the proposal demonstrates the commercial value of De la Vega's urban work and the types of balances street artists commonly strike to control their message and their image. The primary distinction De la Vega makes is thus not around one's engagement in commercial and promotional work or having commercial interests fund or become associated with your message, but rather—and in a move evocative of the concerns of other area artists and activists—whether a message remains autonomous or is tainted and compromised by the commercial involvement. As De la Vega added, whether sponsored by the Hope Foundation or Old Navy, it is he who decides the content and nature of his message and the images he paints. Granted, De la Vega has come a long way since he painted free murals, and unlike other street artists, he can afford a degree of autonomy in his work. Most often, murals commissioned by merchants display more directly whatever services are rendered and products sold; the mural for the pawnshop with the salsa musicians or the mural outside the hardware store are cases in

Figure 14.   Commissioned mural by Delta. Photo by the author.

point. The distinctions he makes, however, underscore the active struggles over artistic legitimacy and representation that are waged around wall space in El Barrio. These struggles revolve around multiple axes, but are largely at odds with outdoor advertising's arbitrary and solely commercial treatment of urban space. And perhaps more centrally so, they are always at odds with marketers' preference for preassembled eightsheet posters over commissioned street art.

Still, De la Vega's overt marketing of himself and his work has not escaped criticism. When his murals were inexplicably vandalized, defaced in black paint in the summer of 2002, rumors spread that far from a personal message or vendetta by another street artist, it was a challenge to his overt marketing practices. Some believed he had crossed the line with his promotion of his work and of El Barrio, indicating residents' awareness of the precariousness of marketing as an assertion strategy. For others, this scandalous act gave them more reason to support De la Vega. An anonymous letter in *Siempre* touted that his murals "belonged to the community, they were no longer of De la Vega," that it was not him, but the "community" that had been damaged by this act.[11] This incident vividly indicates the range of responses and sentiments triggered by the ongoing attempts at marketing culture in El Barrio; although an important resource against the area's gentrification, it is never an uncontested move. Unwritten rules are always at play in regards to how much to market the area, for what purposes, to whom, and for what ends. These are concerns that are shared by street artists and residents, even if different criteria about appropriate artistic recognition and financial return are always at play.

Yet it is his new "new agey art," in the words of another artist, that has attracted most visibility, but also local criticism. Although murals were the catalyst to his success, the artist has since moved away from them to other types of public art, particularly conceptual, didactic, or moralizing chalk and paint inscriptions. And in a context where nationalist icons, flags, and heroes dominate local murals, De la Vega's move quickly attracted attention, hence the "new agey" label. De la Vega explains that this decision was made solely on the basis of his individual artistic trajectory, although his motivations were also tied to changes in the neighborhood itself.

De la Vega had first turned to murals to address the decay and abandonment of East Harlem, which he found "run down," full of empty walls and abandoned buildings that he thought could be improved by a mural with strong symbolic messages, an image or a flag. But in his view, new construction and renovations have rendered this task largely irrelevant. To make his point, he referred to the site of one of his early murals, "In Memory of Sammy," on 102nd Street, which was erased after the building was bought and renovated by Mt. Sinai Hospital. Many of his earlier murals have suffered a similar fate and are now seen only on postcards and other paraphernalia for sale in his studio. De la Vega still paints murals if commissioned, but his primary work revolves around temporary chalk inscriptions painted mostly on the street. This choice is obviously not unrelated to the area's gentrification and antigraffiti legislation, informed as it was by the greater accessibility of streets in comparison to building walls, where permits need to be negotiated with merchants and landlords. Most significantly, De la Vega's artwork and messages have also shifted. As if to stress their universal reach, his works are no longer solely directed at the Puerto Rican community, nor do they touch on political and social issues; they are rather philosophical messages instilling individual progress and well being. In fact, his taglines are a direct invocation of the aspirational dreamworld ethos burgeoning over East Harlem as a result of new developments: "Become your dream," "You are your own best investment," "The struggle for survival in the big city makes you loose sight of your dreams." Moreover, his messages, all signed "De la Vega," are no longer limited to El Barrio, but rather can now be found in white chalk along Park Avenue and in Soho, as well as imprinted in the photographs of his street work and T-shirts for sale in his El Barrio studio/gallery storefront. This move has been interpreted as a reflection of the artist's embrace of middle-class ideology, or even to his conception of dreams as a space of liberation (Fuentes Rivera 2002). Certainly, it also speaks to his artistic aspirations: the supposedly universal appeal and applicability of art prevails over and above its ever present ethnic, cultural, and social content and significance. What I find noteworthy in this larger discussion are the connections between his shift in imagery and style and the processes of gentrification now at play. These processes and his work are mutually related, fueling and affecting one another. This is one of the reasons why De la Vega's "new agey messages" are seen suspiciously by many of his critics as more approving and appeasing of the rapid changes in the area rather than as critical or questioning of gentrification. De la Vega largely shuns these criticisms, maintaining that his objective is to create a context of respect and integration. "What are we going to do, scream to people that they should get out of East Harlem? We can't do that, but we can foster respect of differences," he conceded. What he is unable to affect, however, is the larger context of gentrification, the same context that makes his work so symbolically important and that affects people's reception of his work.

Conversations with the artist, however, reveal that while often criticized for abandoning his roots, as in the move for more "human" images and messages, De la Vega has neither lost nor stopped cultivating an urban Latino/a style that is also an expression of Latinidad. In fact, his new themes and images may be regarded as less "Puerto Rican" or "Latino" within the highly charged context of gentrification, but they are unequivocally seen and consumed as authentic by many locals and outsiders alike. After all, it is De la Vega's renowned El Barrio origins and persona that attract locals and outsiders to his shop, and that sustain his legitimacy as an "urban" public artist. His messages and street art are also very much informed by his involvement in El Barrio. In his words, "I am not painting any gringo faces in El Barrio." Arguably, then, De la Vega and the local reception of this work are best seen as expressions and conduits to debates over the area's gentrification. He is seen by some to promote and condone gentrification, but his work is at best ambivalent about it. Perhaps the best example is the mural he painted along 101st Street close to the yuppie hangout Dinerbar. As if a warning or a call for action, De la Vega's tagline—"Don't think for a minute that we have not noticed that the 96th boundary has moved further north"—is flanked by a rising fist on the left and a flying dove to the right. It speaks both to residents' anger over the area's gentrification and to their aspirations to place, not to mention their determination to stay in El Barrio.

Altogether, though with different objectives, De la Vega and other artists are, not unlike outdoor marketers, centrally involved in promoting and maintaining a distinct Latino feel in the area, acting through overt nationalistic messages, through abstract messages that are nonetheless connected to local aspirations, or through commercial murals that represent the local neighborhood. Insofar as ethnic marketing requires the existence of a culturally specific niche, which can be marketed as such, outdoor marketing will likely continue to reinstate El Barrio's public identity as a Latinized neighborhood, possibly in stark contradiction with its ongoing transformations. What the work and outlook of De la Vega and other street artists suggests—relative to advertising—is that the area's Latinness is never easily reducible to particular images or icons. Instead, it is always tied directly to transformations and specific developments in the community, connected unavoidably to local tensions, in this case, to tensions triggered by processes of gentrification. Their work and their images serve as important forums for debate over

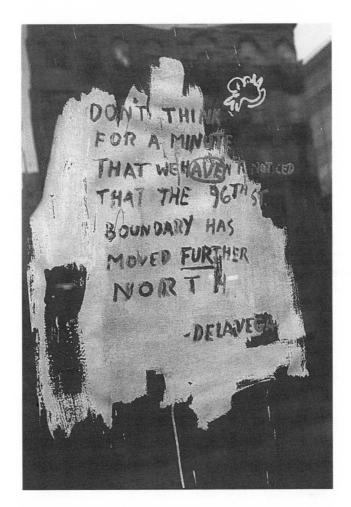

Figure 15. Writing by James De la Vega. Photo courtesy of
Rebecca Cooney.

the future of El Barrio, fostering and feeding into conversations about the
gains and perils of its ongoing transformation. That is, they become a
conduit of protest, expression, competition, and wider dynamics in the
community at large; they are sensitive barometers of local tensions and
changing demographics of their area, which belong to the moment, not

solely to corporations' need for ethnic niche markets and images. For marketers, walls in El Barrio are interchangeable with those of any other "Latino" neighborhood in the city. The goal is to anchor El Barrio for future profit, and this has particular consequences for whatever is involved and for whoever has a right to this space. Once again, in the contest over space, it is not necessarily the promotion or negation of a "Latino content," or the marketing of culture, or, in this case, of street art, that is ultimately at stake, but rather on what basis, who and what is involved in its promotion, and how they can participate culturally and economically in this activity. By necessity, then, the public conversation between advertising and street art should be gauged against the artists that now make a name, a living, and a claim to these walls, as well as on the types of economies and different artistic forms that are fostered in them. Most important, they need to be gauged around the messages, exchanges, and critiques that are facilitated, or hindered, by these analogous, yet starkly different expressive forms.

Some Final Words

El Barrio Unido Jamás Sera Vendido
[A United Barrio Will Never Be Sold]

Chant for antigentrification march
organized by Harlem's Tenant Council

There is no such thing as an "ending" when the everyday struggles of a community facing such rapid transformations as El Barrio are concerned. But one of the most moving meetings I attended prompts me to re-cap some recurring issues around the cultural politics of space in East Harlem/El Barrio, and the multiple issues that are currently at stake. Once again, I start with an exchange taking place at a public hearing, if only to call attention to the everyday debates triggered by neoliberal policies and processes of gentrification. The May 2002 hearing debated the contested eviction of the Rosarios' Gladiators wrestling program from the Thomas Jefferson Park. This program had been held in the park consistently from 1973 to January 2002, when it was swiftly evicted after one written notice and the boxing equipment was quickly removed overnight. This took place amid allegations by the Parks Department of a physical altercation,

Figure 16.   Antigentrification rally organized by Harlem's Tenant Council. Photo by the author.

the inappropriate filings of permits, and failed procedures over the use of the space, and counteraccusations from the Rosarios of harassment and wrongdoing by the Parks Department.

But this time, the hearing was not a contested show of disparate opinions, but a unified show of support for the Rosarios and a condemnation of the Parks Department. The men, both Black and Puerto Rican residents, thanked the couple for the faith and dedication they had invested in them as children. They credited the Rosarios with turning them into the responsible and righteous citizens that now stood before them as professionals, as fathers, and as community leaders. The women spoke on behalf of their children who had no access to public space and recreation due to diminishing after-school programs and recreational resources. They thanked the Rosarios for steering their children in the right direction, for protecting them from drugs and crime. All together the event became symbolic of larger transformations in El Barrio. As district leader

Carmen Quiñones summoned to the audience: "They are taking our home and our land. We are still being sold. We are in a battle every single day. It sends a statement, if we let this happen, that you can come into East Harlem and do whatever you want to do." The program was equated with heart, with life, with culture, and with El Barrio, as residents defended the Rosarios and by extension asserted their claim to space, as well as to services in the community, particularly those provided by its residents with their own needs in mind. In the passionate words of one of the speakers: "Thirty years of giving with the heart are wasted with this decision. The Rosarios gave heart. Every time there is a program that gives from the heart, if people give their life, their culture, if it means something, they take it away. But I say *Viva el Barrio! Viva los Rosario!* [Long live El Barrio and the Rosarios]."

Framing these concerns were rumors that the eviction was guided by the demands for an adult fitness program by the residents of a nearby co-op and by middle-class residents moving to the area as a result of impending new developments. This realization exposed how the needs of middle-class adults and new development initiatives could easily take precedence over those of children and longtime residents. Most of all, the eviction displayed the ease with which governmental approval over the use of public space and social services by neighborhood and community groups can be disregarded on account of technicalities, be they failure to follow proper paperwork procedures, or alleged altercations, or else, some feared, whenever more upscale constituencies asserted a need for a particular space or institution. Indeed, as was amply evident at the hearing, this was not the first time community groups had been ousted from public parks in recent years.

The Gladiators' case has since faded from public view, though it is not forgotten, certainly not by those who were ousted or by their supporters. But the case stood out as a vivid example of the trends and tensions I had repeatedly witnessed in East Harlem. Demonstrated also was the preeminence of the tenets of business and efficiency, even when the space in question, a public park's facility, was not intended for privatization. For among other allegations, the Rosarios were evicted because they had failed to follow proper procedures for the use of space, and because they lacked a board of directors, that is, for being "inefficient" and thus vulnerable targets for eviction. As in other instances described in this work, residents deployed alterative ways of evaluating institutions, services, and programs where "people give from their heart, their life, their culture." But to little avail. Alongside the upscaling of El Barrio there was little room for claims based on any other basis than "efficiency," progress, and profitability.

The preceding chapters showed similar dynamics at play throughout different development initiatives in El Barrio, from home ownership programs, to the Empowerment Zone, to charter schools. On and on, these programs were invariably promoted through the tenets of efficiency, increased accountability, and progress, while the bases on which those services and claims to space had been gained in the past were repeatedly questioned as failed and outdated. Seldom did this quandary result in the kind of outrage aroused by this eviction. Residents were many times critical of their public and social-service institutions, from public schools to housing, not to mention their elected officials, and eager to embrace alternatives for change. People were especially critical of past "empowerment" policies that had done little to bring about lasting change in the community, but in fact had kept them down with social programs, never with lasting infrastructure. Indeed, the current neoliberal moment is only but a new, arguably more aggressive, chapter in a long history of policies and developments leading to El Barrio's marginalization. People were amply aware of this. But as in the Gladiators' hearing, whenever residents defended particular spaces on grounds other than economic sustainability, business, and profits, they were repeatedly challenged.

A variety of factors were involved in promoting the dominance of consumption-based developments as mediums of progress and upward mobility. Among them is the area's history of neglect and of lacks and needs, against which virtually no alternative to privatized-driven development was forthcoming. An attending development ideology favoring consumption-based developments was also at play. In this context, people could only debate, but never challenge, these policies outright. Home ownership programs surfaced as a solution to the lack of housing alternatives, as the purchase of place and the privatization of services, an assurance of their future in El Barrio. Cultural activists, for their part, were told that learning the "right ways" of carrying on cultural work through the development of marketable and self-sustaining cultural institutions would assure the development of tourism in El Barrio, an aim many associated with the broader goal of securing the area's Latino heritage for years to come. Each time, a discourse of business and consumption was circulated, and each time residents were faced with multiple contradictions. Home ownership did little for the displaced and the poor and provided no guarantees that East Harlemites would be the main beneficiaries from these developments. Charter schools would only provide for a few selected children. Meanwhile, the marketing of Latino culture prioritized visitors rather than residents and their needs for entertainment and cultural venues, necessarily limiting residents' freedom and ability to control how culture will be promoted and defined.

The promotion of these consumption-based alternatives was in turn accompanied by a disavowal of ethnicity and identity discourses, long deployed to demand equity and empowerment, in favor of treatments of culture that emphasized its utility for business and industry. Through policy guidelines, in workshops and in meetings, East Harlemites were repeatedly told that it was marketable ethnicity, that is, culture as "sustainable" business and industry, that was the legitimating mode for economic development and political empowerment. All the while, claims based on the rights of Puerto Ricans and Latinos for cultural assertion and cultural rights to place, to institutions and to control of developments, were discredited as discourses of the past that needed to be superseded if real development was to be obtained. The greatest irony here is that ethnic and racial identifications were in effect not in contradiction but in conversation with contemporary developments. In fact, I hope to have shown that while ethnicity and race are increasingly attacked as discourses for equity and empowerment, they are in effect the bases on which spatial transformations in urban cities are being waged. After all, ethnic pride and Puerto Rican and Latino claims to El Barrio were many times at the heart of people's embracing neoliberal logics favoring the privatization and purchasing of place.

This is why I have repeatedly called attention to the culturalist and class underpinnings of contemporary neoliberal initiatives and to the ways they often beguile nationalist and class identifications. I already pointed to the contradictory synergy between outside developers and Puerto Rican residents and their middle-class-centered definitions and aspirations, and the ease by which ethnic pride could be capitalized by politicians and developers. But most directly, in policies such as the EZ's Cultural Industry Investment Fund, residents were asked to think about their culture in marketing terms, triggering debates about what culture, constituency, or institution was more worthy of funding. Such debates were very much triggered by politicians and development enthusiasts. Most important, these policies helped circulate a consumption ethos where purchasing power or particular cultural competencies predicated access to these spaces. As a direct outcome, dreams of Puerto Ricans' class empowerment nourished their ethnic solidarity, but not without simultaneously furthering gaps between the same ethnic-defined constituency, such as those between Puerto Rican development enthusiasts and the poor. After all, the groups most involved with and invested in creating an "identity of place" for El Barrio and in promoting contemporary initiatives (from home ownership programs to tourism) were in effect those who, on account of their background, education, and class, were less dependent on existing state-driven services and structures. That is, they were more likely to benefit from options emphasizing choice and consumption than East Harlem's neediest, and they were in a better position to dream that they could wrest some control of this type of development for themselves and for El Barrio.

Alternative frameworks and seemingly antieconomic values of community and culture used to construct El Barrio as an "inalienable" space for Puerto Ricans and Latinos are never entirely politically or economically disinterested. El Barrio's cultural and historical value was in effect deployed to assert rights to space, to services, to institutions, and to things that could be potentially transferable to money, to resources, and political power, but only by those with some economic capital or political connections. Indeed, culture is always intrinsically bound up in everyday economies. What I have sought to call attention to are the different approaches, bases, and perspectives to the marketing and promotion of culture that are always at play. As pivotal as culture may be for urban economic development initiatives, not all types and manifestations of "culture" are profitably or economically viable. Issues of race, ethnicity, identity, and political disenfranchisement affect the "rentability" of culture, variables that will play out differently in historically and regionally specific contexts. Thus my insistence that a Latino content or Latino-directed cultural urban policy is neither a buffer to gentrification nor a conduit of Latino empowerment. This situation points to the intersection of class, culture, and history in the making and maintenance of social marginality. Put simply, as upwardly mobile as Puerto Ricans may have become in El Barrio, their status is ultimately circumscribed by a "tainted" heritage, one that has yet to be successfully valued and promoted in and of itself without compromising openness. This explains the many difficulties encountered by middle-class Puerto Ricans to "cash" in on their culture, which is limited and never commensurable with projects and development initiatives promoted by unracially marked developers and development initiatives. Whether it is all a matter of time before Puerto Rican culture becomes consumable remains a quandary. For now, these chapters suggest that as popular as Puerto Rican or Latino culture may become, they have yet to translate into lasting infrastructure in the neoliberal city. This task remains a difficult one; the marketability of a culture never comes without a cost.

But there were also hopeful moments in this story. Against the EZ's efforts to promote marketable ethnicity, which would be cleansed from its past and thus attractive to tourism, East Harlemites continued to seek ways to promote culture as a medium of cultural assertion and validation, not to mention as a venue of assuring some participation in the economy of culture. On and on, their attempts prioritized alternative logics for evaluating projects and were never solely about securing El Barrio for private profit. Such is the case with cultural activists intent on cultural programming that was politically informed by the community's history and continued struggles in the present; or with the work of street artists; or with Mexicans' claims for community control of Mexican events; or Puerto Ricans' demands for equity in EZ funding, and with numerous claims by East Harlemites for the use of public space and access to quality services and institutions commensurate to those enjoyed by their prosperous and non-raced counterparts. Each time residents insisted on evaluative criteria that prioritized openness, opportunity, community, history, accountability, and representation, evincing that people can never be entirely, nor so easily, removed from any "cultural" entrepreneurial initiative, be they as actors, participants, or constituencies.

Given this, there is a need to reevaluate, rather than deride and devalue, the validity of discourses of culture identity and community that are deployed by place-brokers and cultural activists in El Barrio. Such discourses were consistently delegitimated as narrow, or out of touch with the economic, political, urban, and cultural policy circles, particularly when used as mediums of assertion, or when used in opposition to policies that did not favor Puerto Ricans' and Latinos' claims to space. Instead I propose that we question and scrutinize the fallacies on which neoliberal discourses and policies are predicated, and the consensus with which they are vested. Here I hope to have shown how the urban neoliberal policies promoted as the solution to East Harlem's problems were based on people, institutions, and programs proving their worthiness, entrepreneurship, and marketability, processes that are always entrenched in social inequalities. Most important, neoliberal policies and developments draw on and capitalize pervasive discourses of race and ethnicity while ignoring them as bases for inequities. In this context ethnic-based claims are significant and necessary. They at least helped reinstate the political importance of ethnic identities and of ethnic-based demands so negated by contemporary urban policies where it is culture as industry and aesthetics (the proper museum, advertisements, and so on) that prevails. Specifically, cultural debates in El Barrio evoke politicized claims while calling attention to attendant inequalities that result from these policies. They bring attention to the fact that developers and marketers of the Upper Manhattan EZ and other urban policies, past and present, do not simply target the raceless poor; they target particular groups with particular histories and previous experiences with policies that failed them, and with developers that always got their way. Most of all, they expose the impossibility for urban policies, developers, and politicians of ever disavowing ethnicity.

That ethnicity and its politicization by residents are so suspect in the current neoliberal moment may therefore suggest that they constitute an important challenge to the attending economic discourses that envelope everyday life in East Harlem and beyond. I say this while fully aware of the challenges always presented by ethnic and nationalist politics. These positions invariably complicated intraethnic and racial relations, as was the case with African Americans and Puerto Ricans, whose debates often obscured that large corporations were the greatest beneficiaries of development proposals for Upper Manhattan communities. But nationalist and cultural citizenship strategies within groups and intra and interethnic coalitions across groups run in parallel ways. Sometimes, nationalist stances even facilitated the organization of different constituencies in ways that later bore collaborations across groups. This was the case of Mexicans and Puerto Ricans, groups that live *"juntos pero no revueltos"* but that nevertheless also reached out to each other, as in the realm of electoral politics, where it is as "Latinos," not as single constituencies, that they hold the most consequence. This was also the case with Puerto Ricans and African Americans. After all, it is as Puerto Ricans and Latinos that Puerto Rican activists have historically negotiated with nearby Harlem and with the area's Black leadership at the level of city and state government. It is through these identities that they struggled, but also cooperated in mutual causes, as in Blacks' and Puerto Ricans' common appeal from the community board over the EZ's treatment of East Harlem, or their shared demand for the improvement of East Harlem's schools and their common denunciation of the Rosarios' park eviction. It is also as particular constituencies that they came together in the Harlem Tenant's Council antigentrification march in 2002. This day, there were few Puerto Ricans and Mexicans in the march, but those present carried their flags, effectively representing two larger constituencies.

Finally, discourses of national identity and cultural citizenship are oftentimes the only recourse left with which to demand political rights, as was particularly evident among Mexicans, who have the least number of openings in the political terrain in which to maneuver for rights and entitlements. Perhaps most important, the outcomes of ethnic claims voiced by and for particular groups were never narrowly limited to particular groups. In calling attention to issues of representation and cultural and economic parity, these claims always had greater repercussions for other Latinos, not to mention for all East Harlemites. Namely, they evoked neoliberalism's investments in ethnic and racial politics, creating disjunctions in the supposedly business-oriented and race- and ethnic-free canons of neoliberal politics, unsettling the pretenses that the market can in fact provide for all, equally and fairly, particularly for ethnic subjects. In so doing people presented a set of demands for cultural equality that can never be easily contained and neutralized by these policies. Hence the need to extricate the different aspirations, identities, claims, and politics that are sustained and communicated by different deployments of culture, even when these may be caught up in the same dynamics of privatized development and, in this case, gentrification.

For while oftentimes entrenched in the same dominant discourses and processes, the dreams and aspirations of Puerto Rican and Latino culture brokers in El Barrio are starkly at odds with the paradigms generalized by the neoliberal policies they must maneuver. Theirs is a vision that impels their rightful inclusion in these new developments, as home owners, planners, and consultants, as artists and creators and equal beneficiaries of economic development. Even if a fleeting dream that is available to few, while embraced by so many, this view communicates a different claim and politics than that associated with neoliberal policies. Specifically, it demands equality and economic empowerment, by and for particularized constituencies who have historically been most deprived from these gains, requests that will not dim while they are left unanswered. The fact is that current ethnic and cultural identifications are being concurrently fueled by a variety of political and commercial interests, and are thus not about to fade, as long as they are profitable, politically marketable, and viable. For worse, or perhaps, for better, the neoliberal city feeds from the symbolic, particularly from culture and identity. For better, because doing so displays its contradictions for all to confront and see, guiding us toward more appropriate and equitable urban and cultural policies.

Notes

INTRODUCTION

1. East Harlem is part of New York's designated Empowerment Zone (EZ), one of the first six urban EZs introduced after the law came into effect in 1994. Additional zones are located in Chicago, Detroit, Baltimore, and the Philadelphia-Camden (New Jersey) metropolitan area and in cities as varied as Pulaski County, Ark.; Syracuse, N.Y.; Fresno, Calif.; and San Antonio, Texas.

2. By "Latinidad," I refer to the enactments, definitions, and representations of Latino culture, widely recognized to be outcomes of social processes of struggle and negotiation.

3. According to the 2000 census, for instance, Latinos comprise 52.1 percent of East Harlem's population, followed by African Americans at 35.7 percent. While whites constitute 7.3 percent, this group is visibly growing in the community. Among Latinos, Puerto Ricans are still the largest subgroup, making up 57.7 percent of the Latino population, followed by Mexicans and Dominicans, at 16.9 and 7.7 percent, respectively.

4. According to Manhattan Community District designations (Manhattan Community Board 11: 2000, 1), East Harlem includes three neighborhoods—El Barrio/Spanish Harlem (East Ninety-sixth to East 125th Street), East Harlem Tri-

angle (East 125th Street to East 142nd Street); Little Italy (Third Avenue to the Harlem River); and Randall's and Ward's Islands. Yet these distinctions are perceived in contrasting ways by different residents of East Harlem. Most often, however, East Harlem or El Barrio is used by residents to refer to the entire uptown area of East Harlem, from Ninety-sixth to 142nd Street. The area's most Latino/a component (its central section from Ninety-sixth to 125th Street), however, is recognized as the one under most intense gentrification.

5. For instance, the city council district includes sections of the Upper West Side, a wealthier section of the city, which local residents consider starkly at odds with East Harlem.

6. Important social science works focusing on El Barrio include Bourgois (1995), Freidenberg (1995, 2000), Lewis (1968), Elena Padilla (1958), and Wakefield (1959). In regards to the representation of the area, see Rodríguez (1995) for a review of the portrayal of Puerto Ricans in historical and social science research. As Rodríguez notes, the colonial situation, the lack of Puerto Rican writers, and the strict and overdetermining application of social science research paradigms and categories all served to pathologize Puerto Ricans in the journalistic, government, public, and academic literature. This representation was most hurtful to communities heavily populated by Puerto Ricans, such as El Barrio.

7. Many of these expressive forms are in fact the products of resistance and appropriation of space by Puerto Ricans' experiences with displacement and urban renewal in New York, as Aponte-Parés (1998) rightly notes in his well-known essay on the *casitas.* See also the works of El Barrio authors Mohr (1986), Thomas (1967), and Quiñonez (2000) for important literary portrayals of Puerto Rican life in El Barrio, and of El Barrio's significance for Puerto Ricans' coming of age.

8. Socioeconomic and housing information is drawn from U.S. Census Bureau, 2000 Census, STF3, SF1, as compiled by the Population Division of the New York City Department of City Planning for 2002 obtained on their Web site in January 2003 (http://www.ci.nyc.ny.us/html/dcp/html/lucds/cdstart.html.). Comparison data for 1980 and 1990 was drawn from New York City Department of City Planning (Socioeconomic Profiles 1993). Regarding its diminishing land, East Harlem still houses a great number of vacant lots in Manhattan (703 of the 2,349 available lots), but East Harlem's real estate is quickly diminishing. In 1995, there were 937 vacant lots, but in 2002 this number had diminished to 703. Compare, for instance, the number of lots listed in Community Board 11 (2000) with those listed in its annual district needs for 2002/2003 (New York City Department of City Planning 2002/2003). Meanwhile, in 1999 rents in stabilized buildings increased 10.2 percent, the highest increase rate in rents for the borough of Manhattan; see New York City Rent Guidelines Board (1999), based on the 1999 Housing Vacancy Survey.

9. See Comaroff and Comaroff (2000), Chomsky (1999), Storper (2000), and

Goode and Maskovsky (2001) for more discussion of the tenets and operations of neoliberalism in the economic, financial, and cultural realms; and Ruben (2001) for how these policies play out in urban development models. Chomsky in particular highlights the fallacies of equating neoliberalism with free markets and with lack of government intervention. As he notes, neoliberal policies thrive on government subsidies, though these are directed to particular sectors and business interests, such as private corporations or to middle classes. And always, these policies entail new techniques of government and new definitions of good citizenship that de-link the citizen from the state. See for instance Brin Hyatt 2001; and Maskovsky 2001. Escobar's telling description of "development" as technology of government, whereby "development policies" are tied to the reproduction of inequalities and marginalization of communities, is also relevant here, where privatization is furthered through the discourse of development (1995). Finally, Lisa Duggan's examination of the perilous effects of neoliberalism on political discourse and its effects on the politics of race and sexuality and her critique of the fallacious separation of economic, political, and cultural fields, on which neoliberal policies are predicated, is also directly relevant to this discussion (Duggan 2003).

10. See for instance Abu-Lughod (1991), Brumann (1999), Segal and Handler (1995), and Ortner (1999), among others, who have explored the ideological precepts of this concept. Briefly, scholars have critically exposed the assumptions of homogeneity and harmony, consensus, authenticity, and other misleading meanings that are continually associated with the term.

11. For instance, middle and upwardly middle-class status among Latinos is often uncritically associated with particular nationalities, such as Cubans, with little critical attention to class as a variable among Latinos, although there are now important exceptions in this area; see, for instance, Valle and Torres (2000).

12. In this context, idioms of ethnicity, multiculturalism, and cultural difference that increasingly supplant those of race are best seen as indexes of enduring practices of racialization, always deployed to the least assimilable groupings.

13. East Harlem's Black population is not homogeneous. It includes West Indian and African immigrants, and differences of citizenship and nationality matter, although they are largely veiled in everyday politics. My interdependent usage of the labels Black and African American and dominant use of "Black" politicians responds to the veiling of such distinctions in everyday politics and practice. See Biondi (2003) for a succinct discussion of the usage of these terms as political categories.

14. This lack of documentation echoes a general void in works looking at relationships among Black and Latinos, a relationship at the forefront of public debate especially after the 2000 census, showing Latinos outpacing Blacks as the biggest minority group. See Mindiola, Niemann, and Rodríguez (2002), an important work looking at Black and Latino politics in contemporary cities.

15. As of 2001, Black elected officials outnumber Latinos in the New York City Council, State Senate, State Assembly, and U.S. House of Representatives, in some cases almost at a rate of two to one. Asian Americans, again, are the least represented minority in elected positions.

16. Sorting out voting patterns around race and ethnicity is extremely difficult and largely speculative, given the lack of information to identify voters around these variables. Still, a recent study on Latino political participation (conducted through Hispanic surname analysis of voter registration records) by the Hispanic Federation (2002), confirms the lower participation of New York Latinos, especially those who live in predominantly Latino neighborhoods, likely due also to the intersection of other variables, such as class and education.

17. Adam Clayton Powell IV is the son of former U.S. Representative Adam Clayton Powell Jr. (1908–1972) and Puerto Rican Yvette Diago, whose father was a former mayor of San Juan in the 1940s. Charles Rangel is known by many Puerto Ricans as the product of a Puerto Rican father and African American mother. In a phone conversation, George Dalley, his chief of staff in Washington, however, denied this. Rangel never knew his father, except that he came from a southern town in Virginia, though Rangel has never denied the possibility of a Puerto Rican background. It helps his politics, but he has not asserted it forthright. Rangel defeated Adam Clayton Powell Jr. in 1970.

18. There are fifty-nine community boards in New York City representing the views of particular communities. Their recommendations are not binding, though they need to be consulted on most land-use issues. They are composed of volunteer members who must live, work, or have particular interests (such as own property) in the district.

CHAPTER ONE

1. See Community Service Society of New York (1998). This involves 40 percent of public housing stock and 22 percent of other publicly funded housing. New Directions: East Harlem, El Barrio, Randall's and Ward's Islands. Manhattan Community Board 11 (2000).

2. Though tenants can also obtain some of these properties, they have not benefited from these disposition programs as much as nonprofit and private developers have. Because the transfer process is between individual entities and parties, rather than among multiple tenants, the transfer of properties runs smoother and faster, leaving nonprofits and private developers as the greatest beneficiaries of these policies.

3. Sánchez-Korrol also notes that as early as the mid-1920s 60 percent of the Puerto Rican migrant population lived in two areas of Manhattan, spanning Ninetieth Street to 116th, between First and Fifth avenues, and 110th Street to

125th Street between Fifth and Manhattan avenues, communities known as El Barrio or La Colonia Hispana (1983, 58).

4. See Sexton (1965) for a more detailed discussion of the distribution of space around ethnicity between African Americans and Italians. She noted in particular the role of the commuters' railroad track on Park Avenue and 102nd Street as a boundary isolating groups from each other, as well as how public housing itself served to further segregate East Harlem around race and ethnicity; the area north of the projects was Black, and to the south, Puerto Rican. She also describes how tenement buildings, and even blocks, were divided between these groups. In other words, she paints a world of neighbors who lived both together and divided.

5. Sexton (1965). A void of research on how housing policies affected Puerto Rican settlements as well as a general lack of research on the history of Puerto Ricans in New York hinders a more accurate assessment of these trends.

6. Sánchez (1990), 436, quoting Anderson (1964).

7. As Sánchez notes, from 1950 to 1980, Puerto Ricans had rates similar to Blacks as recipients of public welfare but were largely behind them as recipients of public housing. Sánchez argues that Puerto Ricans were just as needy as Blacks, but that they lacked political power. This further shows, he argues, that Puerto Ricans were seen as a peripheral labor force, hence their relegation to the more vulnerable and less permanent aid of welfare rather than housing (Sánchez 1990).

8. Such is the case of Taft and Johnson Houses where Blacks constituted 59 and 58 percent of initial occupants versus 35.8 and 25.4 percent for Puerto Ricans (Sánchez 1990, 563).

9. Other housing projects were identified as more or less middle class or working class than others. These distinctions were based on the kinds of subsidies available to tenants, and whether some were co-ops or rentals, or were supposedly bigger or nicer than others. Interestingly, within these hierarchies, tenements, which are now generally most prized for their historic value were placed at the bottom of the hierarchy. More research is needed on how these hierarchies were drawn, and how they play out today.

10. Cultural pluralism, dominant in the 1960s, saw ethnicity as an integrative device, as a depolitized tool for the integration of distinct groups, each with its culture, into a harmonious whole, in terms similar to the policies and discourses of multiculturalism that arose two decades later.

11. Writing in the mid 1960s, at the height of these processes, Sexton (1965) describes the overwhelming power of social workers and clergy in East Harlem. Their power, she notes, stemmed from a variety of sources, such as white Protestant privilege, as well as their identification with the Democratic Party, which represented a challenge to the then powerful Italian and, to a lesser extent, Irish political machine. Sexton's description attests to the conflicts between an emerging leadership who felt controlled, abused, and undermined by social workers.

The social workers' alliances with middle classes and their conciliatory stance toward change was a particular cause of conflict.

12. I do not mean to suggest a commonality in outlook and politics among these Puerto Rican leaders and politicians at this time. They were indeed known to feud and disagree with one another during their tenure and collide over different programs and initiatives. By listing them as important political anchors in East Harlem, I seek rather to highlight the confluence of power they brought to East Harlem during the 1970s and 1980s.

13. See Barrett's exposé of their "kingdom" in the *Village Voice* (1985). More recent debates over Del Toro occurred shortly after Angelo Del Toro's death when a priest-led organization, the East Harlem Partnership for Change, requested to no avail a public audit of all public program funds managed in East Harlem by the Del Toros (Vega 1995). Many charged that they were targeted to deviate attention from corruption within the Koch administration. See González (1995) and McFadden (1995) for accounts of the networks of patronage prevalent then, and the repercussions of their political reign.

14. These include Los Tres Unidos, later renamed for Angelo Del Toro, and the Taino Towers, conceived and spearheaded by an East Harlem Tenants Council struggle in 1965. Both were built in the late 1970s and early 1980s, yet their sites and the struggles over monies long preceded their construction and were greatly aided by the political power attained by Puerto Rican politicians in East Harlem.

15. See Van Ryzin and Genn (1999) for a good overview of the effects of the ten-year plan in New York City. Obviously, there are progressive reasons why mixed-income housing should be promoted, provided displacement does not occur. For one, it provides a higher tax base to support public education. Oftentimes, however, the promotion of mixed-income housing, as well as of programs for residents that "create community," are also directly informed by William Julius Wilson's (1987) conceptualization of the underclass as isolated, where healthy neighborhoods involve the promotion of class- and ethnically diversified communities to counter the "ills" and "pathologies" of the lower classes. In other words, the premises are based on the middle-class "uplift ideology" that associates positive role models exclusively with middle classes while pathologizing the poor as always needy of social and cultural uplift. As shown by Sabiyha Prince's (2002a, 2002b) research with Black professional managerial workers in Harlem, there is ample acceptance of this middle-class uplift ideology among all class fractions, yet differences in how Black professionals interacted with broader community contradicted the facile view that the involvement of middle classes in low-income communities always leads to improvements in the quality of life of low-income community members. See also Lawson Clark (2002).

16. Fueling the debate was Mireya Navarro's (2000) front-page article, "Puerto Rican Presence Wanes in New York," which many believed purposely

disregarded Puerto Ricans and their presence in the city. Similar reports on the census in other newspapers practically erased Puerto Ricans by highlighting their "dwindling" numbers. As Angelo Falcón (2001), states, Puerto Ricans are still the largest Latino ethnic group in the city. That a decrease in their numbers, along with the dramatic growth and diversification of the Latino population, results in their erasure as a political force in the city is detrimental to the political power of the entire Latino community.

17. Michelle Boyd's (2000) description of what she regards as "racial nostalgia" in the redevelopment of Bronzeville, an African American neighborhood in Chicago's South Side, is relevant here. She speaks of how a marginalized past can be easily cleaned and represented in the process of making claims to the neighborhood and its development. The result is the favoring of middle classes, in this case, the Black middle classes, and of values congruent with development advocates while erasing the memories and needs of the poor.

18. Walls don't have to be physical or tangible, though public housing projects constitute both. See Marcuse's (1995) discussion of walls as metaphors and expressions of social divisions that simultaneously reflect and reinforce such divisions. Their ambiguous nature is evident here, where they serve multiple purposes and effects. Originated to contain the poor and consolidate the power of the powerful, they obviously insulate Latinos from prospective gentrifiers, and the area from development.

19. See Maskovsky (2001) for a discussion of how community participatory models can serve as mediums of regulation and government.

20. According to a coordinator of these plans in the city's Planning Office, as of the fall 2001, less than ten out of the fifty-nine existing community boards in the city had filed these plans, and only a few had been approved. Community Boards 9, 10, and 11, which represented Upper Manhattan, had all filed them.

21. This report was drafted by Calvert under commission from CIVITAS Inc., an Upper Manhattan community organization involved in quality-of-life issues on the Upper East Side and East Harlem, while he was also head of Calvert Associates, a real-estate consulting company.

22. It calls in particular for these buildings to be disposed through the city's Housing Preservation and Development Office and its Neighborhood Entrepreneur Program, the Neighborhood Revitalization Program, and the Tenant Interim Lease Program.

23. While community protests were credited for halting the project, it was stalled indefinitely by counterfiled lawsuits between Procter and Gamble and the developer and, in particular, by accusations of fraud, breach of contract, and racketeering (De Palma 1986). I thank Philippe Bourgois for this insight.

24. The rise in property prices is also directly spurred by city ownership programs. This is another negative outcome of these programs that may cause the

displacement of locals who are pushed by rising property and rental prices in the "revitalized" areas (Hevesi 2001).

25. Indeed, it is not surprising that those most enthused about home ownership and local entrepreneurship are those who have political contacts; or they are members of the community board and thus more likely to hear of coming developments and the application process; or they are people who were directly tied to their development and are most able to tap into these very scarce opportunities for home ownership.

26. Complaints about the marketing of home ownership programs were common, particularly developers' practice of counting residents of Community Board 10 (West Harlem) as "community," or East Harlem residents, when they counted the number of residents that bought or were housed in new projects in East Harlem.

27. See Pacenza (2002) for a good exposé on the eviction of immigrants by Hope and the difficulty immigrants face in Housing Court.

28. See Pacenza (2003) for a thorough discussion of the future implications of these trends for most Community Development Corporation initiatives and nonprofit developers.

29. Rates for apartments by Steve Kessner in 1998 quoted in Calvert (1998). Rates for 2001 were obtained over the phone on July 2001.

CHAPTER TWO

1. See http://lmcc.net/programs/indexprograms.html for a description of "Mapping New Terrain: Communities in Transition." It included a series of community dialogues during the summer and fall of 2001 and spring of 2002. Among them were "A Stranger in My Community," held on Jan. 22, 2002; "What Defines a Legend Most," Nov. 11, 2001; and "La Rosa del Barrio," on Oct. 24, 2001.

2. As noted earlier, by emphasizing the objectification of culture onto space I'm not suggesting that East Harlem's history is homogenous. East Harlem, as is also the case with Harlem, has always been more diverse than suggested by its representation and politicization by local actors, although the deployment of this history, not unlike the deployment of strict correlations of culture and space, are never politically insignificant.

3. These dynamics have been documented in relation to multiculturalism and, more broadly, for nationalist processes. Both of these entail essentialized definitions of identities, seen and presented as single, bounded, and identifiable with a unique history and cultural property that corroborates their existence and connects them with a past (See Coombe 1998; Segal and Handler 1995; and Williams 1989, among others who have documented these processes).

4. Readers will find ample evidence of this position in the discussion postings

of "Welcome to East Harlem Online," where it is not uncommon for Puerto Ricans—whether residents or not of El Barrio—to establish their claim to space and contribute to discussions about the status and fate of the area. See http://www.east-harlem.com\forum.

5. See Lefebvre's well-known distinction between the perceived, the conceived, and the lived components of space (as in spatial practices, representations of space, representational spaces), distinctions that foreground the different elements that, in their interconnections, constitute and imbue value to space as "social space" (Lefebvre 2000). Accordingly, space is always socially constituted, though not solely through physical boundaries, representations, or practices, but by the interaction of these various elements, which may sometimes coalesce or oppose one another, but most centrally, are always connected to how one understands, lives, and experiences a particular "space."

6. Anthropological work in material culture is helpful here, particularly Annette Weiner's (1992) conceptualization of the "inalienable," denoting possessions that—on account of their history or association with status—invoke a "transcendent" value to their keepers or owners. As she notes, land is perhaps the most inalienable of possessions, insofar as it "does not move" while it changes owners, underscoring the permanence of meanings, values, and hierarchies vested in particular places, never entirely expunged through their transfer. Specifically, the inalienable is produced through social relations, histories, and representations, and is never a state but a process, though one endowing things with dense cultural meaning and that, once constructed, seems immanent and natural. Most significantly, this meaning is transferable to status and identity for those with access, control, or possession of inalienable things (see Myers 2001).

7. The episode that is generally understood to have marked the political reign of Puerto Ricans was the election of Carolyn Maloney as councilwoman in the early 1980s. She was aided by the feud between two Puerto Rican candidates, Anazagasti and Roberto Rodríguez. who encountered each other in this race, leaving the way open for her election. She remained in office until 1992, when she became a congresswoman.

8. As a gay Black politician well known in AIDS advocacy circles, Reed likely experienced racism and homophobia. Most animosity, however, stemmed from the fact that he had been most favored by the West Side electorate. In other words, he was seen as someone who failed to understand the complicated issues of ethnicity and race that pervaded everyday politics. At the same time, his "outsider" status was also seen as an advantage by many residents who de-linked him from the established power bloc made up of long-time Harlem and East Harlem politicians.

9. Latino/a voters would have decreased from 53.6 to 50 percent (the number of Black voters would have also decreased from 25.5 to 23.3 percent). Extremely contentious was the expansion of boundaries of East Harlem to the west, thereby

increasing the number of middle-class voters from the Upper West Side. While Puerto Ricans bemoaned the potential losses for Latinos, African Americans also rejected the new boundaries contained in this first redistricting proposal on the basis that it would have cut out important sectors of East Harlem, such as the Taft Houses, Johnson Houses, Washington Houses, and even the offices of the present councilman Phil Reed. The final boundaries—going back to the same percentage of Latinos, standing approximately at 53.6—still included important voting blocs in the Upper West Side and the Bronx, although they did not coincide with the community board district, or the borders of East Harlem as residents know them (to be coterminous with the boundaries of the community board, the school district, etc.), and were not regarded equally representative of East Harlem.

10. While highlighting new initiatives, I do not mean to suggest that local activism is new in East Harlem, or that these were the only groups active at the time. Most significant, many groups are not organized around ethnicity or nationality, including religious, block, and tenant organizations. Previous initiatives deserve more attention than I can afford in these pages, as do new ones that continue to evolve in the area.

11. The census event was held in June 2001 and the self-education seminar in November 2001. They included a presentation on the census by the Puerto Rican Legal Defense and Education Fund, which focused on the demographic transformation in El Barrio. The self-education seminar included presentations from housing advocates, legal aid, and funding opportunities for local entrepreneurship.

12. One of the best expressions of the clash with dominant Hispanocentric definitions of culture represented by the Nuyorican movement is provided by the transcript of the conference and workshop on Puerto Rican culture organized by the Center for Puerto Rican Studies in 1974. It gathered anthropologists, historians, professors, and artists from Puerto Rico and New York. Evident in the debate is how the comments of El Barrio–born and raised artists such as Jorge Soto embrace openness, popular culture (salsa, Nuyorican poetry) innovation, and Puerto Rican's African legacy in contrast to the more conventional views of those of the island (Center for Puerto Rican Studies 1976).

13. As Sexton (1965) notes, the Triangle was primarily settled by African Americans migrating from the South and became one of the poorest and most autonomous areas of East Harlem. She describes how no social service organizations had "dared" come into the Triangle. Puerto Ricans, the new immigrants then, seemed to have provided better subjects, similar to the role played by Puerto Ricans in Chicago, that is as a buffer population, or model citizen vis-à-vis African Americans (see Pérez 2000). While this role was short-lived, it points to the fluency of social categories and historical categorizations of Puerto Ricans, another aspect mediating Black and Puerto Rican relations.

14. These are differences that are not only obviated in daily practice, but

oftentimes altogether ignored in social analyses. Consider Sanjek's study of neighborhood politics in New York City (2001). While focusing on one of the most multiculturally diverse neighborhoods in the city, it repeatedly subsumes difference into a conglomerate—"neighborhood New York." Included in this conglomerate are the working, lower, and middle classes, across race and ethnic backgrounds, who gathered in community board meetings and community discussions to debate the community's future. This group is contrasted to the "financial, business, and political elites of the city, or with its upper-middle-class professionals" in terms of its politics, interests, and dispositions (2000, 28). Through this focus, Sanjek concludes that there is hope for multicultural society, that the compromises achieved by people in neighborhoods in Queens can serve as examples for "us all." These auspicious conclusions, however, presuppose that we ignore cultural struggles that coexist within those groups, or the connections between members of "neighborhood New York" and "financial elites." The latter have always known how to tap into local knowledge when it is financially convenient.

15. According to Antonia Pantoja's (1989) description of the development of Puerto Rican community organizations and political leadership from the 1950s onward, the late 1960s and 1970s marks the emergence of professionally staffed institutions and advocacy movements. The "young turks," as she calls the emergent leadership, were indeed young, college-educated, and bilingual, and most important, mostly New York born, and insisted that the future and politics of the Puerto Rican community should be in the hands of Puerto Rican New Yorkers. As she notes, this stance was directly informed by the dominance of island institutions on the affairs of New York Puerto Ricans. Additionally, this time marks the growth of activist groups involved in civil rights and social advocacy as the Young Lords. In this way, the movement provided opportunities for a wide range of Puerto Ricans to reach positions of leadership in ways that are now largely unavailable, or that now demand greater preparation. For instance, in the early 1970s it was common to find school educators functioning as museum educators or curators, as they did in Taller Boricua and Museo del Barrio, and social workers working as directors and administrators of social service organizations. These are some of the positions that have since become professionalized in ways that preclude the involvement of old residents vis-à-vis a hyperprofessionalized, newer generation of "young turks."

16. New York City, Department of City Planning, October 2002. Educational Attainment for the Population Twenty-five and Over.

17. This is not to say that they were not dependent on public sector employment and financial support for their jobs and programs, a trend also documented among the Black middle classes, making them especially susceptible to the privatization of government (Patillo-McCoy 1999). Rather they were not themselves

directly dependent on the public services, such as public housing, which, as I previously noted, were so crucial to the area's Puerto Rican population.

18. I discuss this in greater detail in Dávila (2001b).

19. Program for Julia's Jam for Thursday, April 18, distributed over email, April 14, 2002, by YerbaBuena.

20. See Lippard (1990), Dávila (2001b), Moreno-Vega and Greene (1993) for a discussion of the context framing this cultural movement in the 1970s.

21. I find helpful here Sturken's (1997) description of cultural memory, which highlights the social and collective nature of all memories and engages with history and individual memory, enlarging its scope for cultural production and communication. Another helpful description of the working of memory as site of cultural knowledge is provided by Nora (1989), who writes about its spontaneous nature communicated in gestures, spaces, objects, and performances, as opposed to history, which is always contained in particular narratives or sites. These conceptualizations place memory at the heart of all processes of identity and cultural invention.

22. See *New York Latino Journal* (http://www.nylatinojournal.com).

CHAPTER THREE

1. EZ Heritage Tourism Initiative, Fact Sheet and Current Projects, Jan. 28, 2000.

2. As Throsby (2001) notes, even enthusiasts of systems that correlate value across these fields acknowledge the arbitrariness that unavoidably characterizes quests for definitions and measurement of cultural value along economic standards. He describes a particular troubling divide between the individualistic impulse of economics (revolving around maximization of goods by self-interested individuals) and the collective one of culture; the latter always presupposes value by a group, society, or collectivity, and is not always standardized within or outside a particular group, or even within it. The selection and managing of tangible and intangible cultural goods thus remain arbitrary and unavoidably contested processes.

3. Cultural institutions have been a permanent fixture in East Harlem. Not until the 1960s, however, with the politicization of culture among Puerto Ricans as part of larger civil rights struggles and claims for empowerment, and the growth of state funding for the arts, do we see the confluence of factors that led to the development of some of the most influential institutions in the area. This is documented in a study by the National Association of Latino Arts and Culture of eighteen cultural organizations in the eastern United States (NALAC 1995). Some of the organizations that were founded in the 1970s include the Puerto Rican

Traveling Theater, the Caribbean Cultural Center, the Association of Hispanic Arts, and the Puerto Rican Workshop.

4. See Upper Manhattan Empowerment Zone (2000), 5.

5. See Harlem USA 2 Tourist Map for Harlem and Upper Manhattan for a multilingual introduction to the area; as well as Harlem's 125th Street Map and Guide by the 125th Business Improvement District; Harlem, Your Uptown Spot to Shop, all partly funded by the EZ. The only map featuring East Harlem prominently is "Rediscovering East Harlem" initially organized by the East Harlem Historical Society, which I discuss in greater detail below. This map, however, is not distributed through the EZ offices as are the others. For funding distribution see Upper Manhattan Empowerment Zone (2000).

6. A study by the New York Foundation for the Arts reports the declining shares of state and federal government funds for the arts, and the resulting inequities among organizations (2001). Citing a study by the Alliance for the Arts, it notes that government sources dropped from 28.9 percent in 1982 to 11 percent in 1998. As they note, corporations and private foundations filled the void, though they were unable to meet the growing need for government funding for the arts. One ongoing problem that reverberates with the evidence presented in this chapter is the inability of many institutions of all types and sizes to access city funding.

7. Manhattan Community Board 11 (2000), 73.

8. Rental tenants in the area include La Fonda Boricua, La Cantina, James De la Vega, and the Julia de Burgos Latino Cultural Center. The case of the cultural center is perhaps the most revealing here. The organization is housed in a government-owned facility, obtained after much struggle from the community. The original plan was to house cultural organizations in the building, but few organizations were eligible or able to meet the city's requirements for tenants. In order to meet expenses, the center's administration and the city administration recurred to renting two floors of the facility to the Heritage School, an alterative school run by Columbia's Teachers College; this to the chagrin of many organizations who were shut off from benefiting from subsidized rents (Torres Penchi, 2002a). The Julia de Burgos Latino Cultural Center was conceived and organized in the 1980s, but the center did not open until 1998 because of delays in the funding of the project. This project represents the last upshot of the cultural movement that led to the acquisition of public funds for the formation of Puerto Rican and Latino cultural institutions in the mid 1970s, both in East Harlem and throughout the city, insofar as it constitutes the last large-scale publicly funded cultural project in the area. It was also created out of a community struggle to take over the historic building—an abandoned public school about to be turned into a homeless shelter.

9. Upper Manhattan Empowerment Zone, "Criteria for Funding," Cultural Industry Investment Fund Application guidelines, 2. Materials distributed in East

Harlem Empowerment Zone Forum, held at the Julia de Burgos Latino Cultural Center on Saturday, Mar. 23, 2002.

10. In part, these results reflect a certain bias (for example, the selection of tour-bus passengers and even the use of the term "Upper Manhattan," rather than "El Barrio" or "Spanish Harlem"). Even accounting for these variables, however, the study evidences a general lack of recognized tourist sites in East Harlem.

11. A good description of inequalities in housing stock between West and East Harlem in the later nineteenth century and at the turn of the century is provided by Osofsky (1996).

12. The church was taken over following demands for community space from which to run community programs. It stands as one of the most visible acts of protest by the Lords. For a discussion of the church's takeover by the Lords, see Melendez (2003); see Nunez (2003) for an account of the Poets Against War.

13. See http://nuestromuseo.org for a list for recommendations drafted by community activists calling for, among other things, an artist-in-residence program, policies for distributing catalogues among small organizations, training programs for future curators, and other policies to hold the institution accountable to the communities it sought to represent.

14. See Lee (2002) for an evocative example of how the issue was reduced to facile dichotomies in the media. Residents' demands were made amply evident to the board by artists like José Morales, Diógenes Ballester, Juan Sánchez, and activists like Yolanda Sánchez and others in a well-attended town hall meeting held in August 2002, organized by the community board's Cultural Affairs Committee. The debate over El Museo has a long history and merits more exploration than I can afford in this work, insurmountably marked by enduring issues of class and cultural hierarchies always at play in the evaluation of art and artistic institutions. See Moreno (1997), Dávila (1999, 2001b), and Yasmín Ramírez (2002) for some accounts of aspects affecting this longstanding debate, and Lippard (2002) for a good overview of the context framing politics of representations within museums. See Rita González (2003a, 2003b) for a discussion of the marginalization of Latino art within the Latin American and North American art canon. This campaign led to the allotment of two seats on the board of directors of El Museo for community representation, though the replacement of Debbie Quiñones as chair of the Cultural Affairs Committee impaired processes to assure the selection of members that would be accountable to issues of representation, not solely people that would contribute monies and funds as demanded by the board. The group's demand that board members be replaced with new members, however, remained unanswered.

15. Notably, this use was hindered by limited distribution. The map was not distributed at the EZ office, as were other maps and promotional materials for Harlem, nor at local museums. Many locals interpret this as evidence of the EZ's

and the Museum of the City of New York's lack of interest in promoting the community.

16. This radicalism is particularly tied to the work of Vito Marcantonio, East Harlem's radical congressman who represented East Harlem for fourteen years from the 1930s to the 1950s. See Meyer (1989) for a discussion of his involvement in Puerto Rican politics both in the states and on the island.

17. Harlem Your Way! Tours Unlimited, Inc., "Don't Just Be There, Be Involved," http://www.harlemyourwaytours.com?walking%20Tours.htm (accessed on June 18, 2001).

18. The controversy made it to the *New York Times*. See David González (1997).

19. Flyer circulated in meeting of Boricuas del Barrio, June 15, 2001. The percentage was posted under the category for tourism and cultural industry development funds distributed from 1996 to 1999. This exceedingly low figure was contested by EZ staff who counted help for technical assistance and feasibility studies granted to local institutions in the area.

20. The rise of the Republican Party at the state and federal level was another important factor contributing to the dispersal of the power of Harlem's Black politicians, hurting in particular Charles Rangel's once assured chairmanship of the Ways and Means Committee (Hicks 2003).

21. In addition to Mt. Sinai, Metropolitan and North General hospitals hold great influence in East Harlem as some of the largest employers and stakeholders of housing developments.

22. The eviction of the "Harlem Five"—a bar, bodega, barbershop, pizza place, and Chinese restaurant—longtime commercial and service establishments in Central Harlem, is perhaps the best example of how local merchants have not reaped benefits from the EZ (Waldman 2001). Among the larger ventures receiving loans from the EZ were the development Harlem USA and, most recently, Gotham Plaza. These issues came vividly alive during a conference at the Malcolm X Memorial Museum on June 20, 2002. The conference, Redlining Time and Space: Culture and the Question of Real Estate in Harlem, was organized by Dorothy Désir-Davis from the Lower Manhattan Cultural Council. For a critical assessment of the effects of the EZ on Harlem's local merchants, see Bowens (2001) and Chinyelu (1999).

23. Two such beneficiaries received substantial low-interest loans: $11.2 million for Harlem USA; and $15 million for East River Plaza. See Upper Manhattan Empowerment Zone (2001).

24. Obando, along with Ana Flores, was critical to the museum eventually attaining a provisional charter and IRS nonprofit status.

25. Christopher Montgomery, letter to Efraín Suarez, Aug. 3, 2001.

26. Economic Development Committee of Community Board 11, letter to Roy Board, Assistant Secretary of HUD, circulated to members of economic committee, Sept. 16, 2002.

CHAPTER FOUR

1. Proposal for the Museum for African Art and Edison Schools, presented in public hearing for the project, July 2001.

2. The vote on the Uniform Land Use Review Procedure (ULURP), for no. C010511ZMM (an amendment of the zoning map), twelve in favor, six opposed, with eight abstentions, and for no. C010513HDM (for disposition of city-owned property) twelve in favor, four opposed, and ten abstentions. The chair declared the nays and abstentions to be the majority and denied the proposal, although others contested that abstentions should not be counted as rejections to the project. Minutes of Public Hearing ULURP on July 12, 2001, by Community Board 11.

3. Both meetings were held at the Mt. Sinai Hospital's Goldwurm Auditorium. The first, held on July 12, was called by the local community board. A second and much larger meeting, gathering approximately three hundred people with eighty-seven speakers, was held two weeks later on August 1, organized by the borough president Virginia Fields as a response to heightened public interest on the project.

4. Díaz was recruited by Tonio Burgos, from Tonio Burgos and Associates. Having been born and raised in East Harlem, Burgos had previous contacts with longstanding Puerto Rican leaders in social service organizations and other key power positions. Though Díaz's tenure in the assembly was short (he was elected in a special election in 1995, held after the death of Angelo Del Toro, defeating William Del Toro by running as an independent candidate), his defeat of a Del Toro, amid public debate about the latter's alleged corruption, had vested Díaz with a reputation of a moral leader among segments of the area's Puerto Rican leadership. Many theories abound about the relative guilt of the Puerto Rican leaders accused of corruption. Many residents were greatly empowered at this time, mobilized to vote and to participate in electoral politics. Others believe that they were charged in reprise to the power attained by Puerto Ricans at this time. See Vega (1995), for a discussion of the coalition of churches that was central in bringing these claims to the forefront.

5. See past exhibition and catalogues presented and published by the Museum for African Art, http://www.africanart.org/html/past_exhibitions.htm.

6. See Sze (2003) for a good discussion of the politics of environmental justice and race and how they play out in minority communities throughout New York City.

7. Pedro Pedraza (1997) traces East Harlem's tradition of progressive education to the 1920s, specifically to the work of Italian educator Leonardo Covello, who was a close collaborator of the progressive political leader Vito Marcantonio (1902–1954), who served as representative for East Harlem in the 1930s and 1940s. The development of block schools, parent-controlled schools in the early

1960s, was another precedent for the activism that led to the creation of a Puerto Rican–dominated school district in East Harlem (Roderick 2001).

8. Ironically, these struggles were triggered by pulls toward desegregation. Faced with the prospects that their children would be bused, parents of Black and Latino children insisted that their schools should be improved. They demanded equal educational rights with white schools and, most importantly, a curriculum that is sensitive to children's racial and cultural backgrounds. See Edgell (1998) for an overview of the community control movement in New York City, and Jennings and Chapman (1998) for a discussion of Puerto Ricans' role in that movement and the gains they achieved.

9. See Kirp (1992) for a discussion of these issues by commentators on educational reform; and Teske, Schneider, Roch, and Marshall (2000) for an overview of the implementation of choice in District 4 (East Harlem).

10. These educational needs are succinctly expressed in the "Statement of District Needs for Fiscal Year 2003" (Manhattan Community Board 11 2003). It recommends the construction of a new high school and advises that East Harlem children be given priority in choice programs as a means of addressing the educational lacks of the community.

11. Members of the coalition include Rev. Norman Eddy, Lydia López, LaTommyette Martin, and Mee Ling Eng, who is a member of the school board and conducted the fieldwork that provided the foundation for the report.

12. The debate was held at PS 50 on Sept. 5, 2001. It was moderated by John Rivera and sponsored by ACAB Corp. and Affiliates, the Cultural Affairs Committee of Community Board 11, the East Harlem Chamber of Commerce, the East Harlem Council For Community Improvement, East Harlem Online, and SCAN. It was cosponsored by the Human Service Consortium, Little Sisters of the Assumption, East Harlem Citizen Committee, *Siempre,* Church of GOD of 100th Street, East Harlem Pilot Block, and Taino Towers.

13. See, for instance, discussion of the project in the *New York Times* (Dunlap 2002).

CHAPTER FIVE

1. Sánchez and Gómez (2001).

2. Throughout this chapter I use the term "Mexican" as opposed to "Mexican American" or "Chicano" to refer to Mexican activists in El Barrio because this was the self-designation term used most often by the predominantly Mexican-born first-generation immigrants during the span of my research. This usage will likely change in the coming years.

3. Robert Smith distinguishes four different stages of Mexican immigration to

New York City, beginning with the mid-1940s. The largest phases include that spanning from the late 1980s to the mid-1990s, dominated by migrants from the Mixteca Baja region, and the current period, which is also the most diversified, including a growing number of immigrants from Mexico City, particularly from Ciudad Nezahualcoyotl, one of its poorest sectors (Robert Smith 2001).

4. Robert Smith is the first scholar to look at this community, focusing primarily on transnational politics, racialization, education, youth, and social issues affecting their incorporation in U.S. society (Robert Smith 2003a). Jocelyn Solis (2001) and Alyshia Galvez (2003) address issues of citizenship and cultural citizenship. The lack of research on this community is a primary concern of some Mexican organizations, such as Tepeyac, which promotes a lot of documentation and research looking in particular at the role of the Tepeyac organization (Rivera Sánchez 2003).

5. These groups were undergoing many transitions in the summer of 2001. Thus I am purposefully vague in drawing distinctions among them. During my research, alliances were forged and reconfigured, challenging allies in multiple ways. As I note later, however, they share more commonalities than differences and have participated in meetings seeking a common agenda for Mexicans in New York and beyond.

6. While this stance is particularly relevant for new immigrants groups, it is not dissimilar to that still exhibited by many immigrant groups in this country. See Basch et al. (1994) and Cordero-Guzmán et al. (2001) for a discussion of some of the many variables affecting the maintenance of transnational connections by immigrant groups, as related to issues of history, income, race, and ethnicity, among other variables.

7. For instance, the founding of the Mexican Consulate's Program for Mexican Communities Abroad in 1990, whose goal was to improve and increase relations with both Mexicans and communities of Mexican origin outside the country, started from the growing recognition of immigrants' economic, political, and social contributions to Mexico. See Robert Smith (2003a) for a detailed description of the Mexican government role in the creation of a diasporic public sphere among immigrants.

8. While Latinos are generally Democratic, 35 percent supported George W. Bush in the last presidential campaign, the largest percentage of Latinos supporting a Republican candidate since the election of Ronald Reagan. The rapid growth and greater number of eligible voters in this community will make Latinos a decisive political force in future elections.

9. I don't mean to suggest that struggles over cultural citizenship and visibility by this community are new, but they took a heightened significance after September 11. Such struggles over space have indeed been ongoing, waged at many fronts. A particularly well-publicized debate in El Barrio is that which reporter

Juan González (2000) has termed "the battle of the virgins," over which virgin would adorn the churches' altars: La Providencia, the patron of Puerto Rico, or Mexico's Virgin of Guadalupe. This struggle is not so much about the virgin as it is about issues of recognition and visibility that in El Barrio culminated in an altar for La Guadalupe and a recharged interest in all regional patron saints. See Juan González (1997) and Navarro (2002).

10. By this I mean the first citywide parade (in regards to its organization and momentum, as it was described to me by my informants). Festival politics are always contentious. Centro Mexicano sponsored a previous Mexican festival in the 1960s; a smaller parade had once been held on Madison Avenue.

11. Their mission: "To defend our human rights and those of other immigrants, to promote our human rights, and educate and develop a Mexican community that becomes integrated, not assimilated, in the cultural, religious, educational, economic and political life of this state and this Catholic Church"; see http://www.Tepeyac.org (accessed fall 2001).

12. On this point, see especially Robert Smith's (2003a, 2003b) discussion of Mexicans' "in-between" status in New York's racial and ethnic hierarchy, and on how gender and generation play out into these hierarchies. Similar dynamics have been documented in Chicago; see De Genova and Ramos-Zayas 2003.

13. The event on May 11, at St. Cecilia's Church was part of the public relations campaign of the Spanish TV network Telemundo involving meetings with Latin communities in New York. The event was coordinated with the Asociación Tepeyac, and included folkloric dances, games and raffles. Readers will find more discussion of Hispanic marketing and its treatment of New York Latinos in Dávila (2001a).

14. See Robert Smith (2001) for estimates on the number of undocumented.

15. A good example of how reporters manipulated ethnic strife among groups is provided by Feuer (2003). On closer reading it is evident, however, that the schism is also, if not primarily, about established Mexican business owners and restaurateurs shunning competition from Mexican street vendors.

16. See Galvez (2002, 2003) for a description of the role of Guadalupismo as a political discourse among the Mexican community and of its growing alignment with pro-immigrant and progressive politics.

CHAPTER SIX

1. As Joe Austin notes, the meaning of graffiti is highly contentious. He prefers using the term *writing*, which is the oldest term, the less criminalized, and the more inclusive (2001). I usually encountered the term *graffiti* in my conversations, though I use both terms in this chapter.

2. In this chapter I define outdoor media as billboards, bulletins, street furniture media, and transit media (in buses, subways, etc.). It does not include "out of media," which the outdoor marketing industry uses to define any type of media that reaches consumers out of their home, such as radio or speaker-phone announcements.

3. Though different and smaller in scale, the concessions given to outdoor advertisers are comparable to those given to developers by the city's 1961 zoning resolution, which gave private ownership of public spaces in exchange for the development of plazas and parks for the public. These publicly accessible spaces, however, are seldom as publicly accessible as intended by the legislation (Kayden et al. 2000). While street furniture, which depends on accessibility to the public, is waived from these criticisms, similar questions can be raised about the private/public juncture they represent in regards to control of public space.

4. For instance, the most expensive outdoor media (rotary bulletins) cost $3.90 for 10 GRP (or Gross Rating Point, equaling the number of impressions per a percent of total population). In contrast, thirty seconds of a prime-time television spot may cost $20.54 per thousand viewers.

5. See TDI/Infinity Outdoor Latino marketing brochure, "Impacting the Latino Market" TDI, New York, New York.

6. Marketers need permits from the landlord/owner of the buildings in which they seek to place ads, and they must follow zoning regulations. Illegal ads are considered to be those placed in private spaces without such permits.

7. See Pitman et al. (1998) for a discussion of the community-based mural movement among Chicanos; and Vélez-Ibáñez (1996) for the contemporary repercussions of the Mexican mural movement in the United States. A discussion of the political content and message of murals in New York City is provided by Cardalda-Sánchez and Tirado-Avilés (2001) and Taylor (1999).

8. Graffiti's disrepute is also tied to its persecution and pathologization by local authorities, even at the same time that other forms of street art, such as mural art, were being promoted. See Austin (2001).

9. See Miller (2002) and Austin (2001) for examinations of the larger social and political context that gave rise to writing.

10. See http://www.nyc.gov/html/nograffiti/home.html for the mayor's Antigraffiti Task Force.

11. Anónimo (2002).

References

Abu-Lughod, Janet. 1994. *From Urban Village to East Village: The Battle for New York's Lower East Side.* Cambridge, Mass.: Blackwell.

Abu-Lughod, Lila. 1991. "Writing Against Culture." In *Recapturing Anthropology: Working in the Present,* ed. Richard Fox. Santa Fe, N.M.: School of American Research Press.

Acuña, Rodolfo. 1988. *Occupied America: A History of Chicanos.* New York: Harper and Row.

Anderson, Martin. 1964. *The Federal Bulldozer: A Critical Analysis of Urban Renewal.* Cambridge: MIT Press.

Andreu Iglesias, Cesar. 1984. *Memoirs of Bernardo Vega: A Contribution to the History of the Puerto Rican Community in New York.* New York: Monthly Review Press.

Anónimo. 2002. "Perdió la Comunidad." *Siempre,* July 16–Aug. 5, 2002, 15.

Aponte Parés, Luis. 1998. "What's Yellow and White and Has Land All Around It? Appropriating Place in Puerto Rican Barrios." In *The Latino Studies Reader, Culture, Economy and Society,* eds. Antonia Darder and Rodolfo Torres. Blackwell: Maiden, Mass.

———. 1999. "Lessons from El Barrio: The East Harlem Real Great Society/ Urban Planning Studio: A Puerto Rican Chapter in the Fight for Urban Self-

Determination." In *Latino Social Movements*, eds. Rodolfo Torres and George Katsaificas. London: Routledge.

Appadurai, Arjun. 1996. *Modernity at Large*. Minneapolis: University of Minnesota Press.

Audience Research and Analysis. 2000. "Upper Manhattan Tourism Market Study: A Study of Visitors to Upper Manhattan including their Economic Impact and Local Spending." Prepared for the Upper Manhattan Empowerment Zone Development Corporation, Inc. (Dec.).

Austin, Joe. 2001. *Taking the Train: How Graffiti Art Became an Urban Crisis in New York*. New York: Columbia University Press.

Baca, Eddie. 2001. "Whose Neighborhood Is It Anyway?" *Siempre*, Sept. 5–24, 8.

Barrett, Wayne. 1985. "Barons of El Barrio." *Village Voice*, Feb. 5, 14–17, 93.

Basch, Linda, Nina Glick Schiller, and Cristina Szanton Blanc. 1994. *Nations Unbound: Transnational Projects, Postcolonial Predicaments, and Deterritorialized Nation-States*. Langhorne, Penn.: Gordon and Breach.

Berger, Joseph. 2002. "A Puerto Rican Rebirth in El Barrio." *New York Times*, Dec. 10, metro section.

Biondi, Martha. 2003. *To Stand and Fight: The Struggle for Civil Rights in Postwar New York City*. Cambridge, Mass.: Harvard University Press.

Bonilla Silva, Eduardo. 2001. *White Supremacy and Racism in the Post-Civil Rights Era*. Boulder and London: Lynne Rienner Publishers.

Bourdieu, Pierre. 1993. *The Field of Cultural Production*. New York: Columbia University Press.

Bourgois, Phillipe. 1995. *In Search of Respect: Selling Crack in El Barrio*. New York: Cambridge University Press.

Bowens, Doreen. 2001. "Corporate Culture Comes to Harlem." *African Voices* (fall/winter): 28–30.

Boyd, Michelle. 2000. "Reconstructing Bronzeville: Racial Nostalgia and Neighborhood Redevelopment." *Journal of Urban Affairs* 22 (2): 107–22.

Braconi, Frank. 1999. "In Rem Innovation and Expediency in New York's Housing Policy." In *Housing and Community Development in New York City: Facing the Future*, ed. Michael Schill. New York: State University of New York.

Bressi, Todd. 2000. "Digging into the Grass Roots: New York's Community Planning Process Hasn't Always Lived Up to Expectations." *Planning* 66 (3): 10–13.

Bright, Brenda Jo, and Liza Bakewell. 1995. *Looking High and Low: Art and Cultural Identity*. Tucson: University of Arizona Press.

Brin Hyatt, Susan. 2001. "From Citizen to Volunteer: Neoliberal Governance and the Erasure of Poverty." In *The New Poverty Studies: Ethnography of Power, Politics, and Impoverished People in the United States*, eds. Judith Goode and Jeff Maskovsky. New York: New York University Press.

Brumann, Christopher. 1999. "Writing for Culture: Why a Successful Concept Should Not Be Discarded." *Current Anthropology* 40: S1–S27.

Burgos, Adrian. 2001. "The Latins from Manhattan: Confronting Race and Building Community in Jim Crow Baseball, 1906–1950." In *Mambo Montage: The Latinization of New York,* eds. Agustin Laó and Arlene Dávila. New York: Columbia University Press.

Calvert, George. 1998. *A Call to Action: Rebuilding Main Street in the Village of East Harlem.* New York: CIVITAS Citizens, Inc.

Cardalda-Sánchez, Elsa, and Amilcar Tirado-Avilés. 2001. "Ambiguous Identities: The Affirmation of Puertorriquenidad in the Community Murals of New York City." In *Mambo Montage: The Latinization of New York,* eds. Agustin Laó and Arlene Dávila. New York: Columbia University Press.

Center for Puerto Rican Studies. 1976. *Los Puertorriqueños y la cultura: Crítica y debate.* New York: Research Foundation of the City University of New York.

Chin, Elizabeth. 2001. *Purchasing Power: Black Kids and American Consumer Culture.* Minneapolis: University of Minnesota Press.

Chinyelu, Mamadou. 1999. *Harlem Ain't Nothin' But A Third World Country: The Global Economy, Empowerment Zones and the Colonial Status of Africans in America.* New York: Mustard Seed Press.

Chomsky, Noam. 1999. *Profits Over People: Neoliberalism and Global Order.* New York: Seven Stories Press.

Comaroff, Jean and John. 1999. "Occult Economies and the Violence of Abstraction: Notes from the South African Postcolony." *American Ethnologist* 26.

———. 2000. "Millennial Capitalism: First Thoughts on a Second Coming." *Public Culture* 12 (2): 291–343.

Cooke, Oliver. 2002. "Upscale Neighborhoods." *New York Times,* Apr. 1, sec. A.

Coombe, Rosemary J. 1998. *The Cultural Life of Intellectual Properties: Authorship, Appropriation, and the Law.* Durham, N.C.: Duke University Press.

Cordero-Guzmán, Hector, Robert C. Smith, and Ramón Grosfoguel. 2001. *Migration, Transnationalization, and Race in a Changing New York.* Philadelphia: Temple University Press.

Cruz, José E. 1998. *Identity and Power: Puerto Rican Politics and the Challenge of Ethnicity.* Philadelphia: Temple University Press.

Daily News. 2001. "Harlem Pols' Closed-Door Policy." Editorial, Aug. 18.

Dávila, Arlene. 1997. *Sponsored Identities: Cultural Politics in Puerto Rico.* Philadelphia: Temple University Press.

———. 1999. "Latinizing Culture: Art, Museums and the Politics of Multicultural Encompassment." *Cultural Anthropology* 14 (2): 180–202.

———. 2001a. *Latinos, Inc.: The Marketing and Making of a People.* Berkeley: University of California Press.

———. 2001b. "Culture in the Battlefront: From Nationalist to Pan-Latino Projects." In *Mambo Montage: The Latinization of New York,* eds. Agustin Lao and Arlene Dávila, 159–182. New York: Columbia University Press.

Davis, Mike. 2001. *Magical Urbanism: Latinos Reinvent the U.S. Big City.* New York: Verso.

De Genova, Nick, and Ana Ramos-Zayas. 2003. "Latino Rehearsals: Racialization and the Politics of Citizenship between Mexicans and Puerto Ricans in Chicago." *Journal of Latin American Anthropology* 8 (2).

Delaney, Samuel. 1999. *Times Square Red, Times Square Blue.* New York: New York University Press.

De Palma, Anthony. 1986. "East Harlem TV Deal Unraveling." *New York Times,* June 15, sec. 8

Desmond, Jane. 1999. *Staging Tourism: Bodies on Display from Waikiki to Sea World.* Chicago: University of Chicago Press.

Deutsche, Rosalyn. 1998. *Evictions: Art and Spatial Politics.* Cambridge, Mass.: MIT Press.

Dreier, Peter, John Mollenkopf, and Todd Swanstrom. 2001. *Place Matters: Metropolitics for the Twenty-First Century.* Lawrence, Kans.: University of Kansas Press.

Duany, Jorge. 2002. "Irse P'Fuera: The Mobile Livelihoods of Circular Migrants between Puerto Rico and the United States." In *Work and Migration: Life and Livelihoods in a Globalizing World,* eds. Ninna Nyberg Sorensen and Karen Fog Olwig. London: Routledge.

Duggan, Lisa. 2003. *The Twilight of Equality? Neoliberalism, Cultural Politics, and the Attack on Democracy.* Boston: Beacon Press.

Dunlap, David. 2002. "The Changing Look of the New Harlem." *New York Times,* Feb. 10, sec. 11.

East Harlem Coalition to Improve Our Public Schools. 2001. "Report of the Sub-Committee on Need for Space in School District 4 Public Schools" (July).

Edgell, Derek. 1998. *The Movement for Community Control of New York City's Schools, 1966–1970: Class Wars.* Lampeter, Wales: The Edwin Mellen Press.

EFE. 2003. "Desfile divide a los Mexicanos." *Hoy.* Sept. 16, 4.

Escobar, Arturo. 1995. *Encountering Development: The Making and Unmaking of the Third World.* Princeton, N.J.: Princeton University Press.

Falcón, Angelo. 2001. "De'Tras Pa' Lante: The Future of Puerto Rican History in New York City." Puerto Rican Defense and Education Fund (Jan.).

Feuer, Alan. 2003. "Little but Language in Common: Mexicans and Puerto Ricans Quarrel in East Harlem." *New York Times,* Sept. 6, metro section.

Fincher, Ruth, and Jane Jacobs. 1998. *Cities of Difference.* New York: Guilford.

Fliegel, Sy, and James MacGuire. 1993. *Miracle in East Harlem: The Fight for Choice in Public Education.* New York: Times Books.

Flores, Juan. 2000. *From Bomba to Hip Hop: Puerto Rican Culture and Latino Identity.* New York: Columbia University Press.

Flores, William, and Rina Benmayor, eds. 1997. *Latino Cultural Citizenship: Claiming Identity, Space and Rights.* Boston, Mass.: Beacon Press.

Flores-González, Hilda. 2001. "Paseo Boricua: Claiming a Puerto Rican Space in Chicago." *Centro: Journal of the Center for Puerto Rican Studies* 13 (2): 72–95.

Freidenberg, Judith. 1995. *The Anthropology of Lower Income Urban Enclaves: The Case of East Harlem.* New York: New York Academy of Sciences.

———. 2000. *Growing Old in El Barrio.* New York: New York University Press.

Fuentes Rivera, Ada. 2002. "Barrio, ciudad y 'performance': Cruce de fronteras en el proyecto mural de James De la Vega." *Centro: Journal of the Center for Puerto Rican Studies* 14 (2).

Galvez, Alyshia. 2002. "She Made Us Human: The Relationship between the Virgin of Guadalupe, Popular Religiosity, and Activism among Members of Mexican Devotional Organizations in New York City. Unpublished paper.

———. 2003. " 'The Virgin Wants Amnesty': The Vivification of the Virgin of Guadalupe by New York City's Mexican Migrant Community." Paper, fourth annual seminar of the Hemispheric Institute of Performance and Politics, New York, July 11–19.

González, Damaso. 2003. "Realizan boicot contra 'falso desfile' Mexicano." *El Diario,* Sept. 16, 3.

González, David. 1997. "Creating Pride from an Insult in El Barrio." *New York Times,* Apr. 19, metro section.

González, Juan. 1995. "Del Toro's Gang's Time's Up." *Daily News,* Mar. 8.

———. 1997. "Cultures Clash at Church in El Barrio." *Daily News,* Jan. 10.

———. 2000. *Harvest of Empire: A History of Latinos in America.* New York: Viking.

———. 2002. "Bus Depots' Neighbors Left Fuming." *Daily News,* Apr. 9, sports final edition.

González, Rita. 2003a. *Archiving the Latino Arts before It Is too Late.* Latino Policy and Issues Brief. Los Angeles: UCLA Chicano Studies Research Center.

———. 2003b. *An Undocumented History: A Survey of Index Citations and Art Historical Resources for Latino and Latina Artists.* Latino Policy and Issues Brief. Los Angeles: UCLA Chicano Studies Research Center.

Goode, Judith, and Jeff Maskovsky, eds. 2001. *The New Poverty Studies: The Ethnography of Power, Politics, and Impoverished People in the United States.* New York: New York University Press.

Graeber, David. 2001. *Toward an Anthropological Theory of Value: The False Coin of Our Own Dreams.* New York: Palgrave.

Gregory, Steven. 1998. "Globalization and the 'Place' of Politics in Contemporary Theory: A Commentary. *City and Society* (Annual Review): 47–64.

———. 1999. *Black Corona.* Princeton, N.J.: Princeton University Press.

Grosfoguel, Ramón, and Chloé Georas. 2001. "Latino Caribbean Diasporas in

New York." In *Mambo Montage: The Latinization of New York,* eds. Agustin Laó and Arlene Dávila. New York: Columbia University Press.

Guinier, Lani, and Gerald Torres. 2002. *The Miners' Canary: Enlisting Race, Resisting Power, Transforming Democracy.* Cambridge, Mass.: Harvard University Press.

Hale, Charles. 2002. "Does Multiculturalism Menace? Governance, Cultural Rights and the Politics of Identity in Guatemala." *Journal of Latin American Studies* 34: 485–524.

Halter, Marilyn. 2000. *Shopping for Identity: The Marketing of Ethnicity.* New York: Schocken Books.

Hanson-Sánchez, Christopher. 1996. *New York City Latino Neighborhoods Data Book.* New York: Institute of Puerto Rican Policy.

Harvey, David. 2001. *Spaces of Capital: Toward a Critical Geography.* London: Routledge.

Haslip-Viera, Gabriel, and Sherrie Baver. 1996. *Latinos in New York: Communities in Transition.* Notre Dame, Ind.: University of Notre Dame.

Hayden, Dolores. 1999. *The Power of Place: Urban Landscapes as Public History.* Cambridge, Mass.: MIT Press.

Herbstein, Judith. 1978. "Rituals and Politics of the Puerto Rican 'Community' in New York." Ph.D. diss., City University of New York.

Hevesi, Dennis. 2001. "City Homeownership Plans Lift Neighborhoods, Study Says." *New York Times,* July 30, metro section.

Hicks, Jonathan. 2003. "As Political Lions Go Gray, Harlem Wanes as Center of Power." *New York Times,* Feb. 3, metro section.

Hispanic Federation. 2002. "Latino Political Participation in New York City." A Report of the Hispanic Federation (Mar. 12).

Holston, James, and Arjun Appadurai. 1999. Introduction to *Cities and Citizenship,* ed. James Holston. Durham, N.C.: Duke University Press.

Honig, Bonnie. 1998. "Immigrant America? How Foreigners 'Solve' Democracy's Problems." *Social Text* 56.

Housing First: Affordable Housing For All New Yorkers. 2001. "New York's Affordable Housing Crisis: Context, Principles and Solutions," http://www.housingfirst.net.

Infante, Manuel. 2001. "La Voz del Pueblo: Mexicanos y Dominicanos." *El Diario/La Prensa,* Oct. 9, 10.

Jackson, John. 2001. *Harlemworld.* Chicago: University of Chicago Press.

Jackson, Peter, and Nigel Thrift. 1995. "Geographies of Consumption." In *Acknowledging Consumption: A Review of New Studies,* ed. Daniel Miller. London: Routledge.

James, Winston. 1999. *Holding Aloft the Banner of Ethiopia: Caribbean Radicalism in Early Twentieth-century America.* New York: Verso.

Jennings, James, and Monte Rivera, eds. 1984. *Puerto Rican Politics in Urban America.* Westport: Greenwood Press.

Jennings, James, and Francisco Chapman. 1998. "Puerto Ricans and the Community Control Movement: An Interview with Luis Fuentes." In *The Puerto Rican Movement: Voices from the Diaspora,* eds. Andrés Torres and José Velázquez. Philadelphia: Temple University Press.

Jones-Correa, Michael. 1998. *Between Two Nations: The Political Predicament of Latinos in New York City.* Ithaca: Cornell University Press.

Judd, Dennis, and Susan Fainstein, eds. 1999. *Constructing the Tourist Bubble: The Tourist City.* New Haven: Yale University Press.

Kayden, Jerold, with the New York City Department of City Planning and the Municipal Art Society of New York. 2000. *Privately Owned Public Space: The New York Experience.* New York: John Wiley and Sons, Inc.

Kelley, Robin. 1998. *Yo Mama's Disfunktional: Fighting the Culture Wars in Urban America.* Cambridge, Mass.: Beacon Press.

Kirp, David. 1992. "What School Choice Really Means." *The Atlantic Online (The Atlantic Monthly), http://www.theatlantic.com* (Nov.).

Kirshenblatt-Gimblett, Barbara. 1998. *Destination Culture, Tourism, Museums and Heritage.* Berkeley: University of California Press.

Kreinin Souccar, Miriam. 2003. "El Barrio: Left Behind and Angry." *Crain's New York Business,* Jan. 13, 20.

Kugel, Seth. 2003. "A Bus Depot Will Reopen and Resident Worry." *New York Times,* Aug. 24.

Laó, Agustin, and Arlene Dávila, eds. 2001. *Mambo Montage: The Latinization of New York.* New York: Columbia University Press.

Lassalle, Yvonne, and Marvette Pérez. 1997. "'Virtually' Puerto Rican: 'Dis'-Locating Puerto Rican-ness and its Privileged Sites of Production." *Radical History Review* 68: 54–78.

Lawson Clark, Sherri. 2002. "Where the Poor Live: How Federal Housing Policy Shapes Residential Communities." *Urban Anthropology* 31 (3): 69–93.

Leclerc, Gustavo, Raul Villa, and Michael Dear. 1999. *La Vida Latina en L.A.: Urban Latino Cultures.* Thousand Oaks, Calif.: Sage Publications.

Lee, Denny. 2002. "A 'Museo' Moves Away From Its Barrio Identity." *New York Times,* July 21, sec. 14.

Lefebvre, Henri. 1995. *Writing on Cities.* Trans. Elizabeth Le Bas and Eleonor Kofman. Cambridge, Mass.: Blackwell.

———. 2000. *The Production of Space.* Trans. Donald Nicholson-Smith. New York and London: Blackwell.

Lewis, Oscar. 1968. *A Study of Slum Culture: Backgrounds for La Vida.* New York: Random House.

Lin, Jan. 1998. *Reconstructing Chinatown: Ethnic Enclave, Global Change.* Minneapolis: University of Minnesota Press.

Lippard, Lucy. 1990. "Socio Political Implications." In *Taller Alma Boricua, 1969–1989: Reflecting on Twenty Years of the Puerto Rican Workshop.* New York: El Museo del Barrio.

———. 2002. "Biting the Hand: Artists and Museums in New York since 1969." In *Alternative New York, 1965–1985,* ed. Julie Ault. Minneapolis: University of Minnesota Press.

Llanos, José. 2003. "Los cuates se abren camino." *Hoy,* Sept. 16, 4.

Logan, John. 2000. "Still a Global City: The Racial and Ethnic Segmentation of New York." In *Globalizing Cities: A New Spatial Order?* eds. Peter Marcuse and Ronald van Kempen. Malden, Mass.: Blackwell.

Logan, John, and Harvey Molotch. 1988. *Urban Fortunes: The Political Economy of Place.* Berkeley: University of California Press.

López, Veronica. 2003. "Call Me Puerto Rican." *New York Times,* May 1, sec. A.

MacCannell, Dean. 1999. *The Tourist: A New Theory of the Leisure Class.* Berkeley: University of California Press.

Manhattan Community Board 11. 2000. *New Directions,* Plan 197-A. New York: Community Board 11 (March).

———. 2003. "Statement of District Needs for Fiscal Year 2003."

Manhattan Community Service Society of New York. 1998. "Community Districts with Over 20 Percent Concentration of Federally-Assisted Housing." Public Policy Department, Housing Policy and Research Unit (Mar.).

Marcus, George, and Fred R. Myers. 1995. *The Traffic in Culture: Prefiguring Art and Anthropology.* Berkeley: University of California Press.

Marcuse, Peter. 1995. "Not Chaos but Walls: Postmodernism and the Partitioned City." In *Postmodern Cities and Spaces,* ed. Sophie Watson and Katerine Gibson. Cambridge, Mass.: Blackwell.

Martínez, Miranda. 2001. "The Good Garden: City Power, Community Boards and Moral Discourses of Spatial Use." Paper presented at the Metropolitan Studies Colloquium, New York University, Nov. 29.

Maskovsky, Jeff. 2001. "Afterword: Beyond the Privatist Consensus." In *The New Poverty Studies: The Ethnography of Power, Politics, and Impoverished People in the United States,* eds. Judith Goode and Jeff Maskovsky. New York: New York University Press.

Massey, Doreen. 1994. *Space, Place and Gender.* Minneapolis: University of Minnesota Press.

Matos, Felix Rodríguez. 2001. "The 'Browncoats' Are Coming: Latino Public History in Boston." *The Public Historian* 23 (4): 15–28.

McCarthy, Anna. 2001. *Ambient Television*. Durham, N.C.: Duke University Press.

McCracken, Grant. 1988. *Culture and Consumption: New Approaches to the Symbolic Character of Cultural Goods*. Bloomington: University of Indiana Press.

McFadden, Robert. 1995. "Angelo Del Toro Legislator from East Harlem Dies at 47." *New York Times*, Jan. 2.

Meier, Deborah. 1995. *The Power of Their Ideas: Lessons for America from a Small School in Harlem*. Boston: Beacon Press.

Mele, Christopher. 2000. *Selling the Lower East Side: Culture, Real Estate and Resistance in New York City*. Minneapolis: University of Minnesota Press.

Melendez, Miguel. 2003. *We Took the Streets: Fighting for Latino Rights with the Young Lords*. New York: St. Martin's Press.

Meyer, Gerald. 1989. *Vito Marcantonio: Radical Politician, 1902–1954*. Albany, N.Y.: State University of New York.

Miller, Daniel. 1995. *Acknowledging Consumption: A Review of New Studies*. London: Routledge.

Miller, Ivor. 2002. *Aerosol Kingdom: Subway Painters of New York City*. Jackson, Miss.: University of Mississippi Press.

Mindiola, Tatcho, Jr., Yolanda Flores Niemann, and Nestor Rodríguez. 2002. *Black-Brown: Relations and Stereotypes*. Austin: University of Texas Press.

Mohr, Nicholasa. 1986. *Nilda*. New York: Prentice Hall.

Morales, Ed. 2002. *Living in Spanglish: The Search for Latino Identity in America*. New York: L.A. Weekly Books and St. Martin's Press.

Moreno, Maria Jose. 1997. "Identity Formation and Organizational Change in Nonprofit Institutions. A Comparative Study of Two Hispanic Museums." Ph.D. diss., Columbia University.

Moreno-Vega, Marta, and Cherryl Greene. 1993. *Voices from the Battlefront: Achieving Cultural Equity.*Trenton, N.J.: Africa World Press.

Museum for African Art and Edison Schools. 2001. "Proposal Project on Fifth Avenue and 110th Street (Tito Puente Way)." Proposal presented at Community Board 11 meeting (July).

Myers, Fred, ed. 2001. *The Empire of Things: Regimes of Value and Material Culture*. Santa Fe, N.M.: School of American Research Press.

NALAC. 1995. *Historical Survey and Current Assessment of Latino Arts and Cultural Organizations in the United States*. Ed. Pedro A. Rodríguez. San Antonio: National Association of Latino Arts and Culture, in collaboration with the Hispanic Research Center at the University of Texas, San Antonio.

Navarro, Mireya. 2000. "Puerto Rican Presence Wanes in New York." *New York Times*, Feb. 28, sec. A.

———. 2002. "In Many Churches, Icons Compete For Space." The *New York Times*, May 29, metro section.

———. 2003. "In New York's Cultural Mix, Black Latinos Carve Out Niche." *New York Times*, Apr. 28, metro section.

New York City, Department of City Planning. 1994. *Puerto Rican New Yorkers in 1990*. New York: Department of City Planning, Sept.

———. 2002. District Profiles, Department of City Planning, http://www.ci.nyc .ny.us/html/dcp/html/lucds/cdstart.html.

———. 2002/2003. "Community District Needs. Manhattan. Department of City Planning. 1993. Socioeconomic Profiles. A Portrait of New York City's Community Districts from the 1980 and 1990 Censuses of Population and Housing."

New York City Rent Guidelines Board. 1999. "Income and Expense Study" (April 27).

New York Foundation for the Arts. 2001. *Culture Counts: Strategies for a More Vibrant Cultural Life for New York City*. New York: New York Foundation for the Arts.

New York Times. 2001. "First of Three Middle Income Buildings: A New Co-Op Going Up in East Harlem." July 8, sec. 11.

Newsday. 1991. "Vote for Powell, Avoid Del Toro." Oct. 28.

Nunez, Ismael. 2003. "People's Church: The Struggle Continues." *Harlem Times*, Mar. 22.

O'Dougherty, Maureen. 2002. *Consumption Intensified: The Politics of Middle-Class Daily Life in Brazil*. Durham, N.C.: Duke University Press.

Omi, Michael, and Howard Winant. 1994. *Racial Formation in the United States: From the 1960s to the 1990s*. New York: Routledge.

Ortner, Sherry. 1999. *The Fate of "Culture": Geertz and Beyond*. Berkeley: University of California Press.

Oser, Alan. 2001. "New Roles for Nonprofit Housing Groups." *New York Times*, June 3, real estate section.

Osofsky, Gilbert. 1996. *Harlem: The Making of a Ghetto*. Chicago: Elephant Paperbacks.

Pacenza, Matt. 2002. "East Harlem's Bottom Line." *City Limits* (Apr.): 14–17, 40–41.

———. 2003. "Housing Next." *City Limits* (Apr.): 25–28.

Padilla, Elena. 1958. *Up from Puerto Rico*. New York: Columbia University Press.

Padilla, Felix. 1985. *Latino Ethnic Consciousness: The Case of Mexican Americans and Puerto Ricans in Chicago*. Notre Dame, Ind.: University of Notre Dame Press.

Pantoja, Antonia. 1989. "Puerto Ricans in New York: A Historical and Community Development Perspective." *Centro: Journal of the Center for Puerto Rican Studies* 2 (5): 21–31.

Pattillo-McCoy, Mary. 1999. *Black Picket Fences: Privilege and Peril Among the Black Middle Classes.* Chicago: University of Chicago Press.

Pedraza, Pedro. 1997. "Puerto Ricans and the Politics of School Reform." *Centro: Journal of the Center of Puerto Rican Studies* 9.

Pérez, Gina. 2000. "The Near Northwest Side Story: Gender, Migration and Everyday Life in Chicago and San Sebastián, Puerto Rico." Ph.D. diss., Northwestern University.

———. 2001. "Introduction: Puerto Ricans in Chicago." *Centro: Journal of the Center of Puerto Rican Studies* 13 (2).

Phillips, Susan. 1999. *Wallbangin': Graffiti and Gangs in Los Angeles.* Chicago: University of Chicago Press.

Pitman Weber, John, James Cockcroft, Eva Sterling Cockcroft, and Ben Keppel. 1998. *Towards a People's Art: The Contemporary Mural Movement.* New Mexico, N.M.: University of Mexico Press.

Platt, Larry. 2000. "Magic Johnson Builds an Empire." *The New York Times Magazine*, Dec. 10.

Plunz, Richard. 1990. *A History of Housing in New York City.* New York: Columbia University Press.

Portes, Alejandro, and Alex Stepic. 1993. *City on the Edge: The Transformation of Miami.* Berkeley: University of California Press.

Prince, Sabiyha Robin. 2002a. "Changing Places: Race, Class, and Belonging in the 'New Harlem.'" *Urban Anthropology* 31 (1): 5–36.

———. 2002b. "Making Race and Place: African American Professional Managerial Workers in New York City." Revised version of paper presented in "From Africa to the Americas: New Directions in Afro-American Anthropology," School of American Research, Apr. 11–15, 1999.

Pristin, Terry. 2001. "Hud Scraps Cuomo Remedy for Harlem Housing Scandal." *New York Times*, May 11, metro section.

Quiñonez, Ernesto. 2000. *Bodega Dreams.* New York: Vintage.

Ramirez, Ana. 2002. "Mexicanos tras una Agenda Comun." *Hoy*, Feb. 5.

Ramirez, Yasmin. 2003. *Passing on Latinidad: An Analysis of Critical Responses to El Museo del Barrio's Pan-Latino Mission Statements.* Washington, D.C.: Smithsonian National Research Conference.

Ramos-Zayas, Ana. 2003. *National Performances: Race, Class and Space in Puerto Rican Chicago.* Chicago: University of Chicago Press.

Ravitch, Diane. 2000. *The Great School Wars: A History of New York City Public Schools.* Baltimore, Md.: Johns Hopkins University Press.

Rinaldo, Rachel. 2002. "Space of Resistance: The Puerto Rican Cultural Center and Humboldt Park." *Cultural Critique* 50: 135–74.

Rivera, José and Letticia. 1998. "What in a Name? East Harlem Online Discussion Forum," http://www.east-harlem.com/spanish_harlem.htm.

Rivera, Raquel. 2003. *Nuyoricans from the Hip Hop Zone.* New York: Palgrave.

Rivera-Sánchez, Liliana. 2002. "Searching Expressions of Identity: Belonging and Spaces, Mexican Immigrants in New York." Paper, Indigenous Mexican Migrants in the United States: Building Bridges between Researchers and Community Leaders, University of California at Santa Cruz, Oct. 11–12.

Roderick, Tom. 2001. *A School of Our Own: Parents, Power and Community at the East Harlem Block Schools.* New York: Teachers College Press.

Rodríguez, Clara. 1995. "Puerto Ricans in Historical and Social Science Research." In *Handbook of Research on Multicultural Education,* ed. James Banks. New York: MacMillan.

Romney, Lee. 2001. "Fox Focuses on Migrants' Role Sending Funds Home: Mexico's President Convenes a Meeting of Wire-Transfer Industry to Hone Binational Policy." *Los Angeles Times,* Mar. 5, sec. C.

Rotenberg, Robert, and Gary McDonogh. 1993. *The Cultural Meaning of Urban Space.* Westport, Conn.: Bergin and Garvey.

Rúa, Merida. 2001. "Colao Subjectivities: PortoMex and MexiRican Perspectives on Language and Identity." *Centro: Journal of the Center for Puerto Rican Studies* 13 (2): 116–34.

Ruben, Matthew. 2001. "Suburbanization and Urban Poverty under Neoliberalism." In *The New Poverty Studies: Ethnography of Power, Politics, and Impoverished People in the United States,* eds. Judith Goode and Jeff Maskovsky. New York: New York University Press.

Sales, William, and Rod Bush. 2000. "The Political Awakening of Blacks and Latinos in New York City: Competition or Cooperation?" *Social Justice* 27 (1): 19–42.

Sánchez, José Ramón. 1990. "Housing Puerto Ricans in New York City, 1945–1984: A Study in Class Powerlessness." Ph.D. diss., New York University.

Sánchez, Arturo, and Milena Gómez. 2001. "Mapa Latino con Acento Mexicano," in *Hoy,* June 27, 3.

Sánchez-Korrol, Virginia. 1983. *From Colonia to Community: The History of Puerto Ricans in New York City.* Berkeley: University of California Press.

Sanjek, Roger. 2000. *The Future of Us All: Race and Neighborhood Politics in New York City.* Ithaca, N.Y.: Cornell University Press.

San Juan, E. 2002. *Racism and Cultural Studies: Critiques of Multiculturalist Ideology and the Politics of Difference.* Durham, NC: Duke University Press.

Sassen, Saskia. 1998. *Globalization and Its Discontents.* New York: The New Press.

Scott, Janny. 2003. "Here, Poverty and Privilege are Neighbors." *New York Times,* Mar. 5, metro section.

Segal, Daniel, and Richard Handler. 1995. "U.S. Multiculturalism and the Concept of Culture." *Identities: Global Studies of Culture and Power* 1 (4): 391–408.

Ševčenko, Liz. 2001. "Making Loisaida: Placing Puertorriqueñidad in Lower Manhattan." In *Mambo Montage: The Latinization of New York*, eds. Agustin Laó and Arlene Dávila. New York: Columbia University Press.

Sexton, Patricia Cayo. 1965. *Spanish Harlem: An Anatomy of Poverty*. New York: Harper and Row.

Sierra, Luis. 1992. *Uncertain Futures: Occupied City-Owned Housing in East Harlem*. New York: Community Service Society.

Sites, William. 1994. "Public Action: New York City Policy and the Gentrification of the Lower East Side." In *From Urban Village to East Village: The Battle for New York's Lower East Side*, ed. Janet Abu-Lughod. Cambridge, Mass.: Blackwell.

Smith, Michael Peter, and Luis Eduardo Guarnizo. 1998. "Transnationalism From Below." Comparative Urban and Community Research, vol. 6. New Brunswick: Transaction Publishers.

Smith, Neil. 1996. *The New Urban Frontier: Gentrification and the Revanchist City*. London: Routledge.

Smith, Robert. 1997. "Mexicans in New York: Membership and Incorporation in a New Immigrant Community." In *Latinos in New York: Communities in Transition*, eds. Gabriel Haslip-Viera and Sherrie Baver. Notre Dame, Ind.: University of Notre Dame Press.

———. 2001. "Mexicans: Their Social, Educational, Economic and Political Problems and Prospects in New York." In *New Immigrants in New York*, ed. Nancy Foner. New York: Columbia University Press.

———. 2003a. "Gender, Ethnicity and Race in School and Work Outcomes of Second Generation Mexican Americans" In *Latinos in the Twenty-First Century*. Berkeley: University of California Press.

———. 2003b. *Mexican New York: Transitional Lives of New Immigrants*. Unpublished manuscript.

———. 2003c. "Racialization and Mexicans in New York City." In *New Destinations for Mexican Migration*, eds. Ruben Hernández Leon and Victor Zúñiga. Unpublished manuscript.

Solis, Jocelyn. 2001. "Immigration Status and Identity: Undocumented Mexicans in New York." In *Mambo Montage: The Latinization of New York*, eds. Agustin Laó and Arlene Dávila. New York: Columbia University.

Steinberg, Jacques. 2002. "For-Profit School Venture Has Yet to Turn a Profit." *New York Times*, Apr. 8, sec. A.

Steinhauer, Jennifer. 2002. "As Bloomberg Takes Over Schools, Pataki Takes Center Stage." *New York Times*, June 13, metro section.

Storper, Michael. 2000. "Lived Effects of the Contemporary Economy: Globalization, Inequality, and Consumer Society." *Public Culture* 12 (2).

Sturken, Marita. 1997. *Tangled Memories: The Vietnam War, the AIDS Epidemic and the Politics of Remembering.* Berkeley: University of California Press.

Sze, Julie. 2003. "Noxious New York: The Racial Politics of Urban Health and Environmental Justice." Ph.D. diss., New York University.

Taylor, Diana. 1999. "Dancing with Diana: A Study in Hauntology." *The Drama Review* 43 (1): 59–78.

Taylor, Monique. 2002. *Harlem Between Heaven and Hell.* Minneapolis: University of Minnesota Press.

Teske, Paul, Mark Schneider, Christine Roch, and Melissa Marshall. 2000. "Public School Choice: A Status Report." In *City Schools: Lessons from New York,* eds. Diane Ravitch and Joseph P. Viteritti. Baltimore: John Hopkins University Press.

Thomas, Piri. 1967. *Down These Mean Streets.* New York: Vintage.

Throsby, David. 2001. *Economics and Culture.* Cambridge: Cambridge University Press.

Tierney, John. 2002. "The Big City: The Gentry, Misjudged As Neighbors." *New York Times,* Mar. 26, metro section.

Toro-Morn, Maura. 2001. "Yo era muy arriesgada: A Historical View of the Work Experiences of Puerto Rican Women in Chicago." *Centro: Journal of the Center for Puerto Rican Studies* 13 (2).

Torres, Andres. 1995. *Between Melting Pot and Mosaic. African Americans and Puerto Ricans in the New York Political Economy.* Philadelphia: Temple University Press.

Torres Penchi, Israel. 2002a. "Centro Cultural Latino Julia de Burgos: Balance de sus Contribuciones y sus Limitaciones." *Siempre,* Feb. 6–26, 5.

———. 2002b. "Jose A. Padilla, hijo, juez y parte de la comunidad." *Siempre,* Aug. 6–26, 9.

Upper Manhattan Empowerment Zone. 2000. "Creating Sustainable Economic Opportunities. Report on Operations 2000."

———. 2001. "The Upper Manhattan Empowerment Zone Annual Report 2001."

Urciuoli, Bonnie. 1993. "Whose Quincentenary Is It? Puerto Rican and Italian-American Class Identity in the U.S. in 1992." Unpublished manuscript.

———. 1996. *Exposing Prejudice: Puerto Rican Experiences of Language, Race, and Class.* Boulder, Colo.: Westview Press.

Valle Victor, and Rodolfo Torres. 2000. *Latino Metropolis.* Minneapolis: University of Minnesota Press.

Van Ryzin, Gregg, and Andrew Genn. 1999. "Neighborhood Change and the City of New York's Ten-Year Plan." *Housing Policy Debate* (10) 4: 799-838.

Vega, Maria. 1995. "Piden Investigar a Del Toro." *El Diario/La Prensa,* Jan. 13, 2.

Vélez-Ibañez, Carlos. 1996. "Making Pictures: U.S. Mexican Place and Space in

Mural Art." In *Border Visions: Mexican Cultures of the Southwest United States.* Tucson: University of Arizona Press.

Venkatesh, Sudhir Alladi. 2002. *American Project: The Rise and Fall of a Modern Ghetto.* Cambridge, Mass.: Harvard University Press.

Villa, Raúl Homero. 2000. *Barrio-logos: Space and Place in Urban Chicano Literature and Culture.* Austin: University of Texas Press.

Wakefield, Dan. 1959. *Island in the City: The World of Spanish Harlem.* New York: Arno Press.

Waldman, Amy. 2001. "Insiders Out in Harlem: Despite Good Times, Business Mainstays Face Eviction." *New York Times,* Aug. 29, metro section.

Weems, Robert. 1998. *Desegregating the Dollar.* New York: New York University Press.

Weiner, Annette. 1992. *Inalienable Possessions: The Paradox of Keeping While Giving.* Berkeley: University of California Press.

Weiner, Tim. 2001. "Mexico Seeks Lower Fees on Funds Sent from U.S." *New York Times,* Mar. 3, sec. A.

Williams, Brackette. 1989. "A Class Act: Anthropology and the Race to Nation among Ethnic Terrain." *Annual Review of Anthropology* 18.

Wilson, William J. 1987. *The Truly Disadvantaged: The Inner City, the Underclass, and Public Policy.* Chicago: University of Chicago Press.

Worth, Robert. 1999. "Guess Who Saved the South Bronx? Big Government." *The Washington Monthly* 31 (4): 26–33.

Wyatt, Edward. 2000. "School Managing Company and Museum Plan Harlem Headquarters." *New York Times,* July 20, metro section.

Yudice, George. 2004. *The Expediency of Culture: Uses of Culture in the Global Era.* Durham, N.C.: Duke University Press.

Zentella, Ana Celia. 1997. *Growing Up Bilingual: Puerto Rican Children in New York.* Malden, Mass.: Blackwell.

Zukin, Sharon. 1995. *The Cultures of Cities.* Cambridge, Mass.: Blackwell.

Index

Italicized page numbers refer to illustrations.

Compositor: BookMatters, Berkeley
Indexer: Sharon Sweeney
Text: 10/14 Palatino
Display: Univers Condensed Light and Bauer Bodoni
Printer and binder: Thomson-Shore, Inc.